METHUEN'S
MANUALS OF PYSCHOLOGY

(Founder Editor C. A. Mace 1946-1968)
General Editor H. J. Butcher

An Introduction to the Psychology of Language

An Introduction to the Psychology of Language

PETER HERRIOT

METHUEN & CO LTD
11 New Fetter Lane London EC4

First published in 1970
by Methuen & Co Ltd, 11 New Fetter Lane, London EC4P 4EE
First published as a University Paperback in 1976
© *1970 Peter Herriot*
Printed in Great Britain
by Billing & Sons Limited, Guildford, London and Worcester

ISBN 0 416 85500 8 (paperback edition)

Distributed in the USA by
HARPER & ROW PUBLISHERS, INC.
BARNES & NOBLE IMPORT DIVISION

Foreword

This book is intended as a survey of the field of the psychology of language which will serve as a source for reference. It is hoped that there is also enough evaluative comment for it to stimulate discussion and serve as a class text.

All errors of fact and interpretation, and all infelicities of style are the author's own. That there are not more is due to the kind and patient help of my friends and colleagues David Allerton, David Bruce, John Butcher, Edward Carney, Hazel Hayhurst, Eric Hoyle, Eric Lunzer and Nicolas Perl. The author would also like to thank Methuen for their assistance and encouragement; and his wife, Barbara, for typing the manuscript.

The text does not contain reference to second language learning, linguistic pathologies other than aphasia, reading, or content analysis. All these were considered interesting but tangential to the main theme of the book. Also, it was decided not to use the phonetic script to describe speech sounds, phonemes, etc. This was in order not to make the linguistic section appear too formidable and to save cost.

Introduction to the Paperback Edition

The appearance of a second printing of this book five years subsequent to its original publication requires some explanation. There have been so many new developments in psycholinguistics that the text is outdated in some respects. However, I feel justified in approving a second printing since the main theoretical trends advocated in the book have in fact occurred. More emphasis is being placed on the functions of language as opposed to its structure; the cognitive processes underlying the content of children's and adults' language have been stressed; the processes of retrieval of information from a person's semantic memory have been investigated more fully; and, finally, the abstraction of the meaning in more natural language situations has replaced verbatim recall as a typical experimental task.

Reference can be made only to the major developments of the past five years, and to review articles or books from which further information can be gained. Considerable impetus has been given to psychological research by developments in linguistic theory (Lyons and Wales, 1973).

Transformational grammar emphasised syntax as the deep structure component of the grammar, with concentration upon such features as noun phrase and verb phrase as the elements from which sentences were generated. The more recent case grammar, however, stresses semantic relationships such as that between actor and action, or action and object acted upon. Thus attention is drawn to the function of language in expressing conceptual relationships.

This functional analysis underlies recent attempts to account for the acquisition of language. It is argued (Cromer, 1974) that the early utterances of children are their attempts to express their semantic intentions. Thus their linguistic skills develop in order to express the results of their increasing cognitive sophistication. However, there may be quite a time lag between the cognitive and the linguistic development. As Slobin (1972) puts it, 'new (linguistic) forms first express old functions, and new functions are first expressed by old forms'. Idiosyncratic utterances by young children can thus be seen as efforts to employ their as yet inadequate linguistic skill to cope with the complexity of their ideas. This account is a move away from a nativist approach which suggests that the universals of language are specifically pre-programmed in the infant's brain. It is derived from an analysis based on audio and video tapes of children's interactions with their mother instead of a structural linguistic analysis of transcripts of audio tapes. The exciting possibility that apes can be taught to use language casts yet more doubt on the notion of a language acquisition device specific to humans and necessary for acquisition.

The same change in emphasis is evident in the socio-linguistic literature (Robinson, 1972). Instead of a concentration on structural differences typical of different socio-economic classes, attention is being paid to the ways in which language functions to define roles in particular interactions. Particular interest is being given to the relationship between function and structure: are certain structures used for a particular range of functions, and what are their features which make them suitable?

Continuing with the concept of language as a means of communication, the study of paralinguistic features is growing fast (Argyle, 1974). A corollary is the notion of understanding a message as a parallel-processing operation in which signals of many different types, each with their own rule system, are interpreted. This view appears to be in contradiction to the informative-processing model favoured by many investigators of memory. The notion that language material is processed first in terms of its phonological characteristics, then subsequently coded meaningfully and transferred into long-term store, seems mistaken (Herriot, 1974). Rather, our knowledge of the language, our long-term semantic memory, acts directly on input in such a way as to extract meaning as the message progresses. What is the nature of this knowledge? The study of semantic memory (Johnson-Laird, 1974) indicates that we have to suppose that it consists of very abstract elements and rules for their combination and retrieval. Recent evidence suggests that the listener is expected to make inferences from the linguistic message he hears rather than to interpret only what is actually uttered.

REFERENCES

ARGYLE, M. (1973) *Social Encounters*. Harmondsworth: Penguin.

CROMER, R. (1974) 'The development of language and cognition.' In FOSS, B. (ed.) *New Perspectives in Child Development*. Harmondsworth: Penguin.

HERRIOT, P. (1974) *Attributes of Memory*. London: Methuen.

JOHNSON-LAIRD, P. N. (1974) 'Experimental psycholinguistics.' *Ann. Rev. of Psychol.*, **25**, 135–160.

LYONS, J. and WALES, R. J. (1973) *New Horizons in Linguistics*. Harmondsworth: Penguin.

ROBINSON, W. P. (1972) *Language and social behaviour*. Harmondsworth: Penguin.

SLOBIN, D. I. (1972) 'Seven questions about language development.' In DODWELL, P. C. (ed.) *New Horizons in Psychology* (2). Harmondsworth: Penguin.

Acknowledgements

The author would like to thank the following individuals and publishers for permission to reproduce the diagrams listed below:

Figure 1. Neal F. Johnson, from page 441, Theodore R. Dixon and David L. Horton, Editors, *Verbal Behavior and General Behavior Theory* © 1968. Reproduced by permission of Prentice-Hall, Inc., Englewood Cliffs, New Jersey, U.S.A.

Figure 2. Charles E. Osgood, from 'On understanding and creating sentences'. *American Psychologist*, 18, 735–51, 1963, © 1963. Reproduced by permission of the American Psychological Association.

Figure 3. Merrill Garrett and Jerry A. Fodor, from page 453, Theodore R. Dixon and David L. Horton, Editors, *Verbal Behavior and General Behavior Theory* © 1968. Reproduced by permission of Prentice-Hall, Inc., Englewood Cliffs, New Jersey, U.S.A.

Figure 4. Roger J. Wales and John C. Marshall, from page 55, John Lyons and Roger J. Wales, Editors, *Psycholinguistics Papers* © 1966. Reproduced by permission of the Edinburgh University Press.

Contents

I INTRODUCTION TO LANGUAGE BEHAVIOUR

   1. Approaches to language   *page* 11
     a) *Language as a system*   11
     b) *Language as personal behaviour*   14
     c) *Language as inter-personal behaviour*   15
     d) *Connexions between these three approaches to language*   16
   2. The basic approach and organisation of this book   17

II LANGUAGE AS SKILLED BEHAVIOUR

   1. The psychology of skills   21
   2. Phonological skills – theories of speech perception   24
   3. Phonological skills – the effect of context   27
   4. Phonological skills – articulation   30
   5. Grammatical skills – words and form classes   32
   6. Grammatical skills – syntax   37
   7. Grammatical skills – left-to-right analysis   40
   8. Grammatical skills – top-to-bottom analysis   43
   9. Grammatical skills – interaction   47
  10. Sub-sentence structure   52
  11. Conclusions   54

III GENERATIVE LINGUISTICS AND PSYCHOLOGY

   1. Chomsky's general approach   56
   2. Specific aspects of Chomsky's theory   61
   3. Some transformational experiments   66
   4. The semantic aspects of grammatical constructions   69
   5. Evidence for a syntax-semantics dichotomy   73
   6. Evidence for deep structure   74
   7. Conclusions   76

IV MEANING: BEHAVIOURIST APPROACHES

   1. Introduction   79
   2. The word-word approach   82

3. The response-unit – reinforcement approach   *page* 83
4. Mediation   85
5. The word mediator theory   86
6. The representational mediator theory   89
7. A comparison   91
8. Critique of representational mediation   94
9. Free recall and subjective organisation   95
10. Retrieval   97

V LANGUAGE ACQUISITION

1. Acquisition and generative linguistics   102
2. Acquisition of deep structure   104
3. Acquisition of transformations and inflexions   110
4. The learning of language   114
5. Acquisition of the phonological system   120
6. Biological bases – aphasia   124
7. Biological bases of acquisition   128

VI LANGUAGE AND THINKING

1. Introduction   131
2. Cognitive development   132
3. Thinking as internalised language   134
4. Thinking as a mediated language response   137
5. Language and operational thinking   141
6. Semantics and cognitive development   145
7. Communication and thinking   150
8. Linguistic relativity   155

VII THEORETICAL CONCLUSIONS

1. The nature of theory   158
2. A confrontation   162
3. An alternative   163

Bibliography   169
Appendix   188
Author Index   191
Subject Index   196

I

Introduction to Language Behaviour

The purpose of this introductory chapter is to distinguish a field of study which might be termed the psychology of language from other related disciplines; and to explain the organisation of this book.

1. APPROACHES TO LANGUAGE

(a) Language as a system

Linguists study language as a system of sounds and symbols (see Gleason, 1961, Lyons, 1968). Their data are the sounds uttered by native speakers of the language under investigation. Their aim is to make general statements about the structure of this data, and they carefully distinguish these general statements from the data itself. They use the term *language* to denote the system they infer, and *speech* to denote the utterances of the native speaker. The following account of the linguists' approach is intended to be introductory. Different aspects of their work will receive fuller treatment in the text. The structure derived by linguists from their data is hierarchical in nature; that is, there are different levels of analysis, dealing with units of different size.

Phonetic descriptions of data deal with the sounds as sounds apart from any cultural background; the linguist simply transcribes the sounds the informant utters into phonetic script. This method aims at giving an account of the sounds without the informant's or the linguist's own linguistic habits affecting the transcript.

Phonemic analysis discovers those features of sounds which are the basic building blocks of the language. The linguist substitutes one sound for another in a phonemic context, e.g. 'pit' for 'bit', and asks the informant whether he is repeating himself or not. Other operational procedures are also used. It is worth noting that some sounds which are considerably different are not phonemically distinct; others which have differences barely noticeable when they are presented in isolation (e.g. 'f' as in 'fin', and 'th' as in 'thin') are distinct phonemes. The field of phonology, then, is concerned with the discovery of those features which are phonemic and those which are not.

Phonology is also concerned with the principles which determine the formation of *morphemes* from phonemes (known as morpho-phonemics). Morphemes are minimal meaningful forms. They may be words, e.g. 'cat', or affixes, e.g. plural 's', or parts of words, e.g. 'way' in 'railway'. Linguists are particularly interested in the setting up of morphemes and in the principles by which morphemes are combined into words; for example, they are interested in the order rules which allow 'un' to appear only at the beginning of the word 'unsteadily', and '—ly' only at the end.

Syntactic descriptions aim at specifying the principles which determine the formation of sentences. Informants are asked whether the substitutions made by the linguist into sentences uttered by the informant make the resulting sequence ungrammatical. Other procedures are also used; in particular, linguists frequently invent sentences and question informants on their grammaticality.

Finally, linguists deal with the *semantic* level of analysis. This is termed the analysis of content, and is contrasted with the analysis of expression (phonology, morphemics, and syntax). There is no unified approach to semantics among linguists. They are interested in lexicology (the individual items in a dictionary) and in the relationships of synonymy and antonymy that these items may have to each other. They are also interested in semantic rules which specify which dictionary items are acceptable in combination in a sentence and which are not. They also enquire into the nature of ambiguity and its explication.

There are certain more basic distinctions between the levels just enumerated. Those levels which deal with the *combination* of items (morpho-phonemics and syntax) behave differently from those which do not (phonetics and phonemics).

Firstly, the latter can only deal with units in which the sounds run together. When there are pauses in speech, e.g. between phrases or words, the previous phoneme does not affect the subsequent one in any rule-governed way.

Secondly, morpho-phonemic and syntactic rules give rise to three different types of unit, while phonemic analysis allows only two. In the case of phonemics, a sound either realises a phoneme or it does not ('realise' means 'be an instance of a linguistic category'). However, morpho-phonemic and syntactic rules permit in addition the construction of morphemes and sentences which could be used but are not. For example, 'fland' or 'splob' are acceptable as potential English words, whereas 'tland' or 'spkay' are not. Similarly, 'Pink accidents cause sleeping storms' is acceptable as a grammatical sentence which is never used, while 'Accidents pink storms sleeping cause' is not. Morpho-phonemic and syntactic rules are therefore *productive*; they permit many combinations which could be, but have not yet been, used in the language (it should be noted that there is another, more specialised, use of the term 'productive' by linguists). This feature is in contrast with the limited number of phonemes in any given language. Indeed, some linguists consider that the number of possible sentences is infinite.

Finally, it is worth noting that phonemic changes do not produce any *regular* change in meaning. For example, the change from 'pit' to 'bit' is the same phonemically as the change from 'patter' to 'batter', but there is nothing in common between the changes in meaning accomplished. Syntactic rules, however, do involve regular meaning changes; for example, the reversal of 'the boy loved the girl' to 'the girl loved the boy' produces a similar change in meaning to the reversal of 'the sister hated her brother' to 'the brother hated his sister'.

To discover the structure of a sample of speech which they have obtained, many linguists consult informants. These informants are linguistically naïve (in the sense that they are not linguists). Informants are asked questions about, for example, the grammatical acceptability or non-acceptability of a part of the speech sample which the linguist has altered in a certain respect. The linguist is not therefore analysing speech data; rather, he is experimentally manipulating data, and then asking questions of informants about the manipulations which require a verbal response. The linguist assumes that these verbal responses reflect the informant's knowledge of the language. He is anxious to make inferences about the nature of language, and not about the nature and function of the informant. Therefore he is willing to assume that his own question means the same to him as it does to all his informants, and that their responses are therefore comparable. The procedure thus resembles the classical psychological technique of *introspection*, in that the subject's verbal response is being taken as evidence of his knowledge.

There has been a long tradition of hostility towards introspection in psychology. Its use as an indicator of mental states has been criticised repeatedly and justifiably. However, more recently it has been suggested that such constructs as '*awareness*' are inferable from subjects' verbal reports about how they are planning their behaviour. Thus, for example, subjects may report hypotheses which they are making about what part of their verbal behaviour is being rewarded in an operant verbal conditioning experiment (see p. 84). In this case, however, the 'awareness', 'hypotheses' or other constructs are inferences from verbal behaviour. The making of these inferences is a necessary step for experimental psychologists; linguists tend to by-pass this stage and assume that subjects' reports reflect a 'knowledge of the language'.

However, it should be stressed that many linguists do not see the need for the consultation of informants and the effort to treat their own language as though they had never heard it before. Instead, they treat their own *intuitions* about language as adequate data. Furthermore, some of them (especially Chomsky, 1965) claim that their task is to describe the language user's *competence*. Instead of speaking of language as a system external to its users, they insert their formal system into the language user. They then claim that the actual language behaviour of the user, his *performance*, is but an indirect reflexion of this competence.

One is therefore left with two basic types of inference employed by linguists: first, from an informant's responses to a system; and second, from an intuitively deduced system to human functioning.

(b) Language as personal behaviour

A second approach to language involves the making of inferences from *behaviour* to psychological *function*. It is this approach with which this book will be chiefly concerned.

The types of data and of inference to be made from them are varied. 1. One can deal with speech as data and make inferences about its production. 2. One can deal with other responses made as a result of language input. Inferences can then be drawn about the perception of language. Production and perception can be compared. 3. Some of the independent variables affecting these responses can be discovered, leading to inferences about production and perception (e.g. the grammatical complexity of sentences to be recalled can be manipulated). 4. The paralinguistic concomitants of speech can be investigated, some leading to inferences about production (e.g. gesture and intonation). 5. The connexions between the situational and verbal contexts of utterances and their perception or production can be studied, and inferences drawn about their comprehension and meaning. 6. The effects of language as an independent variable on other behaviour can be estimated, and inferences made about its connexion with thinking (e.g. language and problem-solving).

Such investigation uses familiar *experimental techniques*, in an effort to avoid making inferences of a kind not made in other fields of psychology and dependent on introspection. One therefore finds trials to a criterion of recall, errors in recall, response latency and response magnitude measures, and stimulus discrimination and word association techniques recurring in the experimental literature. The use of such techniques allows inferences about human functioning to be made; it is worth noting that their use does not necessarily imply adherence to the theoretical viewpoint with which they are usually associated. Thus, for example, investigations of the syntagmatic to paradigmatic shift (see p. 36) in children's word associations use an associationist technique to prove a point hard to explain in associationist theoretical terms.

(c) Language as inter-personal behaviour

A third approach to language treats it as a means of *communication* in a *social* situation. This obviously requires the production of a message by the speaker, S, and the perception of that same message by the listener, L. The processes which were treated as separate in section (b) are thus occurring simultaneously. Successful communication implies the perception and comprehension by L of the message produced by S. Perception is here defined in terms of the reception of speech, comprehension in terms of its relation by L to the situation. These terms will receive fuller definition elsewhere. Evidence for these activities must occur in L's response. If S has uttered a command, L indicates that he has perceived and comprehended the message by acting in accordance with it (or by refusing to do so). If S has uttered a question, and L replies with an answer which satisfies S, communication again has been successful. However, if S makes a statement which imparts information, there may well be no behavioural response by L as evidence of perception and comprehension.

It is obvious that there are many more variables affecting performance in this situation than there are in situations where S or L is treated in isolation. For example, S may change his output as he is speaking because of feedback information he receives from L's facial expression about the effect his utterance is having on L. It is also clear that there are more constraints on successful perception and production in the communication situation. The utterance has to be produced by a human being with a limited memory and information capacity; but it also has to be perceived by L whose capacities may differ from S's.

Not only differences in capacity are involved; most important, L may use different meaning categories from S; or he may use slightly different grammatical conventions; or he may find the basic phonemic contrasts of S difficult to perceive because of regional variations, indistinct articulation, or noise. Moreover, it is clear that communication takes place in a situational context in which some sort of behaviour is usually required of L by S. It is therefore likely that S's utterance will need to have reference or meaning for L (leaving these terms undefined for the moment). The constraints on the utterance, therefore, work not only from within the utterance itself (e.g. 'the' needs to be followed by a noun) but also from situation to utterance (e.g. one tends not to talk about philosophy to a child learning to tie his shoelaces).

Experiments designed to analyse the communication situation usually use referents which can be coded in different ways (e.g. a series of colours). They then obtain a message from an encoder, together with the referents which he is coding; they present this message to the decoder and note how far his selection of referents corresponds with that of the encoder (see pp. 156-7).

(d) Connexions between these three approaches to language

This book concentrates on language as personal behaviour, as this approach promises most in terms of inferences about psychological function. However, certain connexions between this and the other two approaches must be examined.

1. Are *linguistic* units *psychologically* real?

The question posed in this form perhaps exaggerates the differences between linguists and psychologists. A better way of phrasing it might be to ask whether methods of experiment acceptable to psychologists lead to the finding of the linguists' units at different levels and of interaction between these levels. The different experimental methods permit the inferences to the language user's functioning which the psychologist is anxious to make.

The linguists' analysis isolated different levels. Historically, linguists have tended to see the relationships between levels as being unidirectional from micro-level to macro-level. To the psychologist, the relationships between levels of a *hierarchical* structure are vital, for the structure provided by the linguist might turn out to be a ready-made model of a *complex skill* (see pp. 21-4). The psychologist is not concerned so much with whether the units themselves are psychologically real as with whether the whole model adequately describes the perception and production of language. Thus, for example, the psychologist does not test the recognition or recall of the phoneme so much on its own as with a surrounding phonemic, grammatical, and semantic context. Such an approach is supported by the hierarchical nature of other motor skills and of the instinctive behaviour in animals discovered by the ethologists (see Miller *et al.*, 1960). It leads to a description of language behaviour as a complex skill made up of the subskills of articulation, selection of morphemes, and grammatical combination (Miller, 1964); but it may not deal adequately with 'the problem of meaning' (see Chapter 4).

2. How do communication requirements affect production and perception?

The psychologist operating in the experimental setting of the laboratory may be tempted to ignore some of the features typical of language as communication. In particular, he may omit the area of *meaning*, since this involves surrounding verbal and situational context which are difficult variables to control. He may also ignore the subjective aspect of meaning which must be considered if two or more individuals with different cognitive categories are communicating (although the conventions of language limit the effect of individual differences in categories upon communication). The importance of feedback information regarding the success or failure of one's communication is also underestimated, as is the effect of the social environment on what the speaker decides to say in the first place.

2. THE BASIC APPROACH AND ORGANISATION OF THIS BOOK

The lack of structure in this text parallels the present disorganised nature of the field. Linguists and psychologists have come together only within the last ten years; moreover, there has recently been a revolutionary series of developments in linguistic theory due to the generative linguists. Add to this the fact that psychological theory itself is undergoing profound change, and one is left with the sort of situation described by Kuhn (1962); old paradigms are being discarded for new, since they do not adequately describe already observed data nor produce fruitful experimental hypotheses. A further cause of change is the fact that the logicians have abandoned the logical positivist philosophical position and the physical scientists have abandoned the methodological limitations it imposed.

The present writer believes that all inferences should be made from observable behaviour, and that there should be experimental control. of the situation. He accepts, however, that inferences to unobservables from behavioural data can be and should be made; he assumes that the problem of investigating these unobservables is not simply the technical one of getting inside the skin to observe 'behaviour' there, so he is not a *descriptive behaviourist*. Further, he allows that these inferences cannot be logically reduced to statements describing the inferred variable in terms of the operational test and the result it yields; he is not a *reductive behaviourist*. Finally, he allows the possibility of S-S and R-R relationships, maintaining that the latter in particular are vital if one is to allow that the human being is capable of learning rules and using them to control his behaviour; the writer is not therefore an *S-R theorist* (if an S-R theorist is defined as one who excludes S-S and R-R relationships).

However, the nature of inference cannot be removed any further from empirical evidence. The writer strongly opposes any effort to instal linguists' models of language as models of psychological processes. Their models can and should be used as fruitful experimental hypotheses. But the grounds for accepting them as psychological must be *experimental evidence* based on the responses of naïve subjects. Subjects should be naïve not in the sense that they don't know their own language but in the sense that they are not familiar with the linguists' model of it. Moreover, when some aspect of the linguists' model is not *in principle* empirically verifiable, it is worth asking whether it is a disguised article of philosophical faith rather than a descriptive hypothesis.

The book is therefore a combination of very different elements; accounts of psychological experiments, and discussions of whether a given hypothesis about language is empirically verifiable. Also, a certain amount of space is devoted to the nature of a theory adequate to encompass findings about language and lead to further research. It is considered that no specifically linguistic theory is required to describe language behaviour, but that a general theory can encompass linguistic and complex non-linguistic behaviour. The question whether certain psychological paradigms are still useful and adaptable or whether they should be completely discarded is also considered.

The basically *empirical* commitment of the writer is therefore one determinant of the structure of this book, together with the acceptance of the need for an adequate and experimentally fruitful theory. A second determinant is the desire to analyse language behaviour in as *comprehensive* a form as possible. Analysis of particular dimensions of language, for example the phonological and the grammatical dimensions, is necessary and useful. But if the basic purpose of language is communication, the problem of meaning cannot be avoided. While a distinction between pragmatic, semantic, syntactic and phonological levels may be desirable for analysis of the language system by linguists, it is likely that the presence of all these levels may be a necessary condition for communication to occur; they may, together, be more than the sum of their parts.

The effect of these two determinants upon the contents and organisation of this text will now be considered. Chapter 2 deals with the experimental evidence for the psychological reality of linguistic hypotheses at the phonological, form class, and constituent analysis levels. An attempt is made to assess the relative contributions of sequential and hierarchical processes to this behaviour. The terminology of the psychological field of skills is applied to the findings, but it is concluded that this attempt to apply a psychological paradigm is not completely successful.

Chapter 3 discusses the basically rationalist nature of the generative grammarians' theories. It analyses the distinction between linguistic competence and performance, and concludes that in its extreme form it is not an empirically verifiable hypothesis. The attempts to prove experimentally that the transformational processes postulated by the linguists are psychological processes are described, and it is concluded that the case is not proven. However, the possible empirical value of the hypothesis of deep structure is acknowledged, and welcomed as a reinstatement of the importance of meaning. Nevertheless, it is argued that generative grammarians neglect the various pragmatic factors which affect perception and production; furthermore, it is possible that speakers and listeners use many pragmatic and semantic short cuts which minimise the need to perform grammatical operations.

Chapter 4 is concerned with meaning. Various findings derived from an associationist approach are discussed, and the need to admit some mediating feature into a theory of meaning is stressed. The promise of the experimental technique of free recall is emphasised, since it provides evidence of the way in which the language user stores the words he uses. However, it is stressed that none of the behaviourist approaches have yet dealt adequately with structural meaning. Meaning is taken as the relationship of psychological systems to each other, not as a philosophical problem.

Chapter 5 deals with the acquisition of his native language by the child, and with the biological basis of language behaviour. The two are connected insofar as the generative linguists assume a considerable innate language faculty. The arguments concerning the relative effects of innate and learned components are outlined, and possible mechanisms of language learning discussed. Language pathology (especially aphasia) is considered, but only so far as it reveals the connexion between the brain and different features of language behaviour.

Chapter 6 skims the surface of the vast field of the connexions between language and thinking. Such connexions are inferred when language behaviour as an independent variable affects complex behaviour as the dependent variable. Two historic theories of the development of thought in children are outlined, and a synthesis suggested. Recent experimental work on children's use of language in discrimination tasks, concept learning, and problem solving are described. Next, the requirements of communication are discussed. The effects of socio-economic class on language behaviour and thinking are assessed, and the effect of different languages from different cultures on thinking (the linguistic relativity theory) is described.

The final chapter discusses whether S-R theory is adequate to describe language behaviour; S-R theory is defined, and the distinctions between a linguistic and behaviourist approach are discussed. It is concluded that a hierarchical model based on behavioural evidence is required, and such a model, incorporating the basic constructs of schemata and strategies, is outlined.

The text concludes with a list of books of readings and records of conferences in the field. Individual articles are placed in the bibliography at the end of the book. Many of the individual articles cited are to be found in the books of readings listed. Omitted from this text are the fields of bilingualism and second-language learning, content analysis, reading, and most of linguistic pathology.

II

Language as Skilled Behaviour

1. THE PSYCHOLOGY OF SKILLS

The psychological investigation of skills has been concerned mainly with tasks which require a rapid sequence of responses to a series of stimuli. The tracking task, for example, requires subjects to follow a path which is continuously changing direction because it is marked on a revolving drum. A favourite example of Bartlett's was a game of tennis in which the stroke-player adjusted the series of movements which composed his stroke to accord with the series of stimuli coming from the other side of the net, viz. the opponent's movements and the ball's flight. Fitts (1964), in a review article, insists on the highly organised nature of skilled performance, while Reed (1968, p. 107) summarises by saying: 'The most profitable approaches to the subject have been those which emphasise selection, organisation, and integration. Such approaches imply a rejection of the view that skill should be studied in terms of habit formation or simple stimulus-response chains.'

It is clear that the usual methods of investigating skills differ from typical instances of language behaviour. In a skilled task like tracking, the performance is judged by its success or failure in responding to the stimulus situation. In language behaviour, language output need not be correlated with stimulus conditions to the same degree. Language may concern future or absent events. The constraints are in terms of the speaker's intentions or the general verbal and social context rather than the specific features of the external situation (except in the case of reference).

There are certain respects, however, in which language behaviour might resemble skilled behaviour. The first is its *hierarchical nature*. Skills have been shown to consist of hierarchies and sub-hierarchies of behavioural elements (see the detailed description of the skill of hammering in Miller *et al.*, 1960). Language behaviour might consist of a hierarchy of skills rising from phonological to grammatical and semantic skills; each level of skill might in its turn form a sub-hierarchy, e.g. syntactical skill might itself involve a sub-hierarchy of units rising from morpheme to sentence. It is worth asking what precisely is meant by using the model of a hierarchy of language behaviour. It is clear that different levels imply a different type of unit, governed by its own rules. At each level, units are comparable, but they are also related to other units at different levels. Thus, for example, the syntactic level of the proposed language skill hierarchy consists of units related by certain rules. These rules differ from those which refer to other levels; the rules of combination are different from the rules of articulation. But the syntactic level is related to the articulatory level in the sense that articulatory skill is a necessary condition for syntactic skill to be exercised in language behaviour; and the syntactic and semantic structure determines which articulatory elements are used and in which order they are used. The degree to which the lower levels of a skill are automated determines the size of unit possible at its higher levels.

The second feature of skills is their dependence on *feedback*. Feedback information is derived from one's performance as perceived by oneself. The information received enables one to correct one's performance to coincide with a criterion of success. This process is known as negative feedback. In the case of the tracking task, the criterion of success is to follow the path without touching its sides. In the case of language behaviour, the criterion is some sort of intention on the speaker's part, to which his output and the listener's response match. The importance of feedback is clear at all levels of language skill. If one cannot hear oneself speak until one-fifth of a second after one has spoken, the articulatory level of skill is disrupted. If one does not receive vocal or expressive feedback from one's lecture audience, communication skills may be affected. At all levels of language production, self-corrections of one's own behaviour are indications of the feedback process at work.

The term *automatisation* has been used to describe another feature of successful skilled performance. It refers to the running off of sequences of behaviour without the need for conscious control. The typist can type words or phrases without paying attention to the sequence of letters. Such automatisation is involved in articulatory and in grammatical behaviour, although it is obviously hard to say whether control is 'conscious' or 'unconscious'. Pausal phenomena give indications when planning is taking place; therefore a rapid and smooth sequence of behaviour may be an indication of automatisation. In language behaviour, production is sometimes smooth and relatively continuous within phrase or sentence units, while between them pauses may occur. It is thus tempting to infer that quite large grammatical units are automatised, together with the articulatory skills which are necessary for their production. The degree of automatisation attained in a skill is dependent on the size of the units, or chunks (Miller, 1956) which the skilled performer uses. This is because of the limited nature of the short-term memory; since only a small number of items can be retained in the short-term memory system at a time, the smooth performance of a skill will be prevented if the items stored are too small. Thus the typist who is typing to dictation cannot keep up if she stores the dictator's words as items in her short-term memory; she has to store much larger units, e.g. phrases. The same may well be true of a person producing sentences of his own.

Anticipation is clearly involved in the tracking task. The ability to predict in which direction the path is going to turn enables planning to occur in time, and a movement to be coordinated with its predecessors. It seems clear that anticipation is similarly involved in language tasks. When perceiving speech, the listener can anticipate what is going to be said so ably that he can often supply the word or words over which the speaker is hesitating. The speaker, too, necessarily anticipates. In such a sentence as 'I'll take my umbrella, if it's going to rain', the second half constrains the first in such a way that the speaker has to plan ahead (anticipate) the second in order to utter the first to accord with his intentions.

It seems from the above summary that skilled behaviour contains certain features which are likely to apply to language behaviour. The difficulty is to sort the evidence into the most rational categories. Many experimental techniques do not allow the production and perception of language to be investigated separately; the technique of recall, for example, involves both the perception and the production of the material to be recalled. Thus it is difficult to discover whether both perception and production are skilled behaviour; and whether, if they are skills, they involve the same sub-skills. As a result, it is difficult to treat language skill in terms of first, input, and second, output; nevertheless, later in the chapter possible relationships between perception and production will be discussed. Another psychologically orientated approach would be to take the features of skill mentioned above in turn, and show how each feature occurred in language behaviour. However, the features are very closely inter-related: for example, the degree of automatisation obviously determines the degree of anticipation possible.

The method of analysis adopted here is therefore to assume that language behaviour is a skilled hierarchy consisting of various sub-skills which are the levels of analysis isolated by the linguists. The sub-skills involved and their relationships will be analysed in turn, in an effort to bring out the features that distinguish them as skills. The difficulty, of course, lies in distinguishing these sub-skills. In fact, the linguistic levels of the phonological, the grammatical and the semantic have been retained; articulation can be subsumed under the phonological level, and various difficulties about units can be resolved within this framework; thus, for example, there may be psychological grounds for thinking that syllables and words are units, although linguists are reluctant to use the terms or give them definitions.

2. PHONOLOGICAL SKILLS – THEORIES OF SPEECH PERCEPTION

Before discussing this lowest level in the hierarchy of language skill, it is worth noting that evidence is required before one can talk about a hierarchy at all. Such evidence would show that different levels interact; for example, that grammatical and semantic context affect the perception of phonemes. This evidence will be dealt with under the separate sub-skill headings. In each case, a short account of linguistic theory will precede an account of the psychological evidence.

It has been mentioned (p. 11) that the phoneme is a perceptual constant. That is, despite various physical differences in the sounds uttered, native speakers perceive sounds realising the same phoneme as being the same. It should also be noted that such features as stress and pitch may be phonemic (as in 'subject', verb or noun). Sounds which differ but which realise the same phoneme in the same context are said to be in free variation. Operational tests include: 1. the informant treats the free variants as being repetitions by the linguist; 2. the informant himself uses free variants in his own 'repetition' of a sound. It is clear that sounds (phones) differ in many ways, but that only a few of these differences are criterial for the perception of phonemes. Certain suggestions have been made regarding the nature of these criterial differences. Efforts to isolate them have resulted in *distinctive feature analysis*.

Distinctive feature analysis originated with the Prague school of linguists. It was suggested that the phonemes of particular languages differ according to certain *articulatory* features. These features refer to the nature of the articulation, e.g. whether it is voiced, like 'v', or voiceless, like 'f'; to the organs which produce it, e.g. whether it is made with the lips, like 'p', or whether it is made with the tip of the tongue, like 't'; or to the method of its production, e.g. whether it is continued, like 'f', or withheld, like 'p'. Phonemes may differ in one or more of these features. Since the major work of Jakobson, Fant and Halle (1952), however, the emphasis has been on the description of distinctive features of phonemes in terms of *acoustic* rather than articulatory correlates (although the two aspects do frequently coincide). Certain beneficial results follow from this change of emphasis. Firstly, potential distinctive features of all languages rather than those of one particular language may be discovered. Secondly, the revised theory of Jakobson and Halle (1956), which suggests 12 distinctive features, allows the possibility of a series of binary decisions occurring in the perception of phonemes. For example, the decisions might be whether a given phoneme was voiced or voiceless, continued or withheld, etc. These binary decisions may be hypothetically linked with the on-off mechanism in neural circuits proposed by many physiologists.

Some psychological evidence for the existence of distinctive features is provided by Miller and Nicely (1955), using the method of perceptual confusions. They found that noise and low-pass filtering (i.e. allowing only sounds of lower frequency to be heard) caused confusion in the discrimination of phonemes. The voiced–voiceless feature was least affected by this interference, but those features depending on place of articulation were most affected. The distinctive feature approach was supported, in that it was found that the features had great discriminatory power despite the interference; moreover, the voiced–voiceless feature was shown to be more efficient in this respect than others. In general, the features were shown to be independent in the way they are perceived. Wickelgren (1966) shows that errors in recall of individual letters of the alphabet are determined by the distinctive features of each letter name (e.g. Eff, Ess, Ell). The less distinctive features by which a letter differs from the letter to be remembered, the more likely it is to be substituted for it in error.

Distinctive feature analysis has isolated units smaller than the phoneme. It has distinguished the perceptual cues for phonemes. It has, very hypothetically, linked these binary decisions with the supposed on-off mechanism in neural circuits. Finally, it has emphasised the acoustic nature of the features; in this respect, therefore, it does not support the *motor theory* of speech perception emphasised by Liberman (1957).

Liberman and the Haskins group suppose that speech perception is performed by means of the 'neural surrogate of articulation' rather than by acoustic cues by themselves. This hypothesis supposes not only that we perceive phonemes in terms of certain features which describe articulatory activity, but also that those features are neurally re-enacted as though for the purpose of articulation.

It is worth noting that, in addition, the Haskins group has verified some of the basic hypotheses about perception of phonemes. It has shown, for example, that it is easier to discriminate sounds which differ by a distinctive feature than those which do not, i.e. it is easier to discriminate two sounds which realise different phonemes than two sounds which realise the same phoneme. This is true despite the fact that these sounds differ by an equal amount in terms of frequency and duration. This indicates once more the psychological reality of the phoneme, and is reminiscent of those experiments where a colour continuum is recognised differently by subjects who use different colour categories in their language (see p. 156–7). In both cases subjective learned perceptual categories are imposed on an objectively measurable continuum.

All these findings were made possible by the advanced technology of the Haskins group. They were able to present sounds differing in only one feature by means of the Pattern Playback. This is an instrument which transforms back into sound visual patterns produced by the experimenters on a sound spectrograph (a device that itself transforms speech into visible patterns). The features which were found especially important were the formants of vowels. These are frequency bands of concentrated energy in the pattern produced by the spectrograph, and the position in the pattern of its first two formants distinguishes one vowel from another. Furthermore, the place of articulation of consonants is discriminable by the transitions in the vowel which follows the consonant, and by the relatively steady states which distinguish consonants. It should be noted, however, that Ladefoged and Broadbent (1957) found that the whole of the preceding context of the sentence affected perception rather than the second formant alone. This supports the emphasis of the next section on the effect of context on perception.

The motor theory of speech perception, as has been stated, suggests that a 'neural surrogate for articulation' mediates between the acoustic stimulus and perception. There is, it is suggested, a feedback link between these *articulatory* events and *perception*. In other words, the perceiver checks his perception of acoustic stimuli against the articulatory codings in the brain. It follows that when phonemes are distinguishable by binary features (e.g. voiced–voiceless), perception too should be categorical between phonemes. Where articulation is continuous (e.g. in some vowels), perception, too, should be less categorical and more constant throughout a continuum. Numerous experiments have demonstrated these facts. However, this neural articulatory mediation is unlikely to be peripheral, since anarthric children can comprehend speech (Lenneberg, 1962). Furthermore, peripheral muscle activity has been found in speech perception only in cases where comprehension was difficult (Sokolov, 1961). Therefore one must assume the process of perception to be relatively 'central' and, this being so, it is worth asking why articulatory matching is necessary at a central level. It is likely that auditory analysis of speech must have progressed a considerable way for such central activity to occur at all. It is therefore unnecessary to assume an extra mechanism for perception when the assumption necessarily implies considerable previous auditory analysis.

3. PHONOLOGICAL SKILLS – THE EFFECT OF CONTEXT

The phonemic level of perception has been assumed to exist psychologically largely on the basis of experiments which deal with phonemes in isolation or in a small phonological context. It is possible to argue, however, as Chomsky (1965) does, that analysis into segmental phonemes is unnecessary in situations where adequate syntactic and semantic cues are available. We do not need to attend to low-level cues when high-level ones, yielding more information, are available. However, there is at least one difference between production and perception of language. The perceiver may not have any syntactic or semantic cues at all at the beginning of a sentence. He may depend on phonemic cues for perception until the grammatical structure and semantic selection have had time to develop. Perception of language may, in other words, be 'from the bottom up' (i.e. from lower levels to higher), at least at the beginning of sentences. Moreover, it is difficult to speak of the effect of surrounding context on the perception of sounds as phonemes, since it is difficult to segment speech into sounds. However, research by the Haskins group (Cooper *et al.*, 1952) shows that formant patterns (which might equally well be considered as belonging to *surrounding* vowels) partly determine the perception of phonemes. It has also been shown that the *duration* of the transition is vital in the perception of a frictional sound as 's' or 'z' after a vowel (Denes, 1955). Further definition of these terms and investigation of the findings would require a description of elementary acoustics.

Some *morphological* context was given by Brown and Hildum (1956). They found that the identification of vowel phonemes was better when they were presented in monosyllabic uncommon English words than in monosyllabic nonsense syllables constructed according to the morphemic rules (e.g. 'skice', 'drate'). These in turn were perceived more accurately than monosyllables with unlawful initial clusters (e.g. 'pshoop', 'srate'). Thus semantic and morphemic contextual factors affected phoneme perception. When linguists were told to transcribe the first two types of material, they succeeded equally well in both. The linguist is trained not to perceive in terms of 'words', but the language user may perhaps do so. In general, then, semantic and syntactic cues usually make those phonemic distinctions which could have been difficult far easier. For example, on their own the words 'subject', 'object', 'digest', 'contract' and 'permit' might be taken either as nouns or as verbs. The cues which do distinguish their function are primarily duration and secondarily intensity (Fry, 1955), and they are also distinguished by vowel quality (with the possible exception of 'permit'). Such cues might be difficult to pick up in isolation. In a grammatical context, however, the noun 'permit' will be clearly signalled by an article or possessive pronoun, and also by its place in the sentence construction as a whole. In summary, it is possible that some immediate perception of speech by its phonemic features occurs, but that the syntactic, and semantic constraints provide expectancy cues and almost immediate confirmation. However, research is needed to confirm this hypothesis.

Information theory has made a mathematically expressed attempt to define more strictly the *effect of context* and probability of occurrence of items on the reception of messages. Experiments have been carried out applying the findings of information theory to the perception of speech items. Miller, Heise and Lichten (1951) varied the total number of items from which the items to be perceived were selected. Information theory predicts that the larger this 'ensemble', the less words would be perceived accurately in noise. The material employed was monosyllabic words, and the signal-to-noise ratio was varied. The predicted effect was found, but only when there was a great deal of noise. In other words, the increase in uncertainty caused by the larger ensemble has no effect when recognition is unimpeded. This implies that subjects' recognition of words is so good that number of alternatives has little effect. In a penetrating analysis of this experiment, Garner (1962, pp. 80–4) further notes that there are few results, if any, which indicate that performance is poorer with larger stimulus ensembles; this holds provided that uncertainty measures are used to describe the possible discriminative responses as well as the stimuli; in other words, responses as well as stimuli are selected from an ensemble of alternatives.

and this variable, too, must be controlled if adequate measures of performance in information theory units are to be obtained.

Further convincing demonstrations of the *effect of context* on speech perception are provided by the *dichotic stimulation* technique. Different messages are presented simultaneously to each ear. Cherry (1953) made subjects repeat a prose passage being read into one ear, and then afterwards questioned them about the prose passage which had been presented to the other ear. All subjects could remember was whether the voice was male or female; they had not noticed that it was a foreign language or speech played backwards. It was inferred that a filter system (Broadbent, 1958) operated whereby both messages were identified according to their physical features, but then only one could be attended to, the other being filtered out. However, later experiments have shown that certain items can bypass the filter and be perceived even when the message that contains them is the one not being attended to. Such items are the subject's name (Moray, 1959), or the next word of an unfinished sentence, the previous part of which has been presented to the ear attended to (Treisman, 1960). Indeed, these items can even disrupt perception of the material presented to the ear attended to (Treisman, 1964). Clearly, the number of alternatives of which the item is one have been reduced by the context. The subjective value of the perception of the item to the perceiver is also a factor affecting the likelihood of its perception; Broadbent and Gregory (1963) have adapted the mathematical theory of signal detection to predict the relative effects of subjective value and predictability due to context. Other work in this tradition is that of Bruce (1958), who showed that the utterance of a key word (e.g. 'politics') can induce a set to perceive sentences in noise as sentences about a particular topic.

The above emphasis on the effect of context on the perception of items should not obscure the fact that there is a considerable literature on the *tachistoscopic recognition* of individual words as a function of their *frequency of occurrence* in the language (Solomon and Postman, 1952). However, it need not be assumed that the reason for shorter recognition times for more frequently used words is more frequent exposure to or use of those words. Rather, the correlation observed may be fairly specific to the experimental situation, and be due to the greater likelihood of a frequently used word being selected as a guess by the subject (Deese, 1961). Other variables have also been shown to affect recognition of tachistocopically presented words; the meaningfulness of a word (the number of word associations it elicits, see p. 82) and its rating on the evaluative scales of the semantic differential (see p. 91) are examples (Johnson, Frincke and Martin, 1961). There is also the voluminous literature on perceptual defence, which may or may not imply that other emotional factors are also involved. Finally, there is the finding of Zipf (1935) that the length of a word is negatively correlated with its frequency of usage, implying that common words may be perceived more easily because they are shorter. The overall position is far from clear. One thing that is obvious is that a word is not perceived better only because it has been experienced more frequently. Results concerning visual perception of words in isolation do not, in other words, justify the assumption that words are responses in a naïve behaviourist sense.

4. PHONOLOGICAL SKILLS – ARTICULATION

Output skill at the phonological level is termed *articulation*. Articulatory skill is described by linguists in terms of the manner and place of articulation; some of the terms used are defined on pp. 24–5 in the description of distinctive feature analysis. The position and action of the various speech organs are investigated by physiological phoneticians (see Gleason, 1961). They study the activity or lack of it in the larynx; the point of articulation, which is the place of maximum constriction in the mouth or pharynx; and the manner of articulation, the type of sound-producing or sound-modifying mechanism in the mouth or pharynx. Physiological mechanisms are invoked to explain certain features of speech. For example, the intercostal muscles between the ribs control, together with the diaphragm, the breathing of the speaker. More breath is required for a vowel than for a consonant, and the pulse of the intercostal muscles varies as the transition from vowel to consonant occurs. These pulses of the intercostal muscles may be the source of phonetic syllables, which usually centre round a vowel, with consonants surrounding it. Phonetic syllables are not necessarily phonemic – that is, they need not figure, as phonemes must, in a description of speech based on substitutionary procedures. Placing the syllable break at some other point in the speech sequence will not necessarily lead to a judgement that the utterance is different. It is clear that even the syllable is a skilled sequence of movements, in which surrounding context affects articulation (Lenneberg, 1967, pp. 103–7). 'Keep cool' presents two different articulations of the 'k' phoneme. Subsequent context determined the position of the tongue on the palate. The two syllables were obviously planned as wholes. Phoneticians have also shown that the interaction of syllables with each other affects their articulation. It should be noted, however, that the above motor theory of the syllable is by no means generally accepted among linguists.

A related psychological field of study is that of *delayed auditory feedback* (Yates, 1963). If a speaker does not hear the sound of his own voice until one-fifth of a second after he has uttered, his articulation is disrupted. He elongates vowels and stutters over consonants. Maximum disruption is caused by the delay of one-fifth of a second, and this may be around the time taken to utter a syllable. Lenneberg (1967) explains delayed auditory feedback in terms of a rhythm of activation and execution of the motor patterns of speech, which usually coincide with the syllables. Consonants occupy the activation stage, which leads to the vowel of the execution stage; meanwhile the feedback from the activation stage serves as a cue to initiate the next cycle. Delayed feedback therefore delays the initiation of the next cycle and results in the lengthening of the vowel in the execution phase.

Another skill involved in articulation is the use of acceptable sequences of sounds and the avoidance of non-acceptable sequences. Each language has acceptable sequences, and the linguists have formulated *morpho-phonemic rules* for generating these sequences. A formula (see Brown, 1965, p. 268) can be derived from the clusters of consonants found at the beginning of English words. This formula can produce clusters of phonemes which are possible according to the rules but do not actually occur (e.g. 'splob', 'sklit'). There is, thus, a double reduction in the number of eligible sequences of phonemes; firstly, by definition, those sequences are not used which are unlawful (according to the rules of the English language); and secondly, there are some sequences which are lawful but not used. This provides considerable *redundancy*; that is, the language user 'knows' that out of a great number of sequences of phonemes only a few are used in the language. Uncertainty on the perceiver's part as to the actual identity of the sounds is reduced because the number of possible alternatives is limited by the rules. Another result of the morpho-phonemic rules is *productivity*; that is, there are many sequences which could be used lawfully but have not yet been exploited.

In the case of *phonological* performance, then, one is justified in using the term *skill*. Hierarchical organisation, automatisation, feedback and anticipation are criterial features of skill, and are present at the phonological level. As has been seen, the perception of phonemes by distinctive features usually involves a series of *binary decisions*. Perceptual and articulatory performance is *automatised*, in the sense that there is no apparent difficulty in planning or perceiving at the phonological level, and in the sense that units such as the syllable allow smooth transition by virtue of their size. *Feedback* is involved, of an internal nature in perception, and of an external auditory as well as internal nature in articulation. *Anticipation* is required if one is to use succeeding phonetic context in perceiving and in articulating. Most important, the influence of semantic and syntactic variables on the perception of speech is evidence for the *hierarchical* nature of language behaviour as a whole, since it was stated to be one of the features of a hierarchy that levels interacted.

5. GRAMMATICAL SKILLS – WORDS AND FORM CLASSES

For the linguist, the grammatical level concerns the sequencing of morphemes in the formation of words and of sentences. *Morphemes* are described as minimal meaningful forms, and consist of sounds realising phonemes or groups of phonemes. 'Quick' is a free morpheme, '——ly' is a bound morpheme, and 'quickly' is an acceptable sequence of morphemes formed by applying morphological rules. 'Boys love girls' is a sequence of morphemes formed into a sentence by the application of syntactic rules. The combinations 'quickdom' and 'bringed' break the morphological rules; the sequence 'boys girls love' is not a sentence, since it breaks the syntactic rules. Morphological rules, in brief, apply to the formation of words, syntactic rules to the building of larger constructions than words.

A more detailed linguistic consideration of *morphemes* and morphological rules reveals certain features. The term 'meaningful' used in the above definition of a morpheme presents pitfalls. It does not imply reference, in the sense that 'cat' refers to a certain class of animal; for the word 'from' is a morpheme too. Rather, a morpheme has a characteristic *distribution*, that is, it can occur only in certain places in a sequence. 'From' can occur in 'I went home from work', but not 'I walked from'. Similarly, 'I bought some toys', but not 'I bought somes toy'. To qualify as a morpheme, however, a certain distribution is not enough. Phonemes, too, can have a distribution. In addition, it must be shown that the supposed morpheme has a regular relationship to some content feature whenever it occurs; and that this feature is absent when it does not occur. For example, it must be shown that whenever plural 's' occurs, there is some sort of plurality feature implied which is absent when it does not occur.

General linguistic statements about morphemes and their combination can be made only when certain *form classes* of morphemes have been established. A form class usually corresponds to a 'part of speech', and is a shorthand way of describing the privileges of occurrence of morphemes. For example, in 'Some —— has spilled on the floor' (where 'some' is stressed), the missing morpheme could only be a mass noun because only a mass noun has the privilege of occurring in that position in a sentence, given the surrounding context. It is stressed that linguists do not define parts of speech in terms of meaning – a noun is not the 'name of a place, person, or thing'. This is because the definitions are inadequate – when is an action a noun and when is it a verb? A further objection to meaning as a basis of form class is that words of similar meaning often have different functions, e.g. 'arrive' and 'arrival'. However, there is a definite probability that nouns are names of observable entities; but a statistical probability is an inadequate basis for a formal definition. And formal definitions rather than statements of probabilities are the aim of the linguist.

Before morphemes are divided into form classes, however, linguists make a more basic distinction between *roots* and *affixes*. A root is a morpheme like 'boy', 'girl', 'man' or 'pretty', 'red', 'nice', two groups of roots which belong to different form classes. Affixes consist of prefixes and suffixes, e.g. '*in*elegant', '*re*-read', '*non*conformist' and 'send*s*', 'post*ed*', 'quick*er*'. Suffixes which cannot be followed by any other phoneme are called inflexions. One cannot say 'post*ed*ly' or 'post*ed*s' or 'post*ed*ness', and therefore past-tense 'ed' is an inflexion. Some suffixes *can* be followed by another phoneme or morpheme. Their function is frequently to change the form class of a morpheme, e.g. 'kind' to 'kind*ness*', 'arrive' to 'arriv*al*'. In the case of inflexions, considerable phonetic differences occur within a given morpheme. Thus the plural 's' is different phonetically in the plural forms of 'house', 'cat' and 'care'.

There are morphemic rules for inflexion, which specify which classes of morphemes may be followed by which inflexions. Only verbs, for example, can be followed by third-person singular present tense 's' inflexion; only nouns by plural 's'; and only nouns by possessive 's'. Further, there are rules of inflexion within form classes; the third person singular of a present tense usually has 's' inflexion, the third person plural does not. English depends far less on inflexions than some other languages. Latin, for example, depended on inflexions to signal subject or object function in a sentence, while English relies more on word order. Inflexions do not only have a meaning content of their own; they also signal the form class of the word to which they are attached.

In linguistics, then, the morphological rules are distinguished by their *functional* nature. Form classes, for example, are described in terms of their privileges of occurrence within a sentence, not in terms of their general meaning. If it is hoped to approach meaning through grammar, then one cannot define one's grammar in terms of meaning. Morphemes themselves are distinguished by their relation to content, but the rules of their combination within words are not. The morphological rules are also distinguished by their *productivity*. New plural nouns can be formed by a child by adding the inflexion to a nonsense word, providing it is clear that the nonsense word is acting as a noun, e.g. 'Here is a wug. Here is another one. There are two . . .' 'Wugs' (Berko, 1958). Finally, morphological rules are distinguished by the *redundancy* they allow. Once again, redundancy is loosely described as reducing the number of possible alternatives which could be perceived or uttered. Redundancy involves the use of additional cues beyond those minimally necessary. In the case of inflexions, one can say that the plural inflexion in 'those boys are playing' is, strictly, unnecessary. If the inflexion were omitted, one still has the cues 'those' and 'are' to indicate plurality; while the form class of the word 'boys' is clear from the sentence structure. However, the presence of all three cues makes uncertainty minimal and a mistake in perception highly unlikely. The morphological rules also allow redundancy in the sense that they only allow certain combinations of morphemes, e.g. 'kindly' but not 'kinded'. Thus, like the rules for the combination of phonemes, they limit the number of possible alternatives and therefore the uncertainty.

These features of the morphological rules would allow one once again to use the term *skill* of performance based on them. For example, the combination of inflexion and root is obviously hierarchical in nature. It should be stressed, however, that the above account (based on Gleason, 1961) depends on linguistic rather than psychological evidence. Experiments indicating the psychological reality of the morphological level will now be reviewed. Many experiments which involve the use of inflexions (e.g. Epstein, 1961) also use function words (e.g. 'the'), however, and will be discussed later under the heading of syntactic level. This is unfortunate, since inflexions seem to perform the most important functions of denoting content (e.g. plurality) and also of signalling form class.

One group of experiments is expressly concerned with form class, however. The *word association* technique (see p. 82) has shown that the responses of adults and children above the age of seven or eight are predominantly *paradigmatic*. That is, their response to the stimulus word is of the same form class as that stimulus word. 'Red' is followed by 'blue' rather than by 'dress'. This latter is a *syntagmatic* response in that it is likely to follow the stimulus word in an utterance. Some associations will be both paradigmatic and syntagmatic, in the sense that the response word will both be substitutable for the stimulus word in a sentence, and also be likely to follow it in a sentence (it need not, of course, be the next word in the sentence). Therefore 'black–white' is both paradigmatic and syntagmatic; the syntagmatic feature is clear in such sentences as 'He sees everything in black and white'. 'White' is a more frequent response to 'black' than 'black' is to 'white', confirming this analysis; for sentences using the words 'black' and 'white' in that order seem likely to be more common than those using the words in the reverse order.

Granted that the two categories paradigmatic and syntagmatic are not mutually exclusive, however, one still has to explain why words of the same form class are chosen by adults. Let us suppose that the word association procedure has something in common with the speaker's perception and production of a sequence of words. Since word associations are usually paradigmatic, one can reject the proposition that sentences are produced in a left-to-right manner with one word acting as a stimulus to produce an association.

Ervin (1961) has tried to explain paradigmatic associations as the result of listeners' erroneous anticipations. When hearing a sentence, a listener makes certain anticipations, for example, what the grammatical object is going to be. Alternative expectations will probably be of the same form class, and one or more of them will by definition be wrong. It is these incorrect alternatives which are produced as paradigmatic responses. This approach allows retention of an associationist view of sentence perception, for it supposes that the alternatives are responses (of different probability of occurrence) to the previous context. McNeill (1963, 1966a) however, produces evidence which argues against the idea that the word association task involves the recall of alternatives. He used sentence frames in which to embed nonsense syllables, thereby providing the same privilege of occurrence for each of a pair of syllables. He concluded that associations are productions by the speaker according to rules; the rules concerned are the morphological and syntactic ones regarding the form class of a word and its function in a sentence. Thus it may be inferred that words are grouped by subjects into functional classes. Such classifications might provide part of a filing system for quick retrieval of items when creating sentences. Other parts of the system would be based on more semantic, less functional categories, e.g. whether an animate or an inanimate item was required. Clark (1968) supposes that the grammatical classes are based specifically on the phrase marker tree (see p. 39); free associations might be words of the same form class as the stimulus word; if not, they might be words of a form class occurring in a phrase of which the stimulus word is a part. For example, the response to 'up' might be 'down' or 'ladder'.

Deese (1962) found different degrees of paradigmatic response for stimulus words of different form class. Nouns and common adjectives produced more paradigmatic responses than other form classes, adverbs produced least. This is paralleled in the finding of Entwisle (1966) that paradigmatic responses occur earlier in children in the case of noun stimulus words than in the case of verbs and adverbs. Deese suggests that nouns are schematic for adults because 'they usually provide the source from which the larger segments of utterances are generated'. These findings may indicate that certain semantic rules are also concerned when adults give paradigmatic associations. Children learn the basic grammatical features of language long before the age of six to eight, which is when the shift from syntagmatic to paradigmatic occurs. Therefore it is tempting to suppose that paradigmatic responses require both syntactic *and* semantic rules to generate them. This may be why noun paradigmatic responses are most common – nouns have a set of semantic features which are possibly the first such features that the child learns; for example, the features animate, human, female, adult, etc. Other work concerning the relations between free associates will be reviewed later (pp. 82–3).

A more general distinction than that between form classes is between *content* and *function* words. Used by the linguists Fries (1952) and Jakobson and Halle (1956), this distinction is difficult to define clearly; function words are those which fall at the structural end of a continuum ranging from structural to semantic function. Examples of function words are 'and', 'but', 'through'; of content words 'table', 'disappear'. Glanzer (1962) found that in a paired-associate learning task, content words were better learned as associates to nonsense syllables than function words. However, function words were learned better when they were placed between two nonsense syllables. In other words, when they appeared to have a structural function, function words were learned better. However, Cofer (1967) showed that the same effect was not obtained when longer presentation times were allowed. This permitted subjects to speak the units more completely. It is therefore suggested by Cofer that the superiority of function words was caused by the greater pronunciability they provided. Since pronunciability is not a function of grammatical structure in any clear way, Glanzer's results are termed 'a rather fragile effect'. Another experiment showing a distinction between content and function words is that of Treisman (1965). She found that when subjects had to guess a word omitted from a passage, the guessing of function words was determined by longer-term sequential dependencies than the guessing of content words. In other words, function words were guessed with the aid of cues derived from words further away in the sentence. She attributes this finding to the dependence of function words on the whole sentence structure.

6. GRAMMATICAL SKILLS – SYNTAX

Linguistically, syntax concerns the principles by which words are formed into larger constructions. It will be remembered that words are either morphemes or combinations of morphemes, and that morphemes in their turn are phonemes or combinations of phonemes.

The major problem in the discovery of these principles is to discover the relative effects of sequential and hierarchical organisation. There is the temptation to regard the relationship between adjacent words as of primary importance. But words separated from each other by other words may be more closely related than adjacent words. For example, in the sentence 'We arrived in a broken-down hearse on the stroke of midnight,' the words 'arrived' and 'on', and the words 'in' and 'hearse' are more closely related than 'hearse' and 'on'. This intuitive analysis leads one to suspect that there are many relationships involved in a sentence, most of them involving units larger than one or two words in size. The role of these units in the perception of sentences can be clearly seen in sentences composed of nonsense words, but with inflexions and function words included, e.g. 'The erenstany cates elendied the edom eptly with ledear and aris'. The reader will find that after one or two readings he will structure this sentence as follows; 'The erenstany cates/elendied the edom eptly/with ledear and aris.'

Linguists have evolved the technique of *constituent analysis* to analyse the principles of syntax. A constituent is defined as any part of a construction which results from its being subdivided. Such division is necessary for the intuitive reasons mentioned above; also, because analysis in terms of such large constructions as sentences is impossible. It is impossible in that the number of sentence patterns needed to describe the corpus of actual (let alone possible) sentences is impracticably large. As Gleason (1961, p. 148) says, 'What a grammar must describe, then, is not sentence patterns, but the smaller units of pattern of which they are constructed. Only thus can a language be described.

. . .' When applying constituent analysis to a sentence, the linguist subdivides the sentence into subject and predicate as a first step (nevertheless, it is not taken for granted that every sentence contains a subject and predicate). The subject and predicate are the *immediate constituents*; an immediate constituent is the segment that results after a construction has been subdivided. The immediate constituents of the sentence 'Those boys loved the dodgems' are the subject, 'Those boys', and the predicate, 'loved the dodgems'. The predicate subdivides into 'loved' and 'the dodgems'; the subject into 'those' and 'boys'. 'The dodgems' subdivides into 'the' and 'dodgems'. Finally, 'boys' subdivides into 'boy' + 's', 'loved' into 'love' + 'ed', and 'dodgems' into 'dodgem' + 's'. The sentence is now subdivided into 'Those + boy + s + love + ed + the + dodgem + s'. These are the individual morphemes, the *ultimate constituents* of a sentence.

The above sequence can, of course, be written in terms of form classes: article + noun (plural) + verb (past) + article + noun (plural). This latter formulation is a sentence pattern – different morphemes could be fitted into the different 'slots' in the sentence frame to generate a new sentence. However, there are too many patterns for this to be an adequate description. It should also be noted, firstly, that discontinuous constituents occur: in the sentence 'Put the visitor off', 'put . . . off' is a discontinuous constituent; secondly, not all linguists agree that subdivision should always be binary. In summary, then, constituent analysis is a hierarchical procedure, subdividing sentences into ever smaller units.

As in the case of phonemic and morphemic analysis, linguists use informants to obtain the constituent structure. In such a construction as 'the boss's wife', the method of *comparison of samples* is used in analysis. There are three possible ways of subdividing this construction in a binary way: 'the boss's/wife', 'the/boss's wife', and 'the/boss's/ wife' (where 'the wife' is a discontinuous constituent). The method of comparison of samples involves presenting the informant with a two-word construction which he supposes to be directly comparable to 'the boss's wife'. 'Joe's wife' is such a construction; it could occur in similar environments to 'the boss's wife', and furthermore has the same features (e.g. possessive ' 's') which mark syntactic relationships. In fact, it is *substitutable* for 'the boss's wife' in many sentences, and will prove acceptable to a native speaker in that position. A further test deals with the *freedom of occurrence* of a constituent unit. If a unit is a constituent, it is more likely that it will occur in other utterances than a unit which is not a constituent. Thus, in the sentence 'Those boys loved the dodgems', 'those boys' can occur in many other utterances, but 'boys loved' would not occur so often. Finally, features such as stress and intonation patterns (supra-segmentals) are used to discover which sub-divisions lead to immediate constituents and which do not.

A linguistic development from immediate constituent analysis is *phrase structure grammar* (Chomsky, 1957). This adopts the principle of generation of the finished sentence by rules. The rules are termed rewrite rules; they are applied to sets of symbols, which symbolise constructions of ever decreasing size. Thus the first rule of a phrase-structure grammar is usually S (sentence) $\rightarrow$ NP + VP (where NP = noun phrase, VP = verb phrase, and the arrow denotes 'is sub-divided into . . .'). The derivation (or resulting constituents) of this first rule are then inscribed. They are, of course, NP + VP. A rule is then applied to one of those constituents, for example, NP $\rightarrow$ Art + N, the derivation now being Art + N + VP, (where Art = Article). A rule is applied to VP, VP $\rightarrow$ V + NP. The derivation is Art + N + V + NP. A rule is applied to NP, NP $\rightarrow$ Art + N. The derivation is Art + N + V + Art + N. One is thus left with a sequence of morpheme classes. The specific memberships and inflexions may be added, to give Art (demonstrative) + N (plural) + Aux + V + Art (definite) + N (plural) (where Aux = Auxiliary). However, it is not clear *how* the correct memberships and inflexions can be added. The derivation of the sentence 'Those boys loved the dodgems' follows the above pattern. It should be noted that the product of this final set of symbols is 'Those + boy + s + ed + love + the + dodgem + s'. A transformation (see p. 63) has to be applied to this product to place the '– ed' after 'love' and thereby produce the final English sentence. This final sentence is to be described in terms of *surface* structure, whereas the symbols used in the phrase marker tree describe features of *deep* structure (see p. 63). The analysis consists entirely of symbols until the selection of lexical items is reached. This follows the semantic rules, a separate component of the linguistic model. A tree diagram may be formed to depict the rewrite rules more graphically. This starts with a node at the top, which subdivides into two branches leading to nodes labelled, respectively, NP and VP. These subdivide into nodes labelled Art and N . . . (etc.).

The linguistic difference between immediate constituent analysis and phrase structure grammar is that the latter is explicitly *generative*. The use of symbols denoting form classes enables the number of possible sentences that might be uttered to be continuously narrowed down until the specific pattern of the sentence in question is generated. Thus

Chomsky would say that the topmost level of the phrase-structure grammar, 'sentence', represents a limitless number of alternatives. The final derivation of morpheme classes still allows an immense number of possible sentences as alternatives. From Art (demonstrative) + N (plural) + Aux + V + Art (definite) + N (plural) could be derived 'those boys loved the dodgems' or 'those dogs savaged the postmen' or many others. Thus immediate constituent analysis and phrase-structure grammars are based on the same principles as each other. They both start their analysis from the sentence as a whole; but the phrase-structure grammar uses grammatical symbols to describe the successive subdivisions of the sentence, and leaves the selection of words and their transformation into surface structure to another part of the model.

7. GRAMMATICAL SKILLS – LEFT-TO-RIGHT ANALYSIS

Behaviourist psychology, in contrast to linguistics, has concentrated on *left-to-right* dependencies. That is, any temporal sequence of responses was treated as a chain. When a chain was being learned, each response was under the control of an external stimulus. However, after some learning, preceding responses acted as stimuli to the next response. This was known as afferent stimulus interaction (Hull, 1930). Lashley (1951) warned that this model was inadequate; overall organisational schemata had to be postulated to account for most skilled performances. However, his warnings did not prevent the adoption by psychologists of the Markov probability model as a description of language behaviour. This model was derived from the work of information theorists in the field of communications. It assumes that the probability of any item is determined by the number of alternatives from which it is drawn; by the possibility of occurrence of the particular item if the items have differing probabilities from each other; and by the predictability provided by the preceding context. These three variables are not independent of each other; for example, the number of alternatives from which an item is drawn is limited by the preceding context (see Attneave, 1959, for an introductory account).

This theory was applied to language by means of the technique of *approximations to English* (Miller and Selfridge, 1950). The preceding verbal context to any word was controlled by the experimenter, and a speaker of English produced a word under these constraints. The different orders of approximation were produced as follows. Zero-order consisted of words chosen at random, first order of words chosen according to their relative probability of occurrence (both from Thorndike and Lorge, 1944). Second-order approximation was produced by presenting a common word, such as 'he', 'it', or 'the' to a person, who is instructed to use the word in a sentence. The word he uses directly after the one given him is then noted, and later presented to another person who has not heard the sentence given by the first person. He, in turn, is asked to use that word in a sentence. The word he uses directly after the one given him is then noted and later given to yet another person. This procedure is repeated until a sequence of 10, 20, 30 or 50 words is constructed. The resulting sequence contains successive pairs of words, each of which could go together in a sentence. Each word is determined in the context of only one preceding word. Higher orders of approximation are produced by people using sequences of a given number of words in a sentence. The word used directly after the sequence would be added, the first word deleted, and the new, but overlapping sequence presented to the next person. Order of approximation is $n + 1$, where n is the number of words in the sequence presented. Examples of different orders of approximation of 10 word sequences are:

zero-order: byway consequence handsomely financier bent flux cavalry swiftness weather-beaten extent
first-order: abilities with that beside I for waltz you the sewing
second-order: was he went to the newspaper is in deep and
third-order: tall and thin boy is a biped is the beat
fourth-order: saw the football game will end at midnight on January
fifth-order: they saw the play Saturday and sat down beside him
seventh-order: recognise her abilities in music after he scolded him before
text: the history of California is largely that of a railroad

Miller and Selfridge, using a measure of number of words recalled regardless of order, found that recall of sequences by other subjects increased as the order of approximation to English increased. This facilitating effect was more pronounced as the size of the sequence presented increased; and there was no significant improvement in recall of text over recall of fifth-order approximation. These results must not be interpreted as showing that subjects used the same techniques to recall the material as the experimenters did to produce it. Miller and Selfridge supposed that sequences increased in meaningfulness (short-range semantic and syntactic associations) as order of approximation increased; and that the higher the order, the more likely it was that these short-term associations learned by subjects in their normal use of language would be preserved. These factors explained the improved recall for the higher orders. However, it is not clear that change in *strength* of association is involved; it may be that for higher orders the *balance* of the constraints is different. For as order of approximation increases, so does the amount of grammatical structure present. Furthermore, higher orders may provide more associations between items not juxtaposed. Marks and Jack (1952) found that when ordered recall was required, there *was* a difference between fifth-order and text material. One would expect grammatical constraints to operate at the sentence level, whereas meaningfulness (in Miller and Selfridge's sense) might reach a maximum by around a fifth-order approximation. Marks and Jack's result may therefore be taken to indicate the presence of long term grammatical constraints. So may the finding of Aborn *et al.* (1959) who reported that a missing word was guessed more proficiently when previous and subsequent context was given than when the same amount of previous context only was provided.

Research on the position in the sequence of the items recalled indicates that the later items were better recalled in zero and lower-order approximations (the recency effect), but the early items in the higher-order approximation (the primacy effect) (Deese and Kaufman, 1957). This finding supports the theory that higher-order approximations are learned better because of the sequential constraints involved; but Mandler and Mandler (1964) indicate that the recall curves for sentences are due to their grammatical structure and not to the serial order of words. Since sequential constraints are used to produce approximations with little regard for grammatical structure, it is hardly surprising that they feature more strongly as cues for recall; but this finding does not require the inference that sentences are processed in the same way. As has been said, different constraints may be operating at different orders, with grammatical constraints strongest at text (or sentence) level. These inferences are supported by Coleman (1963) and Tulving and Patkau (1962), who both showed that the 'learning curve' was not in fact typically negatively accelerated, but was, on the contrary, positively accelerated when different methods of calculating results were used. When chunks of words in the correct order were scored, performance improved more rapidly for the higher orders of approximation; and neither word frequency nor the interaction between word frequency and order of approximation were significant (though they were when results were calculated in terms of number of words correct). The process is clearly therefore not a unitary learning process. Grammatical features play a greater part the more closely the material resembles the sentence. If the greater ease of recall were caused by associations between adjacent words, then one would predict a more linear improvement, since the number of such associations increases in a linear manner.

8. GRAMMATICAL SKILLS – TOP-TO-BOTTOM ANALYSIS

It is therefore clear that *left-to-right* sequential dependencies, either of a Markovian nature or simple word-to-word associations, cannot alone describe adequately the perception, storage, and production of language. Grammatical structure must be incorporated into any psychological model. As has been seen, grammatical structure as described by the phrase-structure grammar is hierarchical, *top-to-bottom* in nature. If the phrase-structure grammar were transferred wholesale and given the status of a psychological model, then the hypothesis would be that all items were produced in a top-to-bottom way by the subdivision of larger constituents. Any adequate theory will have to assess the relative contributions of top-to-bottom and left-to-right dependencies.

Johnson (1965) placed considerable emphasis on top-to-bottom dependencies. He supposed that subjects would organise sentences into chunks when given the task of recalling them. These chunks would correspond to the phrase units isolated by phrase-structure analysis. Analysis of data was by calculation of transitional error probability (TEP). TEP is the probability that a subsequent word is incorrect or omitted given that the preceding word is correct. Highest TEPs were predicted, and found, between phrase units; this was taken to indicate that phrase units were chunks, in the Miller (1956) sense. Support for this conclusion is derived indirectly from Epstein (1961) and directly from Herriot (1967). However, Johnson also found that there was a predictable TEP pattern at a sub-phrase level. In fact, the TEPs from word to word were higher if the subsequent word was the beginning of a constituent unit larger than a word. To illustrate: in the recall of the sentence 'The tall boy saved the dying woman', the highest TEP occurred between 'boy' and 'saved', since this is a major constituent break. However, there was also a higher TEP between 'the' and 'tall' than between 'tall' and 'boy'; and a higher TEP between 'the' and 'dying' than between 'dying' and 'woman'.

These findings led Johnson to postulate a model of sentence production which could be described as the *decoding* hypothesis (see Figure 1). He supposed that subjects completely plan an utterance, then decode it step by step in terms of the phrase structure rules. Therefore the transition from 'boy' to 'saved' is difficult because it is not in fact a word to word transition. Rather, it is a transition from word to predicate. The

transition from 'the' to 'tall' is from word to a unit consisting of
modifier + noun. The transition from 'tall' to 'boy', however, is from
word to word, since 'boy' is not the beginning of a higher-order unit.
These structural effects were further illustrated in an experiment
(1966a) in which associations between 'tall' and 'boy', and 'boy' and
'saved' were learned. This learning of the former pair decreased TEP,
when they were integrated into the sentence, but the learning of the latter
pair did not. Latency of recall was shown (1966b) to differ according to
quite minor changes in the complexity of the sentence structure.

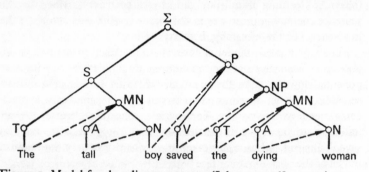

Figure 1. Model for decoding a sentence (Johnson, 1968, p. 441).
Dotted lines indicate decoding operations.
Σ = sentence, subdividing into S (subject) and P (predicate).
NP = noun phrase, M = modifier, T = definite article, A = adjective.

Johnson's experimental procedure may have influenced his theory.
For in a recall task, subjects must analyse structure provided for them
in the sentence, store it in this form, and then decode it when recall is
required. It seems a rash step to suppose that sentences are normally
produced in this way; it is highly unlikely on *a priori* grounds that
sentences are completely planned grammatically before they are uttered.
However, it is possible that Johnson does not intend this inference to be
generalised beyond the recall situation.

Johnson's model also appears to disregard the possibility that
Markovian probabilities are involved in the generation of sentences.
However, the TEPs within phrases decrease as the phrase proceeds, and
therefore could equally well be explained in Markovian as in phrase-
structure terms; for what has been shown is that as the amount of prior
context within a phrase increases, the number of alternative words that
could follow decreases. Moreover, left-to-right constraints are implied
by the TEP analysis itself, which is from left-to-right; when TEP
analysis was applied in reverse, i.e. when the number of correct words

preceded by an incorrect or omitted word was calculated, no correlation with sentence structure was found (Johnson, 1968). Furthermore, Johnson found a primacy effect, in that the earlier parts of the sentence were better remembered than the later. The unlikelihood of complete planning in advance also makes more probable the existence of divergent hierarchies of responses of differing probability.

Furthermore, it is clear that Johnson's model does not preclude the possibility of word-to-word associations being involved in sentence production. His experiment (1966a) requiring prior paired-associate (see p. 86) learning of 'tall-boy' did show a decrease in TEP when the sentence containing those words was learned. This association is at the lowest level of the hierarchy, however.

Finally, Johnson's model is entirely grammatical in nature. It supposes that the analysis of the sentence is into its phrase-structure components. However, it might be equally true that storage is in terms of semantic content; semantic content can clearly agree with syntactic constituents in many cases. For example, one might expect the unit 'tall boy' to be stored in related semantic categories, but not 'boy saved'. Instead, Johnson has taken over into psychology the linguistic model of the phrase-marker tree with the selection of words pictured as occurring after the derivation of the word classes. One is justified in asking what determines the selection of NP $\rightarrow$ Art + Adj + N rather than NP $\rightarrow$ Art + N; in other words, why is the noun qualified in this sentence but not in another? And what determines the selection of 'tall' rather than 'huge' or 'clever'? In both these cases meaning is involved, and if selection of lexical items is left till the end of the structural derivation, no scope is given for meaning until grammar has been determined.

However, despite these criticisms, Johnson's work is of vital importance. It makes it clear that simple item-to-item associations cannot by themselves account for recall of sentences; that the chunks formed correspond to the phrase units of phrase-structure analysis; and that a central integrative process must occur before the generation of a response sequence (but this need not be a complete plan). Moreover, Johnson (1968) is now working on experiments which seem to indicate that the same principles of organisation are applied by subjects to non-language material; these are vital findings, for they suggest that language ability is part and parcel of more general cognitive ability (see chapter VI).

An interesting and totally different technique should now be mentioned, because it provides independent evidence for the psychological reality of units derived from the phrase-structure rules. Ladefoged and

Broadbent (1960) found that when clicks were introduced into sentences being listened to, the subjects reported afterwards that the click had occurred before the unit (often the word) within which it had actually occurred. Fodor and Bever (1965) found that the click was not necessarily placed *in front of* the unit in which it occurred. Rather, it was displaced to the nearest major break between syntactic constituents, whether these were before or after the click. These results could not be attributed to the clicks being attracted to the nearest *acoustic* break. On some occasions acoustic breaks do coincide with constituent breaks, but on others they do not. There was no difference between results for sentences where there was this coincidence and sentences where there was not. Two inferences can therefore be drawn. Firstly, constituent units are perceptual units, in that they preserve their integrity by resisting interruptions. Secondly, the perception involved is active rather than passive; the perceiver applies the structure himself, it is not given him by direct physical signals.

Related to these findings are those concerning *pauses* in speech production. If language is planned as a sequence, then pauses should occur before items of low transitional probability. If, however, it is planned hierarchically, then one would predict pauses before constituent units.

The answers to these predictions have not yet been provided. Goldman–Eisler (1968) and Maclay and Osgood (1959) find that both sequential and hierarchical constraints are operating, and Martin (1967) that decoders of a message placed more pauses at grammatical boundaries, encoders before difficult content words. However, Boomer (1965) reports that when structural units are defined in terms of stress, pauses occur most frequently *after* the first word of such units. He' maintains that this is caused by the speaker having already planned the grammar of the unit but having not yet selected the words; for the first word already constrains the grammatical constructions to follow. Therefore, the lexical selection must occupy the pause. It is clear that this interpretation supports Chomsky (against Osgood, 1968) in his proposal that syntactic structure is applied before semantic selection. It is noteworthy that Boomer does not define his grammatical units in terms of phrase-structure grammar, but in a less formal, more individual way; stress patterns differ considerably between individuals and units based on them may reflect individualistic ways of combining syntax and semantics. Suci (1967) minimised grammatical structure of utterances and found that material consisting of units originally divided by pauses was still more easily learned than material consisting of units not originally so divided. He also found inter-individual differences between subjects. The study of pausal phenomena may, therefore, be a healthy corrective against an over-formalisation of theory.

9. GRAMMATICAL SKILLS – INTERACTION

It is clear that the phrase-structure model cannot be taken over whole-sale from linguistics to psychology. Even a psychological theory such as Johnson's, which leans heavily on it, does not incorporate all its pre-suppositions. Firstly, if a phrase-structure model is taken to be psychological, it omits the possibility of left-to-right dependencies; it has been, and will be, shown that these are involved in sentence perception and production. Secondly, it separates syntax from semantics. The lexical choices are made only after the constituents have been subdivided into form classes. Osgood (1968) maintains that in the psychological process of production, content is selected *before* it is ordered grammatically; and there are good grounds for thinking that the syntactic and semantic features are closely inter-related (see Chapter III). In fact, some linguists' intuitive conviction that syntax and semantics are for analytical purposes distinct is the only reason for incorporating the phrase-structure model as it stands into a psychological model.

Psychological criteria for inclusion of any theory into a psychological model include the following: 1. The units postulated must be response units; that is they usually occur or do not occur, rather than occur partially, and they are affected as a whole by independent variables. 2. The units may be overt or mediational. A mediational response is not observed in behaviour, but inferred from it. It does not necessarily take the form of the overt behavioural response; it need not be pictured for example, as a subvocal repetition to oneself of a word. The important features of mediating responses are, firstly, that they act as stimuli for overt or for other mediational responses; and, secondly, that several external stimuli may elicit the same mediating response, and the same mediating response may act as stimulus for several different external responses. The concept of mediation is more fully discussed in Chapter IV. The speed of response involved in language behaviour seems to require the postulation of higher-order mediational units. If they are mediational, the theory that abstract formulae, such as NP or VP and their subcategories, may be internal response units must be considered (Jenkins, 1965). 3. Relationships between response units must be taken into account. The relative effects of top-to-bottom and left-to-right dependencies must be ascertained, and the possibilities of two-way interaction of levels in top-to-bottom analysis and of interaction of syntactic and semantic features must be considered.

The proposal of a combination of *top-to-bottom* and *left-to-right* dependencies has been made by Osgood (1963) in an article which is essential reading for those wishing to obtain a sophisticated behaviourist model for language behaviour. Osgood suggests that left-to-right sequential dependencies exist at every level (see Figure 2). The left-to-right relationship can occur at the symbolic level, e.g. NP + VP. He

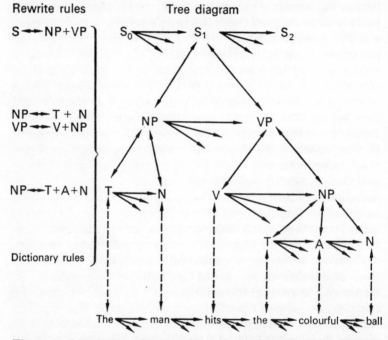

Figure 2. Integration of sequential and simultaneous hierarchies. A phrase-structure tree, with the addition of divergent sequential hierarchies of differing probability and preceding and subsequent sentences (from Osgood, 1963, p. 743). Top-to-bottom directional arrows indicate production; bottom-to-top, perception.

suggests that the relationship is a probability one, and therefore that the + symbol should be replaced by a divergent hierarchy of alternative responses of differing probability. This probability is determined by the frequency of the response itself and its likelihood in the particular context of the previous item or items. As a result of this feature of his theory, Osgood does not need to postulate, as Johnson does, that every detail of a sentence is encoded in advance and then decoded for the purposes of utterance. Another feature of Osgood's theory is that production proceeds from top-to-bottom of the phrase-marker tree, and perception from bottom-to-top. This seems an exaggerated description of the fact that the listener has no grammatical cues right at the beginning of a sentence; for it is clear that he rapidly obtains certain grammatical expectations (for example, if the sentence begins with the word 'the'). Furthermore, unlike Johnson, Osgood does not place the semantic component after the grammatical encoding and decoding; instead, he considers that semantic factors are primary in language production. He supposes (1968) that there is a generating power in the semantic component of the utterance which indicates to what levels of the phrase-structure tree encoding should go. For example, if the speaker wished to speak about boys in general, then the phrase structure tree need not subdivide further than N ('boys') as subject. However, if he wished to refer to one of several boys, he would be forced to form an NP consisting of article + adjective + noun ('the tall boy'). Osgood also considers that there are semantic rules indicating that words can only be used together if they share certain features. For example, 'it shouts' is anomalous because it breaks a semantic rule to the effect that the subject of various verbs such as 'speaks', 'shouts', etc., must be human and animate. Osgood also admits that the speaker stores language items in banks consisting of deep structure units (see Chapter III). The same sort of transitional dependency occurs between these deeper units as between the words within phrases.

Certain experiments which use sentences in an effort to shed light on the relative contributions of these left-to-right and top-to-bottom factors will be described now. Rosenberg (1966) investigated the effects of grammatical structure and associative value on the recall of sentences. Grammatical structure was manipulated by randomising word order. Associative value was assigned to all words of a sentence by selecting a noun which had as common free associates (see p. 82) two adjectives and a verb. An adverbial inflexion was added to one of the adjectives and the four words combined in a sentence, e.g. 'Shrill whistles blow loudly'. For low associative value, uncommon associates were selected, resulting in 'Orange whistles smile harshly'; associative value and grammatical structure were found to have significant and independent effects. It is worth asking, however, what one is doing when one is randomising word order in a sentence. This may be disruptive for several reasons, including left-to-right associative frequency between words and between form classes. Secondly, by forming the sentences from free association norms, it has not been shown that the psychological process involved is that of association between words. It is just as arguable that the high-association sentences are better recalled because they conform to semantic rules (see p. 65); in the case of the above examples, the selection of 'smile' would be prohibited by the semantic rules since it would involve a word with an animate feature ('smile') following one with an inanimate feature ('whistle').

Gladney and Krulee (1967) introduced errors into sentences to be recognised. They found that recognition was impaired more when the main verb was in error than when the subject and object were in error; these in their turn were more disruptive than an adjective or adverb in error. They inferred that these differences were due to the part the different form classes played in making clear the structure of the sentence. The main verb indicates the end of the noun phrase and the beginning of the predicate; however, in the case of the subject and object, determiners such as 'the' remain to indicate phrase structure. Adjectives and adverbs are so closely embedded between determiners and nouns, or after verbs, that they can be supplied in place of the error without much difficulty. Certain grammatical features are more valuable as cues to the phrase-structure of a sentence than others. It is clear that these features tend to occur at the beginning of phrase units; the language, in other words, provides cues to aid the perception of phrase units and probably their recall. Despite this aid, recall is more apt to be incorrect between phrases than within them, as Johnson found. Nevertheless, one must suppose that if the material were divided into non-phrase units, recall between units would be even worse. This would be due to the lack of the cues which inflexions and function words provide at the beginning of phrases. Herriot (1967) provides evidence which supports this suggestion.

Clark (1965, 1966) and Clark and Begun (1968) produce further evidence for both hierarchical and left-to-right processes, in this case in sentence comprehension. When rating sentences of varying degrees of anomaly for their sensibility, subjects rated as having little sense sentences with inadmissible subjects, sentences without verb and object agreement, and sentences without subject and predicate agreement. They concentrated, in other words, on the larger-scale units of the phrase-marker tree in a hierarchical manner. However, when asked to alter one word in the sentence to induce more sense, subjects changed words at the end of the sentence more often than words at the beginning, regardless of whether those words were the logical subject or object. This indicated a left-to-right process, which Clark and Begun explain not in associational terms but as being a result of the first words of a sentence containing the theme of that sentence; subjects are therefore unwilling to change it.

An attempt to tie in the phrase-structure approach with the field of short-term memory has been made by Yngve (1960). Yngve uses the term '*commitments*' to describe the number of coding units which the speaker has committed himself to utter. In the sentence 'My child likes the television', the use of the word 'my' commits the speaker to utter two decoding units. The first is the noun or noun phrase which must follow 'my', the second is a verb phrase to act as predicate. If either of these commitments were unfulfilled, a grammatical error would result: one cannot grammatically say 'my likes the television' nor 'my child'. Yngve's is thus the most parsimonious hypothesis possible: that the speaker only commits himself to those grammatical commitments which are necessary for the production of a sentence. It is not necessary to suppose, on this view, that the whole sentence is planned down to morpheme level before a decoding occurs, and in this respect Yngve's view is preferable to Johnson's.

Yngve has devised a metric for the *depth* of sentences. The number of commitments for each word of the sentence is calculated by adding up the left branches of the phrase-marker tree which describes it. A mean sentence depth is then calculated by dividing the total depth of all words by the number of words. Yngve supposes that commitments have to be stored in the short-term memory until they are fulfilled. He further supposes that a listener has expectations which correspond to the speaker's commitments, and that a similar load is placed on his short-term memory. Add to these grammatical commitments the various semantic constraints, and it is clear that the number of items to be retained in the short-term memory might well approach Miller's (1956) limit of seven, plus or minus two. Martin and Roberts (1966) found that sentences of different Yngve depth were differentially recalled, and explained a finding previously attributed to transformational type (see Chapter III) in terms of phrase structure commitments. It is clear that throughout the subject part of the sentence, the speaker/listener has to retain the commitment/expectation to utter a predicate. Therefore a sentence with a phrase added to the subject is more difficult to deal with than one with the same material tagged on to the predicate (Herriot, 1968*b*).

Objections to a phrase-structure approach include the unlikelihood of sentences being planned completely before they are decoded and uttered. However, Osgood's and Yngve's analyses allow the speaker to produce sub-phrase units as he goes along. Indeed, the indications that left-to-right Markovian processes are at work within phrase units support such a view. Secondly, phrase-structure analyses picture grammatical production as occurring separately from semantic choice of words, although the inclusion of word-to-word associations into the model partly removes this objection. The remaining objections to the phrase-structure formulation are based on theories of *competence* (see Chapter III). Thus, for example, it is supposed that the grammatically competent language user can, *in theory*, produce infinitely long and infinitely embedded sentences. Phrase-structure rules could not deal with such sentences, and therefore it is assumed that they are inadequate as part of a theory of the language user. It is clear that such a view depends on the possibility of a total dichotomy between competence and performance; also on the proposal that no model can serve as part of a theory unless it embraces every type of data, performance and intuition. This will be discussed in Chapter III, together with various other features of language (e.g. transformations and deep structure) which may require more than Osgood's theory by way of explanation.

10. SUB-SENTENCE STRUCTURE

It has been clear from the previous section that there is considerable variance in accounts of structure at the sub-sentence level. 1. Some theorists, mostly followers of Chomsky, maintain that the whole structure of the sentence is to be described in top-to-bottom terms. Each rule of the phrase-structure grammar describes a process of differentiation from a larger to a smaller unit. Therefore the items within a phrase unit are just as much the product of a top-to-bottom analysis as the phrases themselves. These theorists maintain that the units in the finished sentence are derived by means of transformations from the deep structure (see Chapter III).

2. Others (e.g. Rosenberg, 1966; Osgood, 1963) see the need to introduce left-to-right associative dependencies between items. Osgood suggests that this occurs in the manner specified by information theory – the Markov process. Each item produced changes the nature of the source and allows a new set of alternatives from which the next item is selected. This process is supposed to occur within different levels of the phrase-structure tree, not just within the phrase unit level. Jenkins (1965), too, suggests that left-to-right relationships occur between form classes, and probably between higher order units as well (e.g. noun phrase and verb phrase). Thus one expects the association adjective-

noun, in that order, within a phrase, and possibly also the association noun phrase-verb phrase, in that order, within a sentence. These higher-order units are, of course, mediating responses, in the sense that language behaviour is derived from them but does not consist of them. They are taken to be the form-classes discovered by the linguists because these are functionally equivalent, and thereby fulfil the criterion for being a response class.

3. Finally, Braine (1963a) suggests that response units are those sequences of speech which have been observed by the perceiver to occur in a certain position in a larger segment. He emphasises the position of an item in a grammatical construction as being of vital importance. He supposes that grammatical skills are explicable in terms of *contextual generalisation*. That is, the language user hears a segment of speech within a larger construction; each time he hears the segment occupying the same position, he is generalising, until he is able to produce it in the right position in the context of a different utterance of his own. The segment has become a response unit. Such response units are hierarchically organised – one segment becomes a response unit because of its regular position in a larger construction; this construction in its turn becomes a response unit because of its position in a larger unit (and so on, up to sentence level).

Accounts (2) and (3) above are couched in terms of learning theory and therefore to a certain extent are theories of language acquisition as well as of language behaviour. Either way, they face certain objections based on a radical reappraisal of the nature of language (see Chapter III). As theories of language behaviour, they neglect features of language which cannot be described in terms of constituent analysis; as theories of language acquisition, they are alleged to neglect the hypothesis that these deeper features are the first employed by children (see Chapter V). However, it should be stressed that aspects of theory based on experimental findings should not be jettisoned merely because they do not account for all the features of language behaviour.

Experimental evidence not using sentence material for the existence of response units of sub-sentence but supra-form-class size will now be reviewed. Essentially these experiments are concerned with sequential dependencies between adjacent form classes. Gonzalez and Cofer (1959) found that in a free recall task (see p. 95), adjective-noun combinations showed more clustering than other pairs, e.g. verb-adverb. Rosenberg (1965) found that adjective-noun and noun-adjective pairs were better recalled than adjective-adjective and noun-noun pairs. When associative probability of the two words concerned was minimised by the use of low-frequency words, however, adjective-noun pairs were not recalled better than the other pairs; but the adjective-noun pairs did have significantly less words out of place in the recall. Thus associative habit rather than grammatical-class probably accounts for the greater ease of recall of adjective-noun pairs. However, different results may be obtained with different sized units: Rosenberg and his co-workers also found that when words arranged in sentences and phrases were learned with word-frequency equated, there *was* an effect of form class. Adjectives and nouns were easier to learn than verbs and adverbs, but adjectives were no easier than verbs and adverbs when the words were presented in isolation. Moreover, sentences were recalled better than phrases, which in their turn were recalled better than isolated words. Form-class dependencies appear to have a greater effect the larger the response unit concerned.

11. CONCLUSIONS

The term *skill* as defined at the beginning of this chapter is as applicable to the grammatical level of analysis as it is to the phonological. Especially noticeable at the grammatical level has been the *hierarchical* nature of skill; also the preoccupation with response units and their markers, which enable smooth production to occur. However, it must be admitted that the relative importance of top-to-bottom and left-to-right dependencies has not been made clear. A solution probably demands new experimental techniques. The nature and size of the units of each of these types of dependency requires elucidation. Also, the relationship of perception and production is far from clear. Those who favour the competence model of Chomsky (see Chapter III) suggest that perception and production are both based on the same basic knowledge of his language that a native speaker has. However, those who refuse to admit a simple dichotomy between basic competence and actual performance require further evidence. Unfortunately, much of the psychological research is based on techniques which do not permit the parts played by perception and production to be distinguished. Nevertheless, there does seem to be a lot of evidence suggesting that the two are based on the same principles. The motor theory of speech perception is derived from such evidence; so is much of the phrase-structure theorising (e.g. Johnson, Yngve). However, it must be noted that perception demands low level analysis at first by the hearer (Osgood); the level of the syllable, important in production, is of little significance in perception; and it is also true that aphasia may reflect a predominantly receptive or a predominantly productive impairment (see p. 126). Moreover, comprehension is easier for children than production.

It should also be noted that the chapter has concerned perception and production of language only. That is, the attention has been concentrated on the language user's behaviour in terms of utterances or response to utterances; inferences have then been made to his functioning. No attention has been paid to a third factor, that of meaning. The use of the term meaning implies a situational context in which an utterance is made, and a communicative purpose in making it. When this factor is brought into the analysis, attempts to define language behaviour in terms of skill become more difficult. This is because the terminology used to describe skills refers only to the integration of sensory stimuli and motor responses, whereas an adequate account of meaning requires the postulation of representational thinking or cognitive categories. As will be seen from the following chapter, it is probably impossible to separate syntax from meaning, since meaning is involved in every syntactic structure. This is because certain syntactic structures are habitually used in certain situations and are structurally suited to describing them. Syntactic structures and form classes therefore tend to have a meaning.

III

Generative Linguistics and Psychology

I. CHOMSKY'S GENERAL APPROACH

Recently a comprehensive linguistic theory has been formulated by Chomsky (1957, 1965) and his colleagues (Katz and Postal, 1964) based on the productive features of language. Firstly, Chomsky's general assumptions will be described and criticised, and his linguistic theory will be outlined. An immediate problem is whether the theory is linguistic or psychological in nature. It should be made clear from the start that Chomsky and his colleagues are rationalists and not empiricists. They see no objection to the concept of specific innate ideas, and find no difficulty in internalising into the language user the rules of language they have derived by intuitive linguistic analysis. Their procedure therefore differs from the empiricist approach in that they do not derive their inferences about the language user's production or perception from his behaviour. Rather, they derive linguistic descriptions from their own intuitive analysis of language. They seldom use informants, but themselves produce 'sentences' such as 'Colourless green ideas sleep furiously'. Such a sentence is judged grammatical but meaningless on intuitive grounds. Rules are formulated which describe its grammatical nature; these are distinguished from semantic rules which in this case are broken; and the rules are internalised into the language user as his *competence*.

That Chomsky's theory is a psychological one may be inferred from the following: 'A grammar of a language purports to be a description of the ideal speaker/hearer's intrinsic competence' (Chomsky, 1965, p. 4) (the word 'grammar' is used of the set of rules which adequately describes all possible sentences; rules are the individual descriptions which derive one construction from another). 'Obviously, every speaker of a language has mastered and internalised a generative grammar that expresses his knowledge of his language' (1965, p. 8). Yet Chomsky insists that he is not providing a model for a speaker or a hearer.

'To avoid what has been a continuing misunderstanding, it is perhaps worthwhile to reiterate that a generative grammar is not a model for a speaker or a hearer. It attempts to characterise in the most neutral possible terms the knowledge of the language that provides the basis for actual use of language by a speaker-hearer' (1956, p. 9).

This apparent double-talk is probably explicable in terms of Chomsky's basic rationalist assumptions; that innate ideas can be assumed without experimental evidence, and that their effect on behaviour is very indirect. He assumes that there is a level of analysis which deals with *performance*, and which is the sphere of the psychologist and other behavioural scientists. Their concern is with the effects of the limitations of the central nervous system on language behaviour. The language user has, for example, limited channel capacity, limited short-term memory, and limited attention. Although performance is derived from *competence*, the competence model produced by the linguist is not intended for or adequate as a model of the language user.

'No doubt a reasonable model of language use will incorporate, as a basic component, the generative grammar that expresses the speaker-hearer's knowledge of the language; but this generative grammar does not, in itself, prescribe the character or functioning of a perceptual model or a model of speech production' (1965, p. 9).

It seems clear, then, that Chomsky is speaking of psychological entities both when he talks of competence and when he talks of performance. However, he insists on their separation for purposes of definition and analysis. He regards competence as being derived wholly from linguistic considerations; his description of it as 'knowledge' is particularly typical of a rationalist approach, for it involves the assumption of a psychological construct, 'knowledge', without adducing behavioural evidence. Performance, though derived from competence, is of little interest for Chomsky as a linguist; for he sees performance as distorting competence by the limitations it places on it. Competence, according to Chomsky, has unlimited potential output, while performance is only too obviously limited by temporal and physical factors. One must distinguish this use of 'competence' and 'performance' from the sense in which they have sometimes been used; 'competence' as the underlying regularities in performance which must have been learned in order for performance (specific correct behaviour) to occur. In this sense, Harlow's (1949) learning sets are examples of competence.

Chomsky is working 'from the inside out' rather than 'from the outside in'. Two major features distinguish his model from any recent psychological theory. First, he adduces no behavioural evidence to justify its components. Second, no such evidence is logically possible. For if performance always distorts competence, then competence itself can never be inferred. This is because any experimental procedure designed to lead to an inference of competence necessarily involves performance factors; it is logically impossible to control all performance factors in an experiment if one includes as performance such central features as channel capacity. It must be concluded that as it stands Chomsky's model is not in principle empirically verifiable. His separation of competence from performance means that competence is inaccessible to scientific psychology. Chomsky makes a revealing comment which shows the incompatibility of rationalist philosophy and empirical psychology. 'To my knowledge, the only concrete results that have been achieved and the only clear suggestions that have been put forth concerning the theory of performance outside of phonetics, have come from studies of performance models that incorporate generative grammars of specific kinds – that is, from studies that have been based on underlying competence' (Chomsky, 1965, p. 9). In other words, not only is competence not inferable from performance, but also performance cannot be examined without taking competence into account. These are the necessary conclusions of rationalist prior assumptions. They leave the empiricist without the possibility of an experiment; at this point ethical considerations regarding cruelty to the species must be considered!

Another way of expressing the generative grammarians' position is to say (Bever, 1968) that the psychologist's task is the empirical one of discovering the basis of the linguist's own intuitions. However, this assumes that the linguists are right. Since their theory is in principle a psychological one (in the sense that it claims to describe how language users know the rules of their language), such a procedure begs the question. The psychologist's task is to test the linguist's intuitions as experimental hypotheses on naïve subjects. Clearly, subjects know their language; but they are not supposed to know how they know it, and are therefore linguistically naïve. The experimental evidence (see pp. 74–6) that subjects can indeed perceive and recall in terms of deep structure is of vital importance, and its explanation in psychological terms an immediate task. But the existence of such experimental evidence is a sine qua non for the empiricist, while it is not for the rationalist. The rationalist can use arguments for the theoretical possibility of a sentence of infinite length which the empiricist regards as little more than an intellectual exercise.

It is interesting that Chomsky does not see the basic distinction between rationalism and empiricism in the same way. In a section devoted mainly to the acquisition of language, he concentrates on attacking the image of psychology that he has himself set up; he finds it easy to demolish 'the view that all knowledge derives solely from the senses by elementary operations of association and generalisation' (Chomsky, 1965, p. 58). He substitutes a very specific version of a critical period theory (see chapter V), in which he supposes that experience is only necessary in so far as it activates certain neural organisations which reflect the features of language. But the argument is not concerning experience and heredity, as Chomsky appears to think; it is concerning the nature of acceptable evidence and inference.

Other fundamental objections can be raised against those who wish to incorporate Chomsky's model into the language user as a description of the principles underlying his behaviour. First, Chomsky's rules are highly formalised descriptions of what is already an abstraction; for the language Chomsky describes is an abstraction from its context and from its users. Therefore it is unlikely that the linguistic rules are descriptions of mechanisms. At the most, they are descriptions of a system which is part of what a mechanism must account for. There is, in other words, little reason to suppose that formal descriptions of an abstraction are descriptions of actual mechanisms. Yet this is what is assumed when Chomsky's competence model is incorporated into a psychological account; and this is the hypothesis that has led to most of the psycholinguistic research of the last five years. From Miller (1962) on, psychologists have varied grammatical structure of sentences to be recalled; these variations differed in terms of the number of rules required to generate them. It was therefore assumed that differences in recall were due to different demands made on the competence system. Such an approach ignored the effect of aspects of language not included in the transformation rules, for example, its meaning. In brief, it is unlikely

1. that the competence model can be incorporated wholesale into the model of the language user; and

2. that other 'performance' factors do not affect the very nature of the competence part of the model of the language user.

Other results follow from a rejection for psychological purposes of the abstraction of the 'language' which is the generative linguists' data.

For example, when one removes the requirement for infinitely long sentences of an infinite number, one is left with the possibility of a finite number of sentence types. Obviously the number of sentences is immense if one treats two sentences as different which contain different words, though they have the same structure as each other. However, if sentences of similar structure are treated as comparable, the number of sentences which are used or which could be used is certainly not unlimited. This is particularly true if one analyses structure in terms of deep rather than surface structure (see next section). Analysis of the type used by Jenkins and Braine becomes possible (see pp. 52–3).

The sort of problems employed by many psycholinguists in their research clearly reflects their assumption that language is a formal self-contained system. For example, subjects have to rate sentences in order of grammaticality, or they have to perform tasks on such ambiguous sentences as 'I like cooking apples'. The fact that there is considerable agreement on ratings of grammaticality is interesting and requires explanation. But the explanation need not be in terms of a purely grammatical skill available to all native speakers. Ambiguity research centres round the problems of whether subjects compute alternative interpretations of a sentence or not; and whether there is an interaction of such computations or not. Clearly, in most situations there are linguistic and non-linguistic contextual cues which remove ambiguity. However, where there are not, the ability to perceive that there *is* an ambiguity has to be explained. The assumption is the basically incorrect one that a sentence is the unit of meaning, although this is preferable to the assumption that the word is the basic unit (see Chapter IV). However, Osgood (1968) and Olson (1969) make it clear that in many cases the presence of a certain set of non-linguistic alternatives is essential if an ambiguous sentence is to be disambiguated. The reply 'The boy saved the drowning woman' is ambiguous if there are several boys on the beach, but not if there is only one. Experimental evidence showing the existence and importance of pragmatic variables in sentence processing will be presented later.

Finally, the citation of exceptions to rules is used by generative linguists to argue against a proposed description. For example, it may be true that we normally expect the logical subject of a sentence to occur first, except in a passive construction ('Dog bites man', and 'Man bitten by dog'). However, such general probabilistic statements, typical of psychology and experimentally verifiable, are not enough for linguists. Any rule they hypothesise must include every grammatical sentence to which it applies, and be inapplicable to every non-grammatical 'sentence'. Therefore rigorous analysis of structure is typical of the linguist; but it is hardly likely for the language user, since he is apt to use all the probabilistic information he can to ease the load on his perceptual system. Just as the adult might expect the grammatical subject first, so the child might provisionally treat words preceded by 'a' as physical objects, words preceded by 'some' as substances, and words suffixed by '—ing' as actions (Brown, 1957). Such probabilistic inference is not for the linguist, who rightly refuses to define form classes by their reference, and insists on defining them in terms of their grammatical function. The difference is due to a difference of aims. However, this does not deny that the linguists' theories generate valuable hypotheses for empirical research; but it does lead one to expect that experiments trying to demonstrate a direct reflexion of competence (linguistic theory) in behaviour are doomed to failure (many of the criticisms made here are also made in a recent article by Ingram, 1968).

2. SPECIFIC ASPECTS OF CHOMSKY'S THEORY

The previous section has given grounds for rejecting Chomsky's theory as a model for experimental psychology because of the non-empirical nature of the assumptions on which it is based. However, a great deal of experimental work has been based on the assumption that competence *can* be inferred from experimental data (for a sympathetic account of Chomsky's relevance to psychology, see Miller, 1965). It is therefore necessary to describe the linguistic theory of Chomsky in order to be able to describe and evaluate these experiments adequately. This review will be shorter, however, than would have been the case if Chomsky's work did provide a model for psychological research.

Chomsky (1957, 1965) and his colleagues (Katz and Postal, 1964) have provided 'an integrated theory of linguistic descriptions'. It contains several components (see Figure 3). A syntactic component is the basis, consisting of phrase-structure and transformational sub-components. The phrase-structure component operates on fixed strings of symbols, and rewrites a single symbol as a new string (see p. 39). The result of applying the phrase-structure rules is a labelled tree diagram. When no transformational rules are involved in the production of the end-product, the string that results is a deep structure string. When both phrase-structure rules and transformational rules are involved, the result is a surface structure string.

The two other components of the generative system now operate, the semantic component on the deep structure and the phonological component on the surface structure. The application of the semantic component allows semantic readings to be made; the application of the phonological component leads to the production of a phonetically interpreted and interpretable string. Certain comments must be made about the theory as a whole before its individual parts are defined. Firstly, it is a *competence* theory; it does not claim to explain performance. Secondly, the derivations from one component to another are performed by means of *rules*. These rules are descriptions of processes whereby a string of symbols is rewritten as another string. Thirdly,

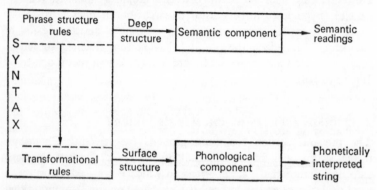

Figure 3. The components of a generative linguistic description (from Garrett and Fodor, 1968).

the derivations are *one-way*; that is, the original string of symbols passes through a temporally ordered sequence of processes. Finally, the emphasis of the theory is very strongly on the distinction between *deep* and *surface* structure. This is in contrast to more traditional approaches, where the semantic component is the origin of sentences and the syntactic component structures them; and where there is usually no distinction made between surface and deep structure.

Firstly, the *syntactic component* will be described, consisting as it does of deep and surface structure sub-components. Deep structure is regarded as a necessary sub-component for several reasons. Sentences may have an identical surface structure analysis but be different in meaning. 'John is eager to please' and 'John is easy to please' are examples. In the former case, 'John' is the subject of the sentence in the deep structure, in the latter the object of the verb. In a surface-structure description the sentences are identical, with 'John' as the subject in both cases. Secondly, sentences may have different surface structure analysis but be intuitively similar in content. 'John is easy for us to please', and 'It is easy for us to please John' are such sentences. The surface structure analysis of a sentence may not distinguish the *logical* subject and object. Chomsky goes so far as to say 'It is also clear that the manner of combination provided by the surface (immediate constituent) structure is in general almost totally irrelevant to semantic interpretation, whereas the grammatical relations expressed in the abstract deep structure are in many cases just those that determine the meaning of the sentence' (Chomsky, 1965, p. 150). Deep structure, then, is a vital feature of generative theory. It consists of such constructions as subject and predicate, verb and object, and modifier and head of a noun-phrase, and is operated on by the semantic component.

The transformational sub-component of the syntactic component also consists of rules, which are applied to the strings produced by the phrase-structure rules. The operations performed by the application of transformational rules are those of substitution, deletion, addition, and permutation of items in the string. For example, the production of the negative construction 'The car doesn't go fast' requires the insertion of the auxiliary verb 'do' and the permutation of the singular inflexion 'es' to 'does', as well as the addition of the negative suffix 'n't'. There are other, simpler transformations. For example, the phrase-marker tree results in a string in which the '-ed' (past tense inflexion) precedes its verb, and a permutation of items has to occur (see p. 39).

It should be noted at this point that transformational theory has been changed. Chomsky's earlier version of transformational syntax supposed that different transformations, e.g. negative, passive, and interrogative, were all optional, and derived from the same deep structure string. This version was used by Miller (1962) in his experiments regarding transformational types, and has predominated in psycholinguistic experiments.

More recently, a radical *revision* of transformational theory has occurred. Chomsky (1965) now maintains that each type of transformational sentence is derived from a kernel string in the deep structure. This kernel already contains the negative element of a negative sentence, the passive element of a passive, etc. Since the negative element is already present, the transformational rules which are applied to the kernel to produce the finished sentence are obligatory; certain rules have to be applied to negative kernels, others to passive kernels. This revision of theory was brought about by the realisation that there are certain meaning features involved in the different types of sentence, which must be accounted for in the deep structure. As a result of the revision, the transformations are not processes *deriving* one construction from another; rather, the negative element is already chosen in the deep structure, and the transformational rules *realise* the type of sentence already chosen. The semantic interpretation of the sentence therefore depends on the deep-structure. However, the actual operations involved in the transformational process are still supposed to be the same as in the previous version of the theory. For example, the introduction of the auxiliary verb 'do' into the negative is still required. As a result, the change in theory does not render valueless the psychological experiments conducted on the basis of the earlier version.

The syntactic component has now been described. Criticisms from other linguists often concern Chomsky's identification of surface structure with immediate constituent analysis. This identification must be rejected because constituent analysis does not claim to be an adequate account of surface structure, but merely an account of the divisions of syntax at different levels. A full account of surface structure would include accounts of various types of construction, classes of morphemes, words, and phrases and their co-occurrence. Moreover, it does not follow that linguists who do not follow Chomsky in his distinction between surface and deep structure must therefore be analysing language in terms of surface structure only. They may include some of the features of deep structure in their own analyses.

It will be recalled (see Figure 3) that the deep-structure is related to the semantic component. This relation between deep structure component and *semantic* component is complex. The 'sentence' 'Colourless green ideas sleep furiously' was used (Chomsky, 1957) to show that syntactic and semantic rules were separate, in that the sentence was grammatical but meaningless. However, a clear distinction between a grammatical and a semantic rule is not so easy. Chomsky (1965, p. 149*b*) distinguishes *strict subcategorisation* features from *selectional* rules. 'John found sad' breaks a subcategorisation rule in that the verb 'found' is transitive and requires an object; a word of a totally incorrect form class has been selected which could not fulfil this function. However, the sentence 'The boy may frighten sincerity' only breaks a selectional rule, that the verb 'frighten' requires an animate object. Such sentences as this can often be interpreted metaphorically, the reason being that they break nothing but the selectional rules; they are 'apparently interpreted by a direct analogy to well-formed sentences that observe the selectional rules in question'. Somewhere between these two examples comes the 'sentence' 'Golf plays John', which is usually termed semi-grammatical. This is because a count noun rather than a proper noun is required after 'plays' and a proper rather than a count noun before it. Clearly, the boundaries of the syntactic and the semantic are ill-defined. The selection of a mass noun rather than a count noun to fill the blank 'Some . . . has spilt on the floor' is a syntactic constraint, to break which would be to violate a subcategorisation rule. The selection of 'ideas' to fill the blank in 'Colourless green . . . sleep furiously' is termed the breaking of a selectional rule; the item chosen should have been from the category 'animate' rather than from the category 'inanimate'. Chomsky supposes that there is a hierarchy of categories, whereby the more basic distinctions (e.g. between verb and noun) are higher than the less basic (e.g. between animate and inanimate). He considers such a hierarchy to be a linguistic universal, i.e. common to all languages.

The *semantic component* also applies rules, the *selectional* rules mentioned above. Before selectional rules can be applied, of course, the syntactic constraints of deep structure must already have been observed. Different levels of deep structure analysis make it clear that what is required in 'Some . . . has spilt on the floor' is a subject, a noun, a mass noun. After these syntactically constrained limitations, selectional rules take over on the basis of categories. It is supposed that certain categories are *features*, e.g. male/female, animate/inanimate, adult/non-adult. It is clear that any item, e.g. 'woman', can be described in terms of certain features – in this case, animate, female, adult, human. A combination of items can be made into a semantically meaningful utterance by selecting only those items which are compatible. One cannot, for example, use the item 'conceive' in association with the item 'man' in the sentence 'The man conceived a baby'. This is because of a selection rule which allows only nouns containing the feature 'female' to occur with the item 'conceive' (when 'conceive' is used literally rather than metaphorically).

It has already been stated that the application of semantic rules to the deep structure strings allows the possibility of *semantic readings*. Semantic readings are part of the ability to interpret sentences, the other part being structural descriptions. Once semantic rules have been applied, it is possible to detect anomalies ('Colourless green ideas sleep furiously') and ambiguities ('Her train was long'), and to observe when sentences are synonymous or are paraphrases of each other. In a similar way, the application of syntactic rules results in the possibility of a *structural description* of sentences; the speaker/listener can tell when a sentence is grammatically well-formed and when it is not, when it can have more than one structural interpretation, and when sentences are grammatically similar or different. It is supposed that the listener can *interpret a sentence* when he pairs the correct semantic reading and structural description. This theory expresses the competence which the language user must utilize for successful performance.

The remaining aspect of Figure 3 which has not yet been dealt with is the *phonological component*. This has been described in Chapter II. It is now proposed to survey those experimental studies which profess to show that competence is reflected in a fairly direct way in performance.

3. SOME TRANSFORMATIONAL EXPERIMENTS

The basic assumption behind the series of experiments beginning with Miller (1962) is that aspects of competence are clearly reflected in performance (see Figure 4); in other words, that the generative rules used by linguists to describe the derivation of a sentence are used by subjects when engaged in a task requiring its analysis. A very direct relationship is being postulated. It is supposed that performance factors such as memory can be controlled to such an extent that the features of competence being investigated are reflected in measures of performance. It has already been argued (p. 58) that competence cannot in principle be investigated at all, since by definition, performance factors cannot be controlled. However, disregarding this argument for a moment, it is clear that the influence of performance on competence is being treated very simply. It is being treated as something which can be controlled experimentally to allow an investigation of pure competence. Instead it might well be argued by Chomsky that competence is far removed from performance in nature; and that any model of the language user would have to postulate complex relationships between performance and competence.

Miller (1962), and Miller and McKean (1964) report experiments which deal with the application of transformational rules to sentence constructions. They gave subjects a task which involved matching the members of one list of sentences with those of another. This matching was to follow a certain transformational rule, e.g. from active to passive, affirmative to negative, or a combination of rules, e.g. from affirmative active to negative passive. It was assumed that differences in the time taken to perform these matches would reflect differences in the time taken to perform the various transformational operations. Predictions were based on the linguistic theory that affirmative active sentences are

basic because they are derived from deep structure by obligatory rules;
other transformations are derived from affirmative active sentences by
optional rules. Transformations from affirmative active sentences should
take less time than transformations from other constructions; and
transformations involving two operations, e.g. from affirmative active

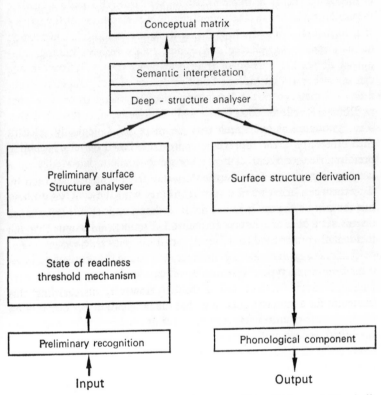

Figure 4. A schema of linguistic performance (from Wales and Marshall,
1966).

to negative passive, should take the sum of the times required for those
transformations singly.

The linguistic theory on which the Miller experiments were based
has been changed. Previously, transformations were assumed to occur
by the application of optional rules, and the need to recover the deep
structure was not recognised. However, the new version insists that
for a transformation to occur from, for example, a negative (N) to a
negative passive (NP) sentence, the deep structure must be recovered

before the transformation can be made. In other words, one has to interpret the N sentence to obtain the deep structure, and then perform the N and the P transformations on the deep structure to obtain the NP sentence. On this basis, the N to P transformation should be easier or certainly no more difficult than the N to NP. However, on the basis of the earlier theory of transformations, the N to NP should be easier; for the N to NP should then simply require the addition of the passive transformation, while the N to P would require in addition the deletion of the negative (see Garrett and Fodor, 1968). Miller's findings supported the earlier version of transformational theory. Therefore one can say either 1. that Miller's findings do not reflect competence (defining competence as the latest version of linguistic theory); 2. that performance reflects competence only indirectly, and therefore that some grammatical operations may be more psychologically relevant than others; or 3. that the whole approach is based on an unscientific premiss: that one can come to conclusions about knowledge of a language without deriving those conclusions from behavioural evidence. To expect the behavioural evidence to agree with the conclusions is to put the cart before the horse. A more moderate approach is to treat the linguists' theories as efforts to formalise a description of language which incidentally provide valuable hypotheses for empirical research.

Mehler (1963) explained his findings concerning the recall of different transformational types of sentence, which closely resembled those of Miller, in terms of the recall of deep structure strings together with 'instructions' to perform the required transformation(s). Those types of sentence (e.g. affirmative active) which are closest to the deep structure, and consequently require fewer instructions, should be most easily recalled. Savin and Perchonock (1965) also found that the number of transformational operations performed on the deep structure affected amount of memory storage space required; storage space was calculated by noting the number of unrelated words subjects could recall after they had recalled the sentence (which had been presented before the words). They also found that any transformation (e.g. to question) occupied the same amount of storage space whatever the type of sentence with which it was associated. The Mehler and Savin and Perchonock experiments provide more convincing evidence than the Miller experiments for some effect of competence on performance; they do not require Miller's assumptions concerning the operations required to derive one type of sentence from another; and since they demanded a recall task rather than a matching task, they are not open to the objection that the psychological processes being postulated were being directly experimentally induced. Rather, their results can be explained in terms of the number of steps required to derive any sentence type from its deep structure. They therefore accord with the revised transformational theory, and support the findings described in section 6 of this chapter, where experiments professing to show a direct perceptual processing of deep structure by subjects are outlined.

It should, however, be mentioned that Martin and Roberts (1966) have shown that Mehler's findings can equally well be explained in terms of Yngve depth (see p. 50). Different transformational types involve different numbers of grammatical commitments as indexed by a phrase-marker tree, and therefore place different loads on short-term memory.

4. THE SEMANTIC ASPECTS OF GRAMMATICAL CONSTRUCTIONS

Several experiments have been carried out which indicate the existence of certain *meaning* features which attach to different transformational types. These experiments required *comprehension* of different types of sentence. Comprehension was inferred from the correct verification of sentences as true or false by reference to pictures. It was found that difficulty of comprehension was not a function of the transformational complexity of the sentence types concerned; for example, it was discovered (Slobin, 1966b) that passives are easier to comprehend than negatives, although they are transformationally more complex. The truth value of the transformational type of sentence rather than its grammatical complexity was the vital factor. These findings would have been difficult to explain in terms of the earlier formulation of transformational theory. However, the later version can deal adequately with them, since it allows a different meaning element for each transformational type.

Other experiments have supported the principle that whenever a task involving meaning is presented, various semantic factors are confounded with grammatical complexity, and indeed, may supersede it. Before these experiments are described, it is desirable to discuss their implications for the findings described in the previous section. The experiments which indicate grammatical processing by subjects all required either matching (Miller) or recall (Mehler, Savin and Perchonock) tasks. The recall task presented several transformational types to each subject; subjects may well have concentrated on the grammatical differences they could perceive in the absence of any instructions to consider the meaning. It may therefore be concluded that only when a concentration on the grammatical features is experimentally induced are the competence features reflected in performance. Much of the evidence now to be reviewed indicates that in any task where meaning must be understood, subjects use all sorts of semantic short cuts to comprehension. The assumptions that performance directly reflects competence and that grammatical operations must always be performed to derive the deep structure for every sentence must be rejected.

Other experiments concerning the semantic aspects of transformational types will now be reviewed. Wason (1961) repeated Slobin's finding of the semantic difficulty in *negativity*, and suggested (1965) that one function of the negative is to point to an exception to a general rule or expectation. Subjects' responses to negative statements were facilitated when the stimuli were described in terms of an exceptional item and a residual class; however, when the stimuli were described in terms of a smaller or larger class, no facilitation was observed. Gough (1965), too, found evidence that in a verification task affirmative-negative and true-false factors interacted; in other words, that the affirmative-negative difference in speed of verification was not simply syntactical, but had a semantic function.

Semantic factors are also involved in the comprehension of the *passive* construction. The passive is supposedly a case in which deep structure has to be perceived before comprehension can occur, since logical and grammatical subjects and objects do not coincide; in the sentence 'The book was read by the professor', 'the book' is the grammatical subject but the logical object. Johnson-Laird (1968) found that one purpose of placing the logical object at the front of a sentence, as happens in the passive, is to emphasise its referent. Clark (1965) discovered that the logical subject was more often animate in active sentences, but the logical object in passive sentences; while M. G. Johnson (1967) showed that subject and object positions in active and passive sentences have different ratings on the activity factor in Osgood's semantic differential (see p. 91); finally, Clark and Begun (1968) (see p. 147) found that logical subjects of real active and passive sentences are less acceptable as objects in anomalous sentences than are logical objects as subjects. All these findings (together with the results of Johnson and Yngve cited in the previous chapter) show that subject and predicate are psychological as well as linguistic entities; but they do not show that transformations are applied to them as deep structure features by experimental subjects to produce surface structures such as the passive. Indeed, the experiments quoted above tend to support

Osgood's (1968) hypothesis of a prior selection of content words from storage banks which permit their use as logical subject or as logical object (or as both), logical subjects probably being a subset of logical objects (Clark and Begun). In other words, deep structure units such as subject and predicate, verb and object, etc., do not have the same psychological as linguistic function; linguistically they are the basis for the generation of sentences by transformational rules, performing a primarily grammatical function; psychologically, they may be a storage system for verbal items which may be actors, objects of actions, or both, performing a primarily semantic function. But clearly grammatical structure is involved psychologically, in that the actor and the object of action are very often the grammatical surface structure subject and object of the sentence.

Slobin (1966*a*), however, emphasised that the difficulty of the passive was due to the non-coincidence of grammatical and logical features described above. Subjects, it was supposed, had to derive the deep structure, the logical subject and object. He distinguished *reversible* and *non-reversible* passives. 'The brother was hated by the sister' is reversible to 'The sister was hated by the brother', but 'The book was read by the professor' is not reversible to 'The professor was read by the book'! Non-reversible passives are such that the semantic rules are broken when they are reversed; a book cannot read a professor because the rules concerning animate and inanimate categories have been violated. A linguistically based interpretation of the ease of non-reversible passives would be as follows; the experimental subject realises that the reversed form would break the semantic rules, and therefore has no difficulty in extracting the deep structure, since there is no doubt which is the logical subject and which the logical object.

However, it may well be that it is not so much semantic *rules* as pragmatic and semantic expectations that determine how one interprets a sentence (defining 'pragmatic' as 'referring to the non-linguistic environment'). Herriot (1969*b*) found that the reversal of such sentences as 'The doctor treated the patient', or 'The bather was rescued by the lifeguard' led to significant increases in response latency and more errors than their non-reversed forms. Clearly, pragmatic and semantic expectations lead us to predict the doctor in the logical subject role, the patient as the logical object. There was no voice (active-passive) effect. However, when reversible sentences with no such pragmatic expectations were presented, there *was* a significant voice effect but no reversal effect; examples are 'The brother hated the sister' and 'The miner was supported by the docker'. Subjects' task was to extract the logical subject and object in that order. There was no significant difference between results for passive sentences in the two experiments. The inference is that pragmatic and semantic expectations are independent of and sometimes perceptually prepotent to grammatical construction. Only when these cues are not available do subjects have to employ grammatical operations to arrive at the deep structure. This could be the explanation of the greater ease of non-reversible sentences. We expect the professor to read the book, rather than note the violation of the semantic rules in the 'sentence' 'The book read the professor'. It should be noted, however, that the expectations need not have been derived from experience of the world; they may originate in the experience of the words 'doctor' and 'patient' being regularly used as logical subject and object when the main verb is such a word as 'treat'. This latter explanation is supported by more recent work which shows that it is the congruity in meaning of the verb with a given noun rather than the noun order itself which determines difficulty.

Other evidence, also, indicates that subjects do not always perform transformations upon sentences before verifying them. Gough (1966) found that even when evidence confirming or disconfirming a sentence was delayed for three seconds after its presentation (allowing time for the transformations to occur), affirmatives were still verified faster than negatives and actives faster than passives. The discovery of meaning, it must be concluded, is not a matter of performing transformations in reverse in order to obtain the deep structure. Other operations are involved.

Pragmatic expectations may be partly derived from childhood learning in which particular constructions are associated with certain types of situation (see chapter V). For example children aged four comprehend 'some niss' as a substance, 'a niss' as an object, and 'nissing' as an action (Brown, 1957). They can select plural objects rather than singular, a past event rather than a future one, and make many other discriminative responses to grammatical cues (Fraser *et al.*, 1963). They may even learn that affirmative sentences often refer to an actor and object situation (Herriot, 1968*b*). Such findings make the hypothesis of initial scanning of input and planning of output by means of pragmatic expectations more probable. They argue against the hypothesis that subjects habitually use transformations when comprehending a sentence; but they do not argue against the need to discover the deep structure when this differs from the surface structure. Moreover, many generative linguistics might deny that the meaning of the grammatical construction is learned by its association with a situation in the child's experience. They might suggest that the results cited above show that children can exercise their innate competence from an early age.

5. EVIDENCE FOR A SYNTAX-SEMANTICS DICHOTOMY

Efforts to prove a distinction between syntax and semantics have been made by Miller and his associates. Mehler and Miller (1964) and Marks and Miller (1964) tested, respectively, recall under conditions of retroactive interference, and free recall of different types of sentences. For the latter experiment, these types were, firstly, meaningful and grammatical, e.g. 'Rapid flashes augur violent storms'; secondly, grammatical but meaningless (termed anomalous), e.g. 'Rapid bouquets deter sudden neighbours'; thirdly, anagram strings, i.e. type one, but with word order randomised, e.g. 'Rapid augur violent flashes storms'; finally, word lists, i.e. type two, but with word order randomised, e.g. 'Rapid deter sudden bouquets neighbours'. Five examples of each type of string were presented, each containing five words. All four types of sentence can thus use the same 25 words, but in different orders. The aim was obviously to control semantic and syntactic factors in an effort to establish the effect of each. The experiments were based on Chomsky's (1957) version of transformational theory, in which he cited the sentence 'Colourless green ideas sleep furiously' as being grammatical but meaningless. More recently however, Chomsky (1965) has stated that he does not believe the distinction is so clear cut (see pp. 64-5).

Marks and Miller (1964) found that in terms of complete strings recalled, the order was normal sentences, anomalous sentences, anagram strings, word lists. In other words, syntax was a more potent cue than semantics. However, in terms of total number of words correct, anagram strings were recalled better than anomalous sentences. This is hardly surprising – grammatical structure aids chunking into phrase units or larger, where word order is important; semantic commonality favours easy learning of a list regardless of order. Two types of error scores were computed: semantic errors ('intrusions', i.e. the misplacing of words from one of the five strings into another) and syntactic errors (inversions of the order of words, and incorrect or omitted prefixes and' suffixes). Semantic errors occurred most frequently in anomalous sentences, in the composition of which semantic but not syntactic rules had been broken. Syntactic errors occurred most frequently in anagram strings, in the composition of which syntactic but not semantic rules had been violated. Both types of error were also frequent in word lists, where both sorts of rules had been broken. However, the randomisation of word order affects semantic as well as syntactic features, since it disrupts any word-to-word associations which might exist in the sentence. Moreover, the anomalous sentences broke grammatical rules also, in the sense that they violated certain subcategorisation features (see p. 64). Therefore semantic and syntactic features are confounded.

Mehler and Miller (1964) found that retroactive inhibition was produced by sentences of differing semantic features or transformational types from those to be recalled. Results were scored according to 'content recall' and according to total correctness, and differences between semantic and syntactic factors became clear. Content recall implies that subjects have recalled the stimulus sentence completely or that their attempt can be transformed into the stimulus sentence by the application of simple transformational rules. Retroactive inhibition was negligible when recall was scored by the content method; but when totally correct recall was required, retroactive interference was considerable. Further, the interpolated material caused more retroactive inhibition when it differed in transformational type from the stimulus sentences than when it differed in semantic content. The authors conclude that 'subjects deal with sentences on two distinct levels; the semantic aspects are coded separately and are relatively free of retroactive inhibition, whereas the syntactic aspects are (in this situation) much more arbitrary, harder to remember, and more subject to retroactive inhibition'. An interesting additional finding concerns the effect of amount of learning. After two learning trials, syntactic interference is zero or facilitatory; only after four trials does it become inhibitory. This might imply that the extraction of meaning was subjects' foremost consideration, and grammatical details were only recalled to fulfil the requirement of the experiment.

6. EVIDENCE FOR DEEP STRUCTURE

Sections 3 and 4 have been concerned with certain experiments from which one might reasonably infer that subjects were analysing sentences down to their *deep structure*. The present section deals with experiments which directly manipulate deep structure as a variable. This is difficult, since deep structure frequently coincides grammatically with surface structure. Blumenthal (1967) using passives found that the logical actor at the end of a passive sentence was a better prompt for recall of the sentence than a noun in the same grammatical position which was not the logical subject. Blumenthal and

Boakes (1967) also showed that 'John' is a better prompt for the recall of 'John is eager to please' than 'eager'; but that 'easy' is a better prompt for recall of 'John is easy to please' than 'John'. Blumenthal and Boakes conclude that 'an analysis of grammatical relations must take place to permit full semantic interpretation of a sentence', and that this analysis is often not of the surface structure, but of the deep structure.

Savin and Perchonock (in press) show that right-branching and self-embedded sentences take up the same amount of storage space in long-term memory. A self-embedded sentence contains a phrase unit nested within another unit of the same type, while a right-branching sentence tags the phrase on after the object. An example of a self-embedded sentence is 'The vase that the maid that the agency hired dropped broke on the floor'. These types of sentence differ in the load they place on the short-term memory, since the self-embedded sentence involves the retention of the predicate commitment while the long subject is being uttered. When a list of words and then these sentences are presented, the types of sentence differ in the amount of storage space required (as indexed by the number of words recalled). However, when the sentences are presented before the words, there is no such difference. The inference is that in the latter case the deep structure is extracted and retained while the words are received; in the former, there is no time to extract the deep structure, and therefore the differential loads on the short-term memory derived from the surface structure have an effect (but cf. Gough, 1966, on p. 70).

Mehler and Carey (1967) showed that deep structure can have a direct effect on perception. They induced a set to expect a certain surface structure, e.g. that describing the sentence 'They are forecasting cyclones' or a certain deep structure, e.g. that describing the sentence 'They are delightful to embrace', by presenting ten sentences of the same type. They then presented a sentence of a different surface structure to those who had received the ten surface structure sentences (e.g. 'they are conflicting desires'). They found that significantly fewer Ss perceived this eleventh sentence correctly in noise than a control group for whom the eleventh sentence had been of the same surface structure as the previous ten. The same applied to the deep structure sentences; when the eleventh sentence was of a different deep structure to the previous ten (e.g. 'They are hesitant to travel'), perception was just significantly worse than when the eleventh sentence was of the same deep structure. However, deep and surface structure were confounded in the surface structure condition.

The point of the experiments indicating the effect of deep structure is not that we always analyse a sentence down to its deep structure in order to decode it. Nor is it proven that we do so by means of formal transformational operations. The point is, rather, that we *can* analyse down to deep structure if an artificially induced absence of other cues forces us to. It is this *ability* which requires psychological explanation. A tentative explanation may be suggested in terms of the constructions in the deep structure acting as storage 'banks' (Osgood, 1968) for particular words or groups of words (see p. 71). Some words might belong, for example, to both subject and predicate banks, others to only one of the two. Thus 'eager' may be predicated of 'John' when 'John' is the deep structure subject, but not when he is the deep structure object. The bank membership of a word or group of words might act as a cue to the identity of the deep structure construction in which it occurred.

7. CONCLUSIONS

The basic gist of the present chapter has been the impossibility of removing considerations of *meaning* when subjects are dealing with grammatical variables. This renders the attempt of the previous chapter to treat grammatical behaviour as a skill somewhat abortive. For a skill implies the S–S and R–R integration into behavioural chunks of sequential behaviour. Redundancies derived from frequency of occurrence in the organiser's previous experience are adequate to account for most skills; these dependencies can occur at any level of the phrase-marker tree, according to Osgood (1963), and as a result, grammatical skills are remarkably flexible. However, it is clear from the present chapter that even out of situational context, every grammatical construction has some sort of meaning. Meaning appears to demand a representational feature (Chapter IV, Sections 6 and 7) although hierarchical features are also required (Section 9).

Another feature of the present chapter has been the realisation that certain aspects of generative grammar seem to be reflected in performance. It has been suggested that this is not true of purely grammatical operations such as transformations, except where all considerations of meaning have been removed from the experimental situation. However, it seems clear that analysis of sentences down to deep structure is a psychological fact when there are no pragmatic cues available. There are alternative ways of dealing with these results. The linguistically oriented psychologist may want to infer that linguistic transformations are performed in order to extract the deep structure; he will conclude that since all existing psychological models cannot adequately describe these linguistic operations, they should be discarded. Other psychologists will try to suggest mechanisms whereby different words or word classes are associated with different deep structure functions (see p. 71). The theoretical question will be considered more adequately in Chapter VII, but it should be noted that the findings on deep structure make it impossible to treat all language in terms of sequences of word classes. The efforts of, e.g., Jenkins (1965) to apply mediational theory to language behaviour by making form classes the mediators were in-adequate as a total theory. But as Jenkins (1968) points out, there is no reason why concentrated work should not be done on parti-cular levels of the hierarchy of language skills. It is merely that the existence of very abstract levels and their effect on other levels must be remembered.

Furthermore the *limitations* of the human organism must be reckoned with in any psychological account of language behaviour. These limit theoretical possibilities and explain some of the features of language (e.g. sentence length, and redundancy). The *experience* of the language user must be taken into consideration. He has heard and used sequences of sounds so often that he has integrated them into units. Such units have different probabilities of occurrence, both as units and as parts of a sequence. He has associated different words and constructions with different features of the world and his experience of it; as a result, he treats certain grammatical features (e.g. subject-object) as cues likely to contain helpful information in his search for meaning. Moreover, the *purposes* of language must be taken into account. There are few cases where language is not used for the purposes of communication. Com-munication may involve primarily the imparting of factual information to another, the manipulation of behaviour, or the arousing of emotional reaction. In all these cases '*meaning*' is involved, in the sense that internal (possibly representational) processes are required to encode and decode the message. This being the case, all the features of language may be treated as cues to meaning. Such features as intonation, duration and volume of utterance, and facial expression will therefore be vital cues to meaning. So will the context of the utterance, both verbal, physical and social. The amazing success of the structural analysis of language should not persuade psychologists to disregard these factors. People need to have something to say before they consider how to say it. The term 'meaning' will be discussed in the next chapter.

Finally, it may be worth summarising the basic requirements of a psychological as opposed to a linguistic theory of language behaviour. Osgood (1963) says

'The thing we must avoid, I think, is "explaining" sentence understanding and creating by simply putting a new homunculus in our heads – in this case a little linguist in every brain. It is true that speakers produce novel sentences all the time, but the semantics and the grammatics cannot both be simultaneously novel, or we fail to comprehend. What is novel is the combination, and this is a familiar psychological problem; ... let us therefore strive for psychological theories of the sentence which are parts of our theories of behaviour in general.'

IV

Meaning: Behaviourist Approaches

1. INTRODUCTION

There are many features of everyday life which a psychological theory ought to be able to explain. But any attempt at psychological explanation should be based on what is known about psychological functions. It should not be derived from the words which are habitually used in the situation to be explained. These words are merely hints that there is something to be explained. They should not constitute an explanation. For example, it is dangerous to take over into psychological theory the term 'meaning' as it is sometimes used in everyday speech, or to take over the assumptions which that use implies. 'What is the meaning of a word?' is an unanswerable question. It is implied that there are two objects or events involved, a 'word' to which a 'meaning' is attached.

This trap has proved fatal to psychological theory and experiment. The notion that 'a meaning' is attached to or lies behind a word, has led to the assumption that words are labels which refer to things. The word 'meaning' can then be used of that to which they refer. Clearly, many words do not refer to tangible objects or events; the referent is therefore internalised, and it is suggested that words refer to concepts. The distinction between connotative and denotative meaning (Evans and Evans, 1957) has then to be invoked to account for the only too obvious fact that not all responses consist of identifying a concept by means of its criterial features (Bruner, Goodnow and Austin, 1956). To the objection that content words may have 'a meaning' in this referential sense but that function words may not, it is replied that function words refer to relational concepts; or that it is the 'meaning' of a sentence of which the function word is a part that is important, not the meaning of the word itself.

Much confusion might have been avoided if analysis had been based on scientific methodology. The distinction made in Chapter I must be insisted upon. Speech, or language behaviour, can be treated in two ways. Firstly as overt behaviour which acts as a cue to behaviour by other people. Secondly as behavioural evidence for the processes which regulate it. If speech is considered as a cue, then the behaviour which results is by definition what is being investigated. The processes involved in regulating the response of the hearer to this cue are obviously of interest. But here again, the assumption of 'a meaning' or 'a content' is fatal. It leads to analysis in terms of a message with information content; but it is clear that 'a content' postulated in addition to behaviour and its regulation is a snare and a delusion. Many types of overt response to speech do not concern 'reception of information' at all. For example, questions might be asked, commands given, jokes cracked or apologies made; to all these utterances, there are appropriate responses based upon their adequate perception. But the important feature of the situation is not that the perception of content is adequate, but that structures are activated which regulate appropriate responses.

Language behaviour is also treated as evidence for the processes which regulate it. It has been made clear in Chapters II and III that these processes are hierarchical in nature; that they involve both the selection of items and the arrangement of those items in a sequence; and that the use of deep structure is evidenced and must be accounted for. Questions concerning 'meaning' may therefore be treated as questions concerning the connexion of parts of this system with other parts. For example, the ability to paraphrase a paragraph or give synonyms for words is considered to raise 'the problem of meaning'. Instead of trying to find 'meaning', however, the solution is to elucidate the connexions between the parts of the system regulating grammar and those regulating choice of words. Many of the experiments described in this chapter may be seen as throwing light upon such connexions or upon individual parts of the system. However, they have tended to disregard the hierarchical nature of the system, since they use the word as the response unit. Only recently has it become clear (see Section 10) that even the organisation of words is hierarchical in nature and therefore requires the postulation of hierarchical regulating systems of retrieval from storage.

Perhaps the most important question, however, does not concern the relations of parts of the system for regulating language behaviour with each other. Rather, it concerns the connexion of that system with others which regulate non-linguistic behaviour. The term 'meaning' is often used in everyday speech when such connexions are implied by behaviour. The importance of non-linguistic cues for perception and production has been made clear by several experiments. It is suggested in Chapter VII that the linguistic system is dependent upon non-linguistic systems for its activation; that the two are connected by feedback mechanisms; and that deep structure provides the vital link between them.

There are thus several experimental criteria which must be met if these relations are to be elucidated. If utterance is treated as a social cue, then the social situation of communication must be taken into account. If utterance is treated as evidence for regulatory mechanisms of a linguistic and a non-linguistic nature, then other environmental cues as well must be admitted. However, in most of the work to be described, such features are absent from the experimental situation. As a result, the data obtained can only be taken to evidence the nature or relations of parts of the system regulating language behaviour; in particular, of the systems regulating word selection. They are no less valuable for having this limited aim. In the account that follows the word 'meaning' occurs frequently. The writer would prefer it to disappear entirely from psychological usage: it has served its purpose in calling attention to a neglected field. However, the workers whose experiments are described use it frequently, and do not share the writer's assumptions about the regulation of behaviour. Therefore the word will be used, defined as frequently as possible in terms of its usage by particular experimenters; but the writer would like to reiterate that he defines the term 'meaning', since he must, as the relations between the systems which regulate behaviour.

Behaviourist experiments will be described in terms of the units of input or output or inferred processes. Detailed criticisms in terms of the above account will not be made, since it is perfectly evident that few of the experiments concern themselves with non-linguistic cues or with structured utterances. 1. The *word-word* approach uses the word association technique whereby input and output units are the word. 2. The *response-unit-reinforcement* approach concentrates on the reinforcing properties of utterances as stimuli of language behaviour, but uses arbitrary methods in deciding the unit of language behaviour to be reinforced. 3. The *word mediator* theory supposes that responses to a word may occur internally and consist of the range of associates it can elicit overtly. 4. The *representational mediator* theory hypothesises that the response to a word is an internalised part of the behavioural response to the word's referent. 5. The *word-list-subjective organisation* approach aims at revealing the categories by which people organise words by employing the task of free recall. Each of these approaches will be reviewed in turn.

2. THE WORD-WORD APPROACH

The basic technique employed by those who favour this approach is that of *free-association*. Subjects are presented with a word, and are required to respond with the first word that comes to mind. Different subjects treat this task in different ways – children usually give syntagmatic responses, adults paradigmatic ones (see p. 34). Some adults nearly always give antonyms as responses, others synonyms (Carroll, Kjelder-gaard and Carton, 1962). Nevertheless, responses are predictable. Russell and Jenkins (1954) showed that for all 100 words used as stimuli, the most common response to each accounted for 37.5% of the total responses. Limitation of the subjects to those who tend towards a certain type of response, or addition of context to the stimulus word (Howes and Osgood, 1954) provide even greater predictability of response.

A variant of this procedure which elicits more than one response for each stimulus word presented is that of Noble (1952, 1963), who uses the term '*meaningfulness*' (*m*) to describe the number of associations made to a given item by a representative sample of subjects during a standard time interval. The emphasis is on the *number* of associates produced. Other factors also have been shown to be experimental variables in the serial learning or paired-associate tasks. (The paired-associate task requires the learning of an item as a response to another. The two items are previously unconnected in the subject's experience, and are pre-sented in such a way that the correct response is shown to the subject after he has made an attempt to respond to the already displayed stimulus item.) These other variables include familiarity, defined operationally as the frequency of the subject's experience of any word as rated by himself; pronunciability; and word frequency, calculated from the Thorndike–Lorge magazine count (1944). Underwood and Schulz (1960) report extensive experiments demonstrating the effects of Noble's 'm' on verbal learning. However, they used nonsense syllables as material, calculating the 'meaningfulness' of the 'nonsense' syllable in terms of the number of word associates it elicited.

Apart from the dissimilarity of the material to language, it must also be noted that the effect of 'm' on verbal learning has only been demon-strated; it has not been explained. The exponents of these techniques would in fact deny that any explanation in terms of inferred psycho-logical processes was required. They would maintain that the elucida-tion of the connexions of 'm' with other independent variables and with experimental performance was the goal of their research. However, there is often the concealed premiss that the experimental technique they employ is in fact an explanation rather than a technique; in other words, it is supposed that meaning is learned by association, i.e. that subjects respond to the stimulus word with the response word because they have experienced the two in temporal contiguity. Even if this premiss is not made, there is the assumption that meaning is the relation between terms, and that this is the operationally defined relation between a stimulus word and a response word. Further, it is often implied that the frequency with which a word is the most common associate to another is an index of habit strength, a word being a response the elicitation of which leads to increased habit strength. This is usually not treated as an intervening variable, but as a way of stating that the response is more likely to occur to the given stimulus in future. Howes (1957) found that the associative probability of any word, as measured by its total frequency as a response in the Kent-Rosanoff norms (1910), is highly correlated with its frequency of usage, as measured by the Thorndike–Lorge count. In other words the association procedure does appear to reflect the emission of words in general discourse.

3. THE RESPONSE-UNIT–REINFORCEMENT APPROACH

This section briefly outlines yet another attempt to describe language behaviour in terms of an experimental paradigm derived from learning theory. The paradigm is that of *operant conditioning*, upon which a very large body of research, starting with the work of Greenspoon (1955), has been based. In brief, it has been shown that a wide variety of features of language behaviour can be conditioned, in the sense that they are more frequently uttered by the subject when he is being rewarded than when he is not. The usual procedure is for the subject to engage in verbal behaviour so that a base-line level of normal performance can be ascertained. The experimenter then rewards the subject with the approving grunt 'uh-huh' on each occasion when the item to be reinforced occurs in the subject's utterance. As a result, the item concerned is emitted more frequently. A large number of types of items have been shown to be subject to stimulus control (e.g. plural nouns, favourable or unfavourable opinions). Moreover, an extremely wide variety of variables, both subject, experimenter and environmental, have been shown to affect ease of conditioning. Reviews of the literature and evaluations of the field are provided by Greenspoon (1962), Williams (1964) and Kanfer (1968).

Lately, the emphasis in the field has been on the question of *awareness*. Some workers (e.g. Spielberger, 1965) have tried to show that awareness of the reinforcement contingencies determines ease of conditioning. Others (e.g. Kanfer, 1968) maintain that awareness in this sense is an inferred intervening variable, and is therefore unnecessary. They suggest that verbal reports or written ratings of awareness are merely additional behavioural variables. The task of the experimenter is therefore to control these variables and observe how they correlate with conditioning. The vast individual differences in speed of conditioning appear to support the awareness hypothesis. The main aim of the radical behaviourists seems to have been to eliminate its effect by discarding subjects who reported it or by careful pre-training. The following quotation from Kanfer (1968, p. 262) illustrates this attitude: 'When care is taken to pretrain human *S*s, much of the variability and the problems of self-instruction hypothesis testing, or other "game playing" disappear and S's behaviour comes under increased control of E's experimental manipulation. . . . In fact, S's attitudes towards E, his awareness of the response-reinforcement contingency, and many other interesting but tangential variables seem to lose their impact.' This is an unedifying confrontation which merely reflects the different research strategies of the radical behaviourist and the more cognitive theorist.

More important, the field of verbal conditioning has told us little about the nature of language behaviour. Awareness of reinforcement contingencies does not appear to be one of the major features of language behaviour. A valuable contribution would be to show that in the same subject, some features of language behaviour were more easily conditioned than others. However, as yet there has been little apparent rationale behind the choice of items to be conditioned; the experimenter has arbitrarily chosen the units rather than obtained them from findings in other research fields which show their importance. Moreover, inferences about the subjective importance of different units of language to the language user cannot be made until the awareness controversy is settled. If subjects do become aware of what it is that is being reinforced, then ease of conditioning will reflect the degree of the subject's awareness of the particular unit being reinforced. However, if such features as hypotheses and awareness are considered irrelevant, then what would have been shown is that some aspects of language can be conditioned more rapidly than others.

4. MEDIATION

Other behaviourist models of meaning owe much to the concept of *mediation*. They may be distinguished into those which insist that the mediation is *representational*, and those which do not. The term 'representational' implies that the mediating response is a part of the overt response made to the referent of the word. The basic paradigm of mediation theory is derived from an experiment by Shipley (1933) (see Maltzman, 1968). He paired a faint light with a tap on the cheek, and, by classical conditioning, the light (CS) elicited a blinking response; the tap was then paired with a shock to the finger, and became the CS for finger withdrawal. On subsequent tests the light evoked finger withdrawal, without even having been associated with the finger withdrawal response in the subjects' experience. The eyeblink, in other words, had become a mediating response. It had 'carried' the finger flexion from one stimulus (tap on the cheek) to another (light). It may have acted in this way because the blinking response produced proprioceptive stimuli which become conditioned stimuli to the finger flexion; or because some equivalent of the blink response in the central nervous system becomes a conditioned stimulus to the finger flexion. Whichever explanation is accepted, the point is that some mediating process must be postulated. This process may be called a mediating *response* if one is willing to assume that it obeys the same laws as overt responses; among other things, this implies that the mediating response is associated with the external stimulus, and the self-stimulation produced by the mediating response is associated with the external response. The evidence of learning by observation, of problem solving, and of delayed response support the same inference of a mediating process.

There are two experimental phenomena in which verbal material is used which also indicate the need to postulate mediational processes. The first is *semantic generalisation* (for review articles, see Feather, 1965, and Maltzman, 1968). Many types of unconditioned response (e.g. salivation to acid drops) have been conditioned to particular words as conditioned stimuli, for example, the written word 'right'. Generalisation has then been shown to occur to the words 'wrong' and 'correct', but not to the word 'write'. This is true of adolescents and adults, but not of children under the age of ten (Reiss, 1946). Clearly, although 'write' is *phonologically* identical with 'right', generalisation of response only occurred to words which were related in *meaning* to the original stimulus.

The second phenomenon, *verbal mediation*, is illustrated by the experiment of Russell and Storms (1955), which used the word-association norms collected by Russell and Jenkins (1954). Russell and Storms found a word which had a very frequent associate, 'soldier' —→ 'sailor'; a further feature was that the associate itself ('sailor') had a common associate (e.g. 'navy') which was not associated with 'soldier' in the norms. Next, they presented to their experimental group the task of learning such paired associates as'ZUG' —→ 'soldier'. Finally, in the test phase of the experiment, subjects had to learn such pairs as 'ZUG' —→ 'navy'. There was a significant difference between the experimental group and a control group which had not learned the first pair. The inference is that the associate 'sailor', common to both 'soldier' and 'navy', had facilitated learning by mediating between them. The important feature of the experiment is that this mediator is implicit – it was never mentioned to the subjects of the experiment.

While these two experiments both illustrate the need to postulate mediational processes, they do not necessarily give any indication as to the nature of the processes involved in the connexions between words which they demonstrate. In other words, because they show that 'right' and 'wrong', or 'soldier' and 'navy' have certain relationships to each other in classical association or paired-associate experimental designs, it does not follow that these relationships consist of or were learned by simple or mediated association or conditioning. Once again, it must be stressed that an experimental technique does not constitute an explanation.

5. THE WORD MEDIATOR THEORY

In word association tests, a stimulus word elicits as the first response a given response word among a certain number of the sample of subjects on whom the test is carried out. As a result, a hierarchy of responses can be composed in order of their frequency of occurrence as first responses. Thus, for example, 'white' is at the top of the response hierarchy to the stimulus word 'black', while 'night' is further down because fewer subjects used it. Many behaviourists have assumed that these associative norms (derived from a large sample of subjects) can be internalised into each individual subject, so that he has a response hierarchy himself to the stimulus word in which some responses are more probable than others.

This highly dubious assumption is incorporated into an explanation of the Russell and Storms experiment (see above), and also of the semantic generalisation phenomenon. It is supposed that in the former case, the mediating response (e.g. 'sailor') is in fact the most probable of the response hierarchy to the training word (e.g. 'soldier'). Then when the test phase of the experiment took place (the learning of 'ZUG' → 'navy'), the response hierarchies to 'soldier' and to 'navy' were activated. Since these both contain as common members the word 'sailor', it was assumed that the words 'soldier' and 'navy' were conditioned to each other by means of the mediator, 'sailor'. As a result, learning of 'ZUG' → 'soldier' generalised to learning of 'ZUG' → 'navy'. The theory is therefore a *chaining* theory, and assumes that mediation takes place during the test sequence. It also assumes that the higher the position of the mediator in the response hierarchy, the stronger mediation will occur and the greater facilitation result.

In a similar way, semantic generalisation is explained in terms of the test word being conditioned to the training word during the test period since both elicit associative hierarchies which have members in common. As a result, the learned conditioned response to the training word generalises to the test word.

There is a considerable body of evidence and theory which argues against this interpretation, however. Firstly, experimenters have failed to find the predicted greater facilitation for mediators of higher associative probability. This is true both of semantic generalisation and of the Russell–Storms paradigm (Carlin, 1958). The hypothesis of a chaining process functioning according to habit strength on the Hullian model is not supported in these cases. However, Peterson (1965) did find that there was a greater mediation effect for nonsense syllables high in Noble's 'm' than for those with low 'm' values. Number of associations in general rather than strength of particular associates might therefore be of importance.

Secondly, there is controversy over the question of the experimental locus of the mediation; at what point in the experimental procedure is the process supposed to occur? Mink (1963) produced evidence which suggested that generalisation occurred not during the test but during the training phase. Using an instrumental learning situation, he found that generalisation only occurred when the training word was the stimulus and the test word the response in the association norms. The word 'bird' is a common response to the word 'eagle', but 'eagle' is not a common response to the word 'bird'; the association is unidirectional. If subjects are taught to press a lever to the stimulus word 'eagle', this response will generalise to the word 'bird'. However, if they are taught to press to 'bird', the response will not generalise to 'eagle'. The implication is that generalisation only occurs when the association is forward, and therefore that it occurs during the training rather than the test phase of the experiment; for in the test phase, the association of the test with the training word was backwards.

Bousfield (1961) suggests that a *verbal representational response* is made implicitly when the subject hears or reads a word – the word 'representational' is used in a different sense here from its meaning in Osgood's theory (p. 90). This response, which is an internal repetition of the word presented, becomes the stimulus to its associative hierarchy of responses, which are elicited. Generalisation of the conditioned response to these associates is assumed to occur during the training stage of the semantic generalisation experiment. For example, while the training word 'right' is being conditioned as a CS to elicit a galvanic skin response (GSR), the word 'wrong' is also being elicited and conditioned to the GSR. Generalisation to the test word 'sin' would result, since 'wrong' is also in the associative hierarchy of the word 'sin'. Bousfield assumes that the test word elicits its own hierarchy, and that the generalisation occurs because several of the items of the hierarchy have already been conditioned by association with the training word. The amount of commonality in associative hierarchies is measured by the index of generalisation (IG). The IG is derived from the association norms, and has been shown to correlate highly with mediated generalisation in a paired-associate task (Bousfield, Whitmarsh and Danick, 1958) and in a semantic generalisation situation (Whitmarsh and Bousfield, 1961).

A primary objection to Bousfield's theory is that it supposes that all the associates to a word are elicited each time that word is presented. Whether this occurs or not is probably a function of the instructions given to subjects, and of the nature of the experimental task. For example, if subjects are especially primed to make associations before the experiment proper, such mediation may be more likely to occur. Also, as Jenkins (1963) remarks, subjects tend to use associative mediators when they are rewarded for doing so, and when the mediators are common overlearned responses (Earhard and Mandler, 1965a and 1965b). The corrollary is that many so-called mediation effects where the mediating links are not common overlearned words are in fact pseudo-mediation and the result of interference.

Secondly, the assumption that the response hierarchy of the training word has to be associated with the response to which the training word is being conditioned has been questioned (Maltzman, 1968). For example, Maltzman and Belloni (1964) found that the simple presentation of the training words, unassociated with any behavioural response, could produce generalisation in an operant test situation.

Thirdly, Maltzman insists on the complexity of autonomic responses, noting that few semantic generalisation experiments use more than one index of autonomic activity; if they did, it would be clear that correlations found between measurements of meaning and autonomic measures were not due to the supposed mediating responses. Rather, the autonomic responses themselves may change during the conditioning procedure, particularly when a noxious UCS is used. At an early stage in conditioning, the response may in fact be an orienting reflex (OR), but may later take on the features of a defensive reflex (DR). As a result, the semantic generalisation will be to an OR in the early part of the training procedure and a DR in the later part, with different results (Luria and Vinogradova, 1959).

Maltzman, discarding the mediation theory, maintains that the concept of the OR needs to be included in any theory of semantic generalisation. An OR is elicited when any word is presented which contradicts subject's expectations based on previous words presented. This is precisely the situation which occurs in the test phase of the semantic generalisation experiment, where a large number of neutral control words are presented as well as the test words predicted to lead to generalisation. The test words elicit the orienting reflex, possibly because subjects are categorising all words in terms of similarity to the training word (Razran, 1949a), and test words appear more similar. They may appear more similar because they are associates (Bousfield), and, indeed, the judgement of similarity need not be conscious (Razran, 1949b). The use of the concept of the OR provides an opportunity to justify the inference of such intervening variables as anticipation and awareness, or, at the least, to define them operationally.

6. THE REPRESENTATIONAL MEDIATOR THEORY

The previous section concerned theories of meaning which supposed that mediation consisted of an implicit verbal response or a series of such responses. The section concluded with Maltzman's attack on mediation theory which denied that the association of stimulus and response by means of mediating responses was a necessary condition for semantic generalisation. The approach of Osgood to be discussed now supposes that the mediation hypothesis is necessary and that it requires association between stimuli and stimuli, and stimuli and responses. However, it differs from non-representational theories in that it suggests that an adequate account of meaning must include reference to the non-verbal situations in which the words were learned. Osgood (1961) therefore rejects such theories as that of Bousfield, arguing that the mediating response to the word 'bad' cannot be itself an implicit repetition of the word. If it is, argues Osgood, how is the mediating response originally learned? It surely cannot be assumed that the original non-verbal experience elicited a verbal mediator of this sort.

Osgood, Suci and Tannenbaum (1957) therefore supposed that a mediational *and representational* model was required to deal adequately with meaning. The term 'mediational' is used in the same way as in the previous section. The term 'representational' indicates that the mediating response *is a part of* the original response to the non-verbal stimulus with which the word under consideration was originally associated. The paradigm is diagrammed in Figure 5. Osgood (1963) states 'Whenever

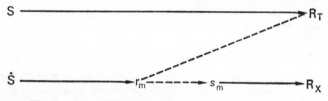

Figure 5. Two-stage mediation model.

some originally neutral stimulus (sign-to-be), $\dot{S}$ is repeatedly contiguous with another stimulus (significate), S, which regularly and reliably elicits a pattern of total behaviour, R_T, the neutral stimulus will become associated with some portion, r_m, of this total behaviour as a representational mediation process.' 'R_X represents the mediated response to the sign, which may be either linguistic or non-linguistic' (Osgood, 1968). The r_m consists of the 'most readily conditionable, least effortful, and least interfering components of the total original reaction' (Osgood, 1963). It is an anticipatory response, derived from Hullian theory, with the function of preparing the subject for overt behaviour. Osgood uses r and s for the mediating terms to indicate that the decoding aspect of meaning, $\dot{S} \rightarrow r_m$, and the encoding aspect, $s_m \rightarrow R_X$, are both subject to the laws of single stage learning theory (e.g. habit-formation, generalization, inhibition). The dependency between r_m and s_m is consequent on automatic motor-sensory feedback. Clearly, r_m and s_m are essential constructs, since the response to a sign, $\dot{S}$, cannot be taken to be the same as the response to its referent, S. This would be the implication if a simple one-stage classical conditioning model were applied to meaning, with UCS as S and CS as $\dot{S}$.

Osgood insists that the theory does not presuppose anything about the physical nature of the mediating response, and inclines to the view

(1968) that it is a central and not a peripheral process; what was originally a peripheral process, he suggests, might have become internalised. However, his use of the term 'automatic motor-sensory feedback' to describe the relation between r_m and s_m makes him appear to support a peripheralist interpretation. Osgood's insistence is necessary because Fig. 5 above represents a situation superficially similar to that obtaining in semantic generalisation. There, too, a stimulus already associated (in this case reflexively) with a response is paired with a neutral stimulus (a word). The word, and words related to it, become conditioned to the UCR. However, semantic generalisation is a special case. The $S \rightarrow R_T$ part of the paradigm is chosen by the experimenter, and the word used as a CS will therefore by definition be a stimulus to an autonomic response. Once again, an experimental technique is not an explanation.

7. A COMPARISON

An experimental test of the representational versus the non-representational theory is difficult. This is because most results are explicable in terms of either theory. However, Osgood, Suci and Tannenbaum (1957) have provided a measuring tool, the *semantic differential*. This technique demands that the subject rates a given concept (the S of Figure 5) on a rating scale of seven points, at either end of which is one or other of a pair of adjectives which are antonyms, e.g. 'good–bad', 'strong–weak', 'cold–hot', 'hard–soft', etc. The response of rating the concept is an R_X which provides evidence as to the r_m. When ratings were factor-analysed, results indicated three basic types of response factor – *evaluation*, *activity* and *potency*. The adjectival pairs 'good–bad', 'pleasant–unpleasant' loaded high on the evaluative factor, 'passive–active', 'slow–fast' on the activity factor, and 'hard–soft', 'severe–lenient' on the potency factor. Many other pairs of adjectives were used as well. These results support a view of the r_m as being a connotative response which reflects the three basic elements of response structure of all organisms to the environment. These are approach-avoidance, rate, and strength. The *nature* of the mediating response to a concept is therefore to be gathered from an analysis of the direction of the ratings on certain adjectival pairs. The *strength* of the response is to be gathered from the degree of polarization on the seven-point scale. The connexion of the evaluative factor with overt approach-avoidance behaviour is supported by Solars (1960), who found that there were shorter latencies for approach movement responses to pleasant words and avoidance responses to unpleasant words than for the converse condition.

As Carroll (1959) in his penetrating critique remarked, the semantic differential does not measure denotative meaning – a kitchen can hardly be described as severe or lenient, nor can these features be supposed to be defining attributes of the concept. Secondly, the nature of the sample of concepts rated will influence the factors found in the responses. Miron and Osgood (1967) emphasise that a large heterogeneous group of concepts must be tested for the three factors to be discovered.

Osgood (1961) claims that semantic generalisation should be explained in terms of representational mediating responses, being the result of overlap between the r_ms of training and test words; he maintains that purely verbal association is not adequate to account for such phenomena. He further quotes the demonstration of *semantic satiation* (Lambert and Jakobovits, 1960). They found that semantic differential ratings became less polarised to certain words after fifteen seconds' repetition by subjects of those words. This indicates the effect of inhibition and could be explained in terms of verbal *or* of representational mediation theory. However, they also found that 'negro' and 'canoe' were satiated in this way, but 'groni' and 'nuka' were not. Bousfield's theory would predict that both sets of words would be satiated, since 'groni' and 'nuka' when repeated rapidly have the same sound as 'negro' and 'canoe'. If the mediating response is the same as the overt expression of the word, then satiation of this mediating response would occur equally to both sets of words. Nevertheless, repetition of 'nuka' and 'canoe' may not be identical; and on certain of the scales, words increase rather than decrease in polarisation after repetition (Yelen and Schulz, 1963). However, this finding may simply reflect differences in the speed of arousal of different types of mediating response (Pollio, 1968).

Bousfield (1961) attempts to explain the results of the semantic differential technique as due to the fact that some of the bipolar adjectives are associates of the concept being rated. Johnson, Miller and Wall (1965) demonstrated that the more polarised a word is on a particular rating scale, the more likely that word is to be associated with the adjectives defining that scale. However, this does not prove that verbal associations are the main necessary and sufficient condition for mediated generalisation. Osgood showed (1961) that many of the adjectives used in the semantic differential scales were not associates of words which were rated at the extreme end of a scale in the Atlas of Semantic Profiles for 360 Words (Jenkins, Russell and Suci, 1958). These two apparently contradictory findings may perhaps be reconciled. Johnson *et al.* compared words of differing degrees of polarisation of response for their association with the defining adjective. Osgood merely noted that of all words which *were* extremely polarised, less than half were associated with the defining adjective. In other words, the overall effect of association between concept and adjective on semantic differential ratings is small, but with that qualification, association is likely to be correlated with polarisation of response. It is also worth noting that Bousfield's theory leaves unexplained the *directionality* of ratings on the semantic differential. Both of the bipolar adjectives may be common associates of a particular word; how then is it that ratings consistently fall towards one end of the scale rather than the other?

It is thus possible that both verbal association *and* representational responses are involved in generalisation of meaning. Staats and Staats (1963) demonstrated that a word can take over the representational response to another as a result of being associated with it. They found that a previously neutral nonsense syllable can resemble a word with which it has been associated in its rating on the evaluative scale of the semantic differential. They also noted (1959) that common associates of a word tend to have similar ratings. They therefore explain the correlation between the word association measures and semantic differential polarisation as follows: the pairing of a word with an associate strengthens the association itself and also conditions the representational reaction to one to the other.

Mowrer (1954) sought to apply representational theory to sentences of an affirmative active type. He supposed that the r_m to 'Tom' in the sentence 'Tom is a thief' became conditioned to the r_m to 'thief'. The r_m to 'Tom' is therefore changed to incorporate elements of that to 'thief'. In other words, the mechanism of predication is assumed to be the same as that of reference: simple association. The only difference is that in the case of predication, the items associated are both words, whereas in that of reference, they are object and word. Perhaps, too, the r_m to 'thief' is changed as a result of the well-loved Tom being included in that category. The explanation is in terms of conditioning by contiguity. Its possibility is supported by the finding of Staats and Staats (1963) that r_m can be conditioned in this way. However (Fodor, 1965), there are many types of sentence which are not of an affirmative active type. What happens in the case of the negative sentence 'Tom is not a thief' (or in the attempted denial by two film stars that they are anything more than just good friends)? And how is it possible to disbelieve the assertion 'Tom is a thief'? More important, the language user's ability to distinguish subject and predicate is a necessary precondition for any such conditioning process to occur.

8. CRITIQUE OF REPRESENTATIONAL MEDIATION

Some basic objections to representational mediation theory have been specified by Fodor (1965). These objections are founded on arguments concerning the nature of language and on certain logical objections to Osgood's arguments. Taken together with the insistence of Maltzman (1968) that association by contiguity is not a necessary condition for semantic generalisation, they constitute a formidable critique.

Fodor argues that the assumption that a word must be associated with a specific situation in order to obtain an r_m is patently false. We do not need 'to keep bad company to fully master the meaning of the word thief', nor do we need to have met Tom to know what the sentence 'Tom is a thief' means. We know that 'Tom' is a name, and therefore understand that someone named 'Tom' has stolen something.

Fodor also claims that the r_m to each sign will have to be different, since signs refer to different entities. Fodor is supposing that mediation theory must include the fact of reference. He argues, in detail, that the $S \rightarrow R_T$ of Figure 5 has to be interpreted in terms of functionally different R_Ts. If all R_Ts are functionally different, then the r_ms which are proper parts of them are also likely to be functionally different. Moreover, r_ms must all be functionally different if different $\dot{S}$ s are to refer to different Ss. This is because $\dot{S}$ is only connected with S by means of r_m. If r_ms were not functionally different in this way, continuous ambiguity would occur. Fodor therefore claims that there is a one-to-one correspondence involved between R_T and r_m and between r_m and R_X which renders mediation theory equivalent to single-stage S–R theory in all respects except observability of response. Fodor's argument is a dilemma: an r_m is simultaneously part of several R_Ts corresponding to distinct Ss or it is part of only one R_T. If the former, r_m will not have one unambiguous referent. If the latter, it will be superfluous and add nothing to a one-stage model.

Osgood (1966) argues that each R_T must have a different r_m, but maintains that the r_m is composed of a number of different components which can combine in many different ways. As a result, biological economy is achieved, since few components are required and r_ms can differ from each other by only one component. Berlyne (1966) introduces further economy into the model by supposing that R_T itself is the sum of the common elements of *all* the Rs associated with that S.

Secondly, Osgood argues that each r_m does *not* have the one-to-one relationship with R_X that it does with R_T, and therefore r_m theory is necessary to distinguish the $\dot{S} \rightarrow r$ stage (decoding) from the $s \rightarrow R_X$

stage (encoding). R_X frequently does not occur; when it does, it need not be a linguistic response in any way corresponding to s_m. It may indeed be another mediating response, r_{m2}. In answer to Fodor's other criticisms, Osgood agrees that we don't have to keep bad company to know what 'thief' means. We learn this by assign learning, the association of words with other words. But both Osgood and Berlyne argue that words are more likely to occur in the presence of their referents than in their absence.

The interesting point about Osgood's reply is that he accepts the need for r_m to be in one-to-one correspondence with R_T and therefore in direct relation with S. He accepts, in other words, that r_m theory has to adhere to the conventions of reference, and meet the requirements of denotative as well as connotative meaning. It follows that the semantic differential is not in its present form a complete indicator of r_m, since the pattern of response on the semantic differential could be the same for two words with different denotations. It is worth asking if a semantic differential technique could be applied to some of the denotative features of language. It seems likely that denotative rating would require a hierarchical model incorporating categories and sub-categories (see Section 9). Such a non-linear model would not allow such easy translation from the rating procedure to statements about the direction and strength of response.

9. FREE RECALL AND SUBJECTIVE ORGANISATION

Results in many fields of verbal learning have indicated that subjects impose their own organisation on material presented to them. For example, Battig (1966) succinctly remarks of paired-associate learning '. . . there can be no more convincing a demonstration of the magnitude and generality of coding processes than to find them under conditions explicitly designed to preclude their occurrence . . .'. A technique designed to allow the occurrence of such processes is that of *free recall*.

For this type of experiment: 1. E may present a list of unrelated words selected at random. S is instructed to recall the list in whatever order he pleases, and several trials are allowed. On successive trials S may respond with two or more words grouped together in a different order from that in which they were presented. 2. E may present a list in which the order of the words is random, but they have been selected as belonging to certain associative pairs, or to categories. S often recalls these words in the pairs or grouped under the categories. 3. E may present the list already ordered according to association or category, not random. Clearly, there is an increasing degree of control by E over the coding performed by S as one progresses from technique 1 to 3 above.

In view of these differences, it is hardly surprising that the principle exponent of technique 1, Tulving (1968), lays most stress on the subjective nature of the organisation of the recalled lists. However, he does not give any account of the nature of this subjective organisation. Sometimes, the units have clear associative or categorical bases (e.g. 'rubber, iron, sand; argument, settle'). But on other occasions, no clear connexion is apparent (e.g. 'conquest, ornament, demand; spoon, chimney'). Battig (1966), suggests that this organisation is based on degree of learning; words that have been learned to the same degree are recalled together. However, as Deese (1968) remarks, Tulving is wrong to assume that it is easier to account theoretically for the recall of single words than for that of subjective units. In fact, the artificial nature of E defined units (words) renders them *less* amenable to theoretical treatment.

Experiments using the more experimenter-controlled techniques (2) and (3) have mainly been concerned with arguing the basis for *clustering* (distinguished from subjective organisation by Tulving, 1968, on the ground that E controls the organisation of the list). One thing is immediately clear: clustering does not occur as a result of the order of presentation of words being kept constant and the consequent association of one item with the next on the list; Waugh (1961) found that results are identical for constant and variable order lists. It must therefore be inferred that already existing ways of organising the material are employed by Ss. Items are perceived and remembered, not learned. Many behaviourists consider it unlikely that any processes other than those of *association* are involved. Others, however, maintain that some results cannot be explained except in terms of *categories* and instances thereof.

Experiments which supply one sort of organisation or the other in the list are not crucial. Thus, for example, Jenkins and Russell (1952) found that associates separated in the list were recalled together. Bousfield (1953), on the other hand, presented lists containing four categories of words – weapons, cities, animals, and articles of clothing. Although presented in a random order, these words were found to cluster in the recall protocols. Relationships between superordinates and subordinates were inferred. However, only when association value and category membership were controlled variables within a single experiment could more decisive inferences be drawn, since clearly both of the above results could be explained in terms of either association or category.

To remedy this defect, Bousfield, Cohen and Whitmarsh (1958) studied clustering for lists in which the items were all examples of categories; some lists contained frequent associates of category names, others infrequent associates of the same names. The frequent associates showed marked clustering, and the infrequent lists relatively little. This result clearly supports an association 'explanation'. However, Marshall (see Cofer, 1965) controlled association value and compared clustering of pairs of categorised words with that of uncategorised words. He varied degree of associative overlap between words, and found that both category and degree of association had significant effects, with a significant interaction effect; at high levels of association, categorisation had no effect, but at low levels an appreciable one.

Cofer (1965) in an exhaustive review article, concludes that experimenter-produced relations provide a basis for clustering alternative to the type of idiosyncratic clustering found by Tulving, provided they are sufficiently prominent. He admits the possibility of categories, but such an admission still allows the possibility of their description in terms of mediating responses. A category word could be described as an associate of a stimulus word which mediated a divergent hierarchy of subordinate words. However, Cofer (1966) goes to great lengths in his efforts to 'explain' results implying categories in terms of associations.

Tulving (1968) maintains that the distinction between associative and mediational mechanisms of clustering emphasised by Cofer is futile, for the following reasons: 1. Association is not an explanation but an empirical fact which has not yet been explained. The fact that a word is commonly given as a response to another word in the free association situation and the fact that the two words are recalled together in the free recall situation need not mean anything more than that the two situations are in some respect similar. It certainly need not mean that the two words were learned through having been experienced in temporal contiguity. 2. It is not possible to control category and vary association, since categories vary in inclusiveness to such an extent that almost any pair of words may be subsumed under some category or other (e.g. 'things'). 3. Finally, there are a great many subjective organisations which are impossible to classify into associative groups, category groups, or any other classification.

10. RETRIEVAL

Tulving's approach has led to some important results. For example, if recall is demanded at different intervals after presentation, one half of the words recalled were recalled on only one of the three occasions when recall was demanded (Tulving, 1968). This result indicates that the distinction between *storage* and *retrieval* emphasised by Melton (1963) is valid, since it shows that much can be stored which cannot be retrieved. The fascinating 'tip of the tongue' experiment by Brown and McNeill (1966) highlights this distinction. The state of knowing a word but being unable to produce it was induced in subjects, and it was found that the most common retrieval cues were letters, number of syllables, and primary stress, primarily at the beginning and end of the word. These features are similar to those noted by Ehrlich (1965) as being cues for clustering in free recall (phonetic and letter structure similarity); it is tempting to infer that the free recall procedure can highlight some of the cues needed for efficient retrieval, or, as Asch and Ebenholtz (1962) term them, *availability* cues.

However, perhaps the most important retrieval cue is *category* membership, and the resultant label that is available for grouping purposes. Tulving and Pearlstone (1966) presented both words belonging to categories and the category names themselves in the list, but demanded recall only of the words. One group of Ss was given the category names as retrieval cues in the recall phase, and was superior to the other group which was not given such cues. Analysis of the results revealed that improvement was due to an increase in the number of categories recalled, not in the number of words within each category. That is, word recall within units and unit recall are independent; the improved recall in terms of number of words that results when units are provided is entirely a result of more units being recalled. This finding is reminiscent of the findings of Johnson (see p. 43) that more errors in recall occur at the junctions between phrase units. It supports Tulving's explanation of the free recall findings in terms of Miller's 'chunks'.

A recent influential approach has been that of Deese (1966). Instead of defining association in terms of the frequency of response as a first associate to a word, Deese uses a measure of the total distribution of associative responses to that word. He insists (1968) that 'the important fact in the manifest organisation of associations is not that 'mother' leads to 'father', 'hot' to 'cold', and 'sleep' to 'dream', not that these superficially similar pairs are contiguous or derived in any form from the law of contiguity, but that they in their obvious differences . . . reflect different organisational processes at work' (p. 99). Deese treats associative data merely as indices of underlying patterns of relation, but does maintain that associative norms are useful tools for revealing such patterns. He therefore agrees with Tulving that associative data are facts, not explanations (since he does not assume that they derive from contiguity of the associates).

Deese analyses the relations between words in terms of the overlap of their respective associative hierarchies. He concludes that a word is to be defined psychologically by a type of distinctive feature analysis. According to this approach, the features defining any item are binary; the intersection of features means that one word may differ from another by only one feature. Associative data are then explained in terms of differences in one or more features: responses which are antonyms of the stimulus word differ from it in one feature only, while responses which are not antonyms are the result of a principle of exclusion or inclusion which is determined by many features. Such features of responses as response strength are superimposed on this basic structure. Deese's theory therefore has much in common with distinctive feature theory in phonemics (see p. 24). There, too, features are binary, but must be fewer in number than the features proposed by Deese. Osgood's (1966) description of the r_m also employs a type of distinctive feature analysis. Its attraction is clearly the number of different items (words, phonemes, meanings) that can be derived from combinations of relatively few features. This behaviourist concept, therefore, has much in common with the generative linguists' emphasis on the productive feature of language.

Mandler (1966, 1968) maintains that the use of distinctive features by Deese makes allowance for the limitations of the human *storage* system which are in fact not so important as the limitations on the *retrieval* system. Mandler suggests that word-equivalents are the theoretical units in a model of word usage, not distinctive features. These would not take up a great deal more storage space than distinctive features, and would lead to far more rapid retrieval. Their limited demands on *storage* space are ensured by an efficient hierarchical filing system, which, for example, subsumes under the category 'acquaintances' the subgroups 'family', 'social', and 'professional'. Each of these subcategories in its turn has its own subcategories, e.g. 'professional' contains 'peers' and 'students'. Each such subcategory might then contain a list of items – their names.

More important, such a filing system also allows rapid *retrieval* by a series of decisions. The number of items in the lowest subcategory, and the number of subcategories in each higher category is limited by the span of short-term memory; so is the number of levels of category in the hierarchy, since one must remember at what level one entered the system in searching for an item. Mandler also states that hierarchies can interact, in that words can be members of many different systems. He suggests that there is another hierarchical organisation which subsumes each of these hierarchies. This allows the language user to perceive the connexion between different uses of the same word, and to select according to context. There is other evidence (e.g. Brown and McNeill, 1966) which suggests that retrieval may also follow the principles of the dictionary, to the extent that the first sound has been shown to be an important cue. Perhaps (Lunzer, personal communication) dictionary retrieval is from long-term storage, while category retrieval is from an easy access store.

Mandler's theory has much in common with the notions of plans and strategies (Miller, Galanter and Pribram, 1960) and with the stimulating integration of the theory of the schema (Oldfield and Zangwill, 1942) and ethological and developmental findings achieved by Lunzer (1968). It reflects the results of Tulving and Pearlstone (1966), who found that the number of categories recalled increases, but not the number of words within each category when category names are provided as retrieval cues. This demands at least a two-level hierarchy, and Mandler (1966) provides evidence that the number of categories recalled from a set of categories of a given size is constant also. A multi-level hierarchy, such as that provided in Mandler's theory, is therefore required.

The implications of such a theory are immense. Many of the problems of experimental psychology and of linguistics may be defined in terms of the position of a word in a hierarchy and the interaction of this hierarchy with other hierarchies of which the word is a member. For example, the nature of synonymy may be explicated in terms of similar position. However, the theory is preliminary, and does not deal with how the language user chooses the point in a hierarchy at which to begin his search; nor does it explain how some hierarchies and categories within hierarchies are more available than others (is it because of frequency and recency of use?).

One may object that Mandler often uses an inference lacking an empirical basis to 'explain' the results of experimental techniques. But it is to his credit that these techniques are not treated merely operationally. When they are, separate bodies of theory grow up because of the different effects of other variables on performance in each experimental situation. As a result, paired-associate learning, mediation theory, and verbal operant conditioning have developed as separate fields. Mandler's theory is not operationally defined, for it contains hypothetical constructs which are inferred from *different* types of experimental behaviour. It is truly theoretical.

The significance of free recall is considerable. 1. It is a development from a field of research which was based on inadequate theoretical foundations (those of association by contiguity). It has therefore given rise to new theoretical assumptions which are direct challenges to the older assumptions. This would not be so if the experimental technique employed had little connexion with previous experimental work, for in this case the adherents of the old paradigm would have dismissed the new evidence as 'unscientific'. 2. The field of free recall has recognised the need in the area of meaning of hierarchical concepts which have been found necessary to describe grammatical and other skills and instinctive behaviour in animals. 3. The distinction between word association as an experimental technique and as an explanation has been highlighted. 4. The distinction between experimenter units and subject units has been revealed; both types of unit are subjective, and both are amply evidenced – the former in the many thousands of experimental designs employing arbitrary experimental units, the latter in the free recall protocols.

The approach of behaviourists to 'meaning' has developed astonishingly in recent years. The realisation that contiguity is not the basis of language behaviour; that subjective organisation is more important than stimulus control; and that psychological structures are hierarchical as well as linear in nature, are indications of this progress. However, there has been little effort to show how non-linguistic cues are related to these processes. The writer believes that the connexion of non-linguistic cues with language behaviour is of vital importance. It allows the inference of a connexion between the regulatory systems of linguistic and non-linguistic behaviour. Such a connexion is the key to an explanation of the acquisition of language (Chapter V) and its relation to thinking (Chapter VI). The whole 'problem of meaning' so-called is concerned with the connexion between non-linguistic and linguistic schemata.

V

Language Acquisition

1. ACQUISITION AND GENERATIVE LINGUISTICS

A disproportionate amount of space will be devoted to the application of generative linguistics to language acquisition, since it is this area of study which has expanded so rapidly recently. Certain other findings concerning the effects of various variables upon the acquisition of language will be described in Chapter VI pp. 153–5. The distinction between *competence* and performance was described and criticised in Chapter III. If one accepts the distinction in the sense in which it is employed by Chomsky, certain implications for language acquisition necessarily follow. If competence is a necessary and sufficient condition of performance, then competence must be present before comprehension or production of language by the child can take place. Its acquisition cannot therefore be explained in terms of learning by behaviour, since the behaviour which would be necessary for its acquisition is supposed to be dependent upon its prior existence. It has therefore been concluded that competence is based on *innate features*, a Language Acquisition Device (LAD) (Chomsky, 1965).

Furthermore, since competence is defined as generative theory (deep structure and the transformational operations which lead to surface structure); and since generative theory is specific about the nature of these features of language; then the conclusion must be that the innate competence is specific, and consists of the universal features of language – the distinctions between subject and predicate, verb and object, and modifier and head. It further follows that the evidence adduced to support these hypotheses must consist of proof that all the early utterances of children can be described in terms of deep structure (even this is not proof positive, since, as performance is the only possible evidence for competence, it is as logically possible to infer that competence is dependent on performance as the converse).

If the earliest utterances of children do give evidence for deep structure, then it becomes plausible to describe the rest of the acquisition process in terms of Chomsky's account of adult sentence production (see Chapter III); this supposes that transformational operations act upon deep structure strings and produce surface structures.

If transformations occur (in the child's utterances) at a later stage than deep structure, it is tempting to infer that the earliest utterances exemplify deep structure acted upon directly by the phonological component; surface structure only becomes part of the child's competence when he has mastered transformations. In other words, the assumption is that at the earlier stages of development, there is little gap between competence and performance. As a result of this supposed correspondence between linguistic description and the process of acquisition, it is the habit of generative theorists to describe the child's acquisition process as being similar to that of a linguist writing a grammar of a language (Donaldson's (1966) thorough critique of this extravagant figure of speech should preclude its further use).

The purpose of the above paragraphs is to show how this account of the acquisition process necessarily follows from prior assumptions of dichotomies between competence and performance and deep and surface structures. McNeill (1966b) has logically carried through his thinking to the conclusions described above. His position is paraphrased by Fraser (1966, p. 116) as follows '... it is now proposed that, first, children are born with a biologically based, innate capacity for language acquisition; secondly, the best guess as to the nature of the innate capacity is that it takes the form of linguistic universals; thirdly, the best guess as to the nature of linguistic universals is that they consist of what are currently the basic notions in a Chomskian transformational grammar.'

The above account is in direct contradiction to an account based on *learning*, which would suppose that any more abstract features of behaviour result from experiences of concrete features; for example, learning sets (Harlow, 1949) result from successful solutions of discrimination problems. As McNeill puts it (1966b, p. 52):

'If children begin their productive linguistic careers with a competence limited to the base structure of sentences, it is difficult to see how it can be explained by any theory of language acquisition that restricts attention to what a child might obtain from the observable surface characteristics of parental speech. Such theories would have to predict the opposite course of development: first, surface structure; then base structure. Most behaviourist theories have assumed this order, with notable lack of success; failure is inevitable when children produce only the base structure, and behaviourist theories produce only the surface structure of sentences. What is needed is either a child who commences acquisition with surface structure or a theory that focuses on base structure. Since it is easier to change theories than children, the latter course has been followed here.'

McNeill's case therefore depends on the description of the earliest utterances of children in terms of deep structure. However, before this most important question is discussed, certain other arguments frequently used to support the generative position will be examined. Firstly, it is alleged that the *speed* with which the skills of language are acquired indicates a strong and specific innate basis. However, such a statement is a relative one; in comparison with what other skilled performance is language acquisition rapid? If one thinks in terms of cognitive skills, it is tempting to infer that language acquisition is indeed faster than, for example, the stages of intellectual development described by Piaget. However, Piaget does not describe these operations in terms of transformations. If he did, it might be found that such early achievements as size constancy or conservation of the object require such description. Indeed, the same processes might underlie linguistic and non-linguistic performance. What is innate, in other words, may not be *content* (the universals) but *process* (Slobin, 1966*b*). McNeill (1968) insists, however, that even if this is the case, the general (cognitive) process must include all the complexity evidenced by the special (linguistic) case. Another argument against the assumption of great speed of acquisition after the utterance of the first two connected words, is the existence of the earlier period in which the child has been exposed to and has possibly comprehended his parents' language.

A second assumption used by the generative linguists to indicate a large innate component is that the child masters the structure of his language as a result of '*mere exposure*' to often incomplete samples of adult speech. But, as will be seen in Section 4, adults often do a lot more than speak *in the presence of* children; for a start, they sometimes actually speak *to* them! And the incomplete nature of many adult sentences may be one source of the unusual orders of combination of children (e.g. 'all gone lettuce').

2. ACQUISITION OF DEEP STRUCTURE

The crux of the generative linguists' arguments, however, is the assertion that all the earliest utterances of children are describable in terms of *deep structure*. The approach to the analysis of young children's utterances has radically changed within the last decade. Instead of applying adult criteria to children's utterances obtained in laboratory conditions, investigators have obtained tape-recorded samples of children's speech in their homes and analysed the transcript as though it were a novel language. Pioneers were Brown and Fraser (1963), Braine (1963*b*), and Ervin (1964). An important collection of reports was edited by Bellugi and Brown (1964). The child's own utterances and those of its mother when she was involved in conversation with the child were recorded, as was the non-linguistic context of the child's utterances. But the latter was not employed explicitly in the subsequent analysis of data.

Brown and Fraser (1963) give an exhaustive account of the process of writing a grammar for this data. Of course, the child cannot report his intuitions as to the grammaticality of sentences presented by the investigator. Instead, the investigator has to analyse the data in terms of the *distribution* of different items. Certain types of word were found to have certain privileges of occurrence: they could only occur in certain positions in the utterance, and not in others.

As a result of this analysis, considerable consensus has been reached concerning the nature of the earliest utterances of more than one word (mostly two words long, and first produced at the age of eighteen to twenty-four months). They are described in terms of two classes, *pivot* and *open* (Braine's (1963*b*) terminology). Pivot class words always occur in one of the two possible positions of a two-word utterance; open class words are not tied in this way. Furthermore, there are different *subclasses* of pivot words; pivot words are said to belong to the same subclass if the words which they precede or follow in the two-word sentences have the same function. In other words, pivot words of the same subclass have the same privileges of occurrence. However, the decision as to which open class words have the same function is not clearly explained. The following examples should clarify the distinction between pivot and open words and also the nature of a sub-class of pivot words. The words 'this' and 'that' are members of the same pivot sub-class in the following utterances of a child observed by Ervin: 'this arm', 'this baby', 'this pretty', 'this yellow', 'this come', 'that arm', 'that baby', 'that pretty', 'that yellow'. However, 'the' and 'a' are a separate sub-class of pivot words, since, although they occur in the same position in the sentence as 'this' and 'that', they do not precede words of the same function; e.g. 'the other, a other'. A two-word sentence can be composed of two open class words, a pivot and an open, or (less frequently), an open and a pivot. Pivot class words are fewer in number than open class words, and each pivot word is consequently used more frequently than individual open class words.

This *statistical imbalance* is a very important feature of two-word sentences. If the pivot words were function words (see p. 36), it would parallel the greater frequency of function words in adult usage. However, pivot words are not usually function words, and therefore it must be inferred that the child has imposed his own structure on his utterances. Such a conclusion is supported by the many utterances which could not be abbreviated imitations of adult utterances, for example, 'allgone milk', 'that doed'. McNeill therefore regards the use of the word 'telegraphic' to describe these utterances as misleading, since it implies that they are merely reductions of adult utterances, not novel creations.

Instead, McNeill (1966b) claims that the basis of the child's utterances is a *productive* rule. The child is using one of the linguistic descriptions assigned to his utterance by the linguist, e.g. $S \rightarrow (P) + O$ (where S = sentence, P = pivot, O = open, and brackets indicate that P may be omitted). McNeill is unwilling to distinguish telegraphic English from novel utterances, the one a result of imitation and the other a novel creation. He maintains that *all* the child's utterances are produced by rules. However, granted that this inference is justified, McNeill still has to show that this rule and other such descriptions of early utterances are based on *innate linguistic universals* rather than on the child's experience of features of language and situation. This is a particularly difficult task, since in terms of form classes, the pivot and open classes contain different parts of speech for different children. Moreover, the *same* child may use the same form class in both the pivot and the open class. This makes it very difficult to infer that a *PO* sentence 'represents' a universal of the form verb-object or subject-predicate.

Nevertheless, McNeill maintains that the pivot and open classes later *differentiate* into the class distinctions available to adults (e.g. that between mass and count nouns), and therefore 'a child honours in advance some of the distinctions on which adult classes are based' (McNeill, 1966b, p. 28). For example, within five months, the pivot class of one of Brown's subjects had differentiated into articles, adjectives, demonstrative and possessive pronouns, and a remaining pivot class (criterion for class membership once again being privilege of occurrence). McNeill maintains (1966b) that this differentiation must be due to innate universals. The adult distinctions do not derive smoothly from the original pivot-open distinction, since the same form classes appear in both pivot and open classes. McNeill (1966c) therefore hypothesises that the child categorises words which he hears in parental speech in terms of their position with respect to the universal features evident in the utterance; the child perceives these universal features as a result of his innate propensity. Thus, for example, a word might be categorised in terms of its position after the noun phrase subject of a sentence, or before a noun. In the former case, it would become an open class word, in the latter a pivot. Some words might occur in both positions and therefore occur in both pivot and open classes.

The previous paragraphs have discussed the *differentiation* of grammatical features from the all-embracing binary categorisation of pivot and open into some of the form classes and features distinguished in adult speech. McNeill's arguments for the existence of innate universals derive, however, from the *productive rules* employed by children. A rule, it will be recalled, is a linguistic description of a supposed process whereby a construction is derived from another. The derived construction is described in greater detail.

Brown and Bellugi (1964) showed that the earliest rules are often $S \rightarrow P + N$ (where S = sentence, P = pivot, and N = noun); e.g. 'that coat'; or $S \rightarrow N + N$; e.g. 'Adam coat'. Later utterances required the rule $S \rightarrow P + NP$, where NP (noun phrase) consisted of $N + N$; e.g. 'that Adam coat'. Brown and Bellugi suppose that the NP constituent occurs as a result of prior use of the $P + N$ or $N + N$ sentences. McNeill, however, argues that this interpretation is impossible, since sentences composed of VNN occurred among the earliest utterances of the child; sentences of this pattern must be generated by an $NP \rightarrow N + N$ rule, so it follows that an NP constituent was available to the child at the earliest stages of his grammatical development. Since NP is the form of the subject of the sentence, and since the subject-predicate distinction is one of the universal features of language, McNeill has argued that the pivot and open classes are in fact of little importance in themselves; they merely reflect the application of the innate universals.

Another early rule, 1. $S \rightarrow$ Pred P (predicate phrase), 2. Pred $P \rightarrow V + NP$, 3. $NP \rightarrow N + N$ or $P + N$ (e.g. 'want Adam coat') shows that the predicate phrase is also available at an early age, with the result that the child has available the two basic components of the fully formed adult sentence – $NP +$ Pred P. Sometimes (in 10 to 15% of cases) the earliest sentences reflect this $NP +$ Pred P structure; for there are sentences of form NV ('Bambi go'), NNV ('Adam panda march'), and NVN ('Adam change diaper').

McNeill's (1966*b*, 1966*c*, 1968) 'tour de force' is to show that, at a stage when one child's grammar included only the classes P (pivot), N and V, that child produced in 400 sentences only 12 of the 36 possible two and three word combinations. All of those 12 combinations were consistent with the deep structure grammatical relations (for example, $P + N$ is consistent with the relation modifier + head noun, $N + V$ with the relation subject + predicate). Of the other 24 combinations which were not uttered, none was consistent with the deep structure relations. Thus the child used every possible combination that expresses the grammatical relation; further, he uttered none of those that did not, although he must have heard many such (e.g. VVN, 'come and eat your breakfast').

However, as Fraser (1966) points out, more needs to be known about 1. what the admissible combinations were, and 2. how it was decided whether a particular utterance was an example of an admissible or inadmissible type. For example, is a VNN sentence automatically admissible? Does 'eat chair mummy' (VNN) reflect the universal features? And why should the example quoted by McNeill ('change Adam diaper') reflect the verb-object relation rather than the subject-verb-object relation in the (wrong) order verb-subject-object?

A more basic objection to McNeill's general approach concerns his use of the terms N, V, NP, etc., in their adult significance. If the single word utterances uttered by a child before he begins combining words are taken to be holophrastic (i.e. contain the meaning of a sentence), why should the words of a two or three word utterance belong to the adult form classes? True, in terms of privilege of occurrence, the child may substitute one item for another in the same position in the utterance. But to call the resulting classes noun or verb is to imply that they fulfil the same functions as the adult form classes of that name: and the essential ambiguity of so many of the children's utterances makes this implication highly dubious.

The generative linguists therefore conclude that a considerable portion of linguistic competence is innate. The child, they say, knows what distinctions are relevant to his future development of an adult differentiated system. The only function of experience is to correct one or two incorrect hypotheses about language which might result from the universals. For example, the child might put predicate before subject until he realised from experience that the order was the reverse.

There is therefore not much support among generative linguists for the theory of Braine (1963a) (see p. 53). Braine's theory of *contextual generalisation* hypothesised that the position of an item relative to surrounding items was learned at every level of the hierarchy of the phrase marker tree of adult speech. For example, the position of a certain phrase in a sentence, or a certain word in a phrase, could be learned, and the item used in the same position but with different context in a novel utterance. Admittedly, Braine's theory does not explain how the important regularities of position are learned and unimportant ones ignored. However, this objection can be dealt with by bringing non-linguistic context into the explanation. The child might notice that a word appeared in a certain position in a certain *situation*. For example, the demonstrative 'that' occurred at the beginning of a sentence when the speaker was pointing at something and naming it.

The same explanation might be adduced to meet the objections of Bever, Fodor and Weksel (1965) to Braine's theory. They allege that contextual generalisation does not allow the existence of transformations or deep structure, since it supposes that the learning of grammar is based only on utterances that the child hears. However, this objection is based on the presupposition that deep structure is innate and a necessary condition for grammatical performance. But there may well be situations operating during adult utterances which permit the child to infer the elements of deep structure. For example, the subject-predicate distinction may be learned from parental sentences uttered in situations in which properties are related to things, the main verb-object relation from sentences uttered in situations in which something is done to something or someone.

However, this suggestion does not wholly answer the objection. The ability to derive deep structure from surface structure plus situational context *when deep and surface structure differ considerably* must also be explained, perhaps as follows. It is possible, for example, that the child comes to learn that when a noun follows a passive verb form in an actor-action-object situation, that noun is the actor. The child can see that the dog's biting Jane, that the dog is the actor and Jane the object; however he hears the sentence 'Jane's being bitten by the dog'. He recognises that the usual sentence order of actor first and object last is reversed in this case, since the evidence in front of his eyes assures him that Jane isn't doing the biting. After experience with other such instances, he comes to realise that this reversal only occurs when the verb has certain passive grammatical features about it. As a result of this learning, he can comprehend the passive construction in the absence of the situation to which it refers. The perception of position in the sentence, of grammatical inflexions, and of the non-linguistic context of utterance is therefore necessary for such learning to take place.

It may be objected that the young child does not possess the capacity for such complex perceptions. But it should be stressed that the stock examples of linguists are especially chosen for their exemplification of the point in question. The sentences about John (see p. 62), for example, differ grammatically only in their deep structure. There is no evidence concerning the age at which children can make distinctions between such special cases. The more general cases where surface structure differs (e.g. in active and passive forms) obviously occur far more often, and comprehension of such forms occurs sometimes at age three (Fraser, Bellugi and Brown, 1963) and certainly at six (Slobin, 1966a). It is therefore tempting to conclude that *comprehension* of grammar is the main contributor to successful language production (see Section 4).

3. ACQUISITION OF TRANSFORMATIONS AND INFLEXIONS

'If children's earliest syntactic competence comprises the base structure of sentences, then obviously the major portion of syntactic acquisition after this point will be taken up with the growth of transformations' (McNeill, 1966b, p. 53). The quotation illustrates the assumption that since transformational rules are necessary in a descriptive linguistic system to account for the derivation of surface from deep structure (see p. 63), they will also be acquired by children before surface structure can be inferred. The child's earliest utterances are supposed to be produced by the action of the phonological component directly upon deep structure strings. At the stage when transformations are about to be learned, sentences derived from deep structure should occur with the transformational element prefixed to the sentence.

This is apparently what occurs. Bellugi has concentrated upon the acquisition of transformations, and, together with Ervin (1964) and Menyuk (1964) provides the majority of the data. A sophisticated presentation of her findings on the negative and interrogative transformations is to be found in Klima and Bellugi (1966). Bellugi distinguishes certain stages in the growth of transformational skill. For example, the negative and interrogative functions are supplied in the earliest stage by the simple prefixing of a negative or interrogative word in front of the sentence or even by intonation alone, e.g. 'no singing song', 'no play that', 'no fall', 'who that?' 'where kitty?' 'ball go?'. It is worth noting, incidentally, that several of these utterances could be taken as either imperative or declarative. Not only is the negative morpheme placed at the beginning of the sentence rather than within or after it, but also a negative uttered in the latter position in the mother's speech is not comprehended.

At a later stage, the negative morpheme is placed in its correct position, but the auxiliary verb is still omitted (e.g. 'He not little, he big'. 'I no want envelope'). Auxiliaries are sometimes used, but only in the negative, not in the positive forms (e.g. 'I can't catch you', 'I don't want it'). 'I can . . .' and 'I do . . .' do not occur in the child's utterances, so 'can't' and 'don't' are to be considered special cases of the negative, not auxiliary verbs plus negative. In the case of the interrogative, the child at this second stage produces sentences like 'Where my mitten?', 'What the dolly have?', 'What me think?'. These utterances reflect the fact that the object of a question is an *N* or *NP*, and it is clear that children understand mothers' questions as demanding such answers; e.g. 'What do you need?' – 'Need some chocolate'.

At a later stage still, children use the negative morphemes and the auxiliaries in the right position e.g. 'I can't see it', 'You don't want some supper', 'It's not cold'. The words 'can't' and 'don't' are taken to be composed of the auxiliary plus the negative morpheme rather than to be simple forms because 'can' and 'do' are used in other utterances. At a similar stage in the interrogative, sentences such as 'Did I saw that in my book?', 'Where I should put it when I make it up?' 'Why kitty can't stand up?' are produced. The auxiliary verbs are now used freely, and it is only the position of the auxiliary relative to the subject that needs correction for the result of the transformational operation to be identical to adult examples.

What principles determine this development? It is clear that the acquisition of transformational rules does not follow the same sequence as the rules describing adult transformations. For example, the derivational order of the indefinite and indeterminate pronouns is 'something → anything → nothing', (Klima, 1964), but for children the developmental order is 'something → nothing → anything'. Furthermore, it is clear that the individual rules of adult transformations do not occur as single and clearly recognisable stages in acquisition; for example, the introduction of the auxiliary verb into the negative construction does not occur at one period, in an all or none manner, for at any given time some sentences may contain an auxiliary, others not. These facts would clearly argue against any attempt to consider the transformational operations as innate, but in fact the attempt is not made, since specific transformations are not universal; each language has its own. However, McNeill typically insists (1966*b*, p. 62):

'We can suppose that a child wants to escape the mess into which his base-structure grammar places him, but escape to where? By now this is a familiar problem. Once again we can appeal to linguistic universals to guide the child. This time we must evoke formal universals: some will specify the general form that base structure rules . . . must take; others will describe in a general way the form of transformations. One part of the formal universals pertaining to transformations presumably would be a characterization of appropriate input, viz., a phrase marker from the base structure.'

The 'mess' to which McNeill refers above is the supposed 'cognitive clutter' obtaining in the earlier stages of the development of transformations. According to an analysis in terms of rules, the child has to remember at least five different possible contexts for the negative morpheme at the second stage of development. For example, at stage 2 negatives appear at the beginning of the sentence, in the forms 'don't' and 'can't', in the question form 'why not', as an imperative 'don't', and in a copular sentence e.g. 'That no fish school'. The development of transformations is then seen as an attempt to reduce the number of these rules to the two or three transformational rules required in the adult grammar.

The child's own rules may be derived from an inductive process similar to that evidenced in the case of inflexions. For example, just as the past tense 'ed' morpheme is overgeneralised to all verbs, so the negatives 'no' and 'not' are always placed at the beginning of the sentence (where they often appear in adult utterances to the child). However, exceptions have to be allowed for – 'Why' also appears at the beginning of sentences, probably more frequently than 'no' and 'not', so the child has to make an exception to his first rule and say 'Why not'. By the time the adult degree of skill has been attained, the position of the auxiliaries and the negative and interrogative morphemes will have been mastered. A series of transformational operations performed on deep structure does not need to be inferred. Once again, then, the child's early utterances appear to be explicable in terms of Braine's theory concerning position of an item within a linguistic context; also, the child will have had to learn the non-linguistic contexts in which each transformation is appropriate. The complexity of the negative and interrogative constructions makes it highly probable that they will occur late in development. It should not be supposed that they are *typical* of sentences which can be described in terms of surface structure. Therefore, the inference that surface structure is not available to the child until these transformational types have been mastered is to be rejected.

Interesting work has been done on the production of inflexions. Berko (1958) tested the generalisation of several inflexions, including the plural morpheme 's' and the past morpheme 'ed'. She used nonsense words and pictures, so that both the referent and the utterance would be novel, thereby fulfilling the criterion of productivity. For example, she showed a picture of a weird creature, saying 'This is a wug'. Then, producing another, 'Here is another. Now there are two . . .'. The child responds to the interrogative rise in intonation with the utterance 'wugs'. Similarly, 'Here is a man wugging. Today he is wugging; yesterday he . . .' 'Wugged'. The child has heard the morpheme 'ed' used when events he knows to be in time past are being referred to; he has also heard it in such verbal contexts as 'yesterday'; and he has always heard it tagged on to the end of a word class which he already recognises as having certain privileges of occurrence and meanings. He therefore produces it when required by a new demand in his environment to do so. Berko also found that the differences in difficulty between elements were probably due to their phonological complexity; for example, the allophones of the plural and the possessive ('gutch*es*' rather than 'wug*s*') were particularly difficult.

This tendency to generalise the rules to new instances is also evidenced in such over-generalisations as 'bringed' and 'mouses'. It is interesting to note that the irregular forms of the past tense (e.g. 'came', 'went', 'sat') are often correctly produced early on in the child's development, but later they become 'comed', 'goed' and 'sitted' (Ervin, 1964). In other words, 'came' is learned as an individual item, but as soon as the regular rule of adding 'ed' is mastered, 'came' falls into disuse and 'comed' is generated. The reason for the child's overgeneralisation is that he has learned that 'ed' refers to the past, that it occurs regularly in one position, and that it is useful when he wishes to refer to a past event. The earlier occurrence of the irregular forms in the child's language may be due to their occurrence as whole words rather than as suffixes, which are more difficult to perceive. However, the attraction to the child of the general rule which embraces all instances cannot be denied; it eliminates a lot of items difficult to store and retrieve; and the child's reluctance to admit exceptions to it can be judged from the occurrence at a still later stage of such monstrosities as 'broughted', 'camed', 'caughted'. Limitation on storage space in itself does not appear to make the over-generalisation necessary, however, for some children (e.g. those speaking French) learn to master without much difficulty an arbitrary gender system for each noun. If the generalising rules required for the production of inflexions can be derived by children from adult models, there is no reason to suppose that rules cannot be derived for other syntactic features from the same source.

The importance of *inflexions and function words* in acquisition has been underrated. Such inflexions as plural 's', past tense 'ed', and participial 'ing' are used regularly in certain types of *situations* (where there is more than one item, where the event being referred to is past, and where something is going on). Therefore they aid the identification of nouns as words which denote items, verbs as words which denote action (Brown, 1957). Furthermore, they always occur after specific form classes, so they aid their recognition also by being experienced in certain *positions* in the sentence. Since they aid the recognition of form classes, they also serve to make the structure of a sentence clear (see p. 50). Inflexions are not produced until relatively late in the grammatical development of the child; but this may be due to the limitations of short-term memory, the inflexion being an additional item to be stored in space occupied by the essential semantic components of the sentence. However, comprehension may well precede production by a long period in this case (see Section 4). Brown and Berko (1960) showed that older children could use a nonsense word as a form class in a sentence after they had heard it so used in another sentence. This illustrates the combined effects of sentence position and inflexions on comprehension and, as a result, on production.

4. THE LEARNING OF LANGUAGE

The term '*learning*' will be used in this context to refer to some more features of experience (as opposed to innate features or their activation) which might be necessary conditions of language acquisition.

Attempts have been made to describe the learning of language by children in terms of operant and classical *conditioning* paradigms. For example, the word 'drink' might be learned as a CS to the UCS of the bottle, while an operant response 'drink' might be learned if the reward was experienced as a result of the response. Skinner (1957) supposes that these early operant responses take the form of 'mands', 'tacts', or 'echoic responses'. A mand is a demand, rewarded by the child obtaining what he asks for; a tact is a naming response, in which the child names some feature of his environment and is rewarded by his mother's pleasure; and an echoic response is simply a repetition of his own or an adult's utterance, the reward being self-stimulation. The discriminative cues for these responses may be features of the external or the internal environment (e.g. the sight of a milk bottle or the feeling of a griping pain). The responses may be shaped to approximate more and more closely in phonological and grammatical features to adult utterances by the withholding of reward from inaccurate responses. The formation of such specific responses is not an adequate account of the growth of language (Chomsky, 1959). It does not account for the structural features which abound in phonological, grammatical and semantic fields; but it does have the advantage of specifying some of the features of the communication situation which motivate and possibly structure early verbal behaviour.

However, some features of children's experience are of vital importance to the learning of the structure of language. These features may be summarised as three behavioural processes, *imitation, comprehension and production*. The relationships between these three processes are of more importance than their individual contributions.

Imitation of adult utterances as a whole is well described by Brown and Bellugi (1964). The child repeats utterances produced by his mother, although he does not reproduce them perfectly. In fact, he *reduces* them by omitting inflexions and function words, e.g. 'There goes one' – 'There go one'. 'He's going out' – 'He go out'. Sometimes, the mother *expands* the child's imitation or another utterance of the child which was not an imitation, e.g. 'There go one' – 'Yes, there goes one', 'Pick glove' – 'Pick the glove up'. Occasionally there are imitations by the child of these expansions, in which some of the inflexions and function words which have been added by the mother are incorporated into the imitation. However, it has not been proved that expansions are a necessary condition for acquisition, and, indeed, Cazden (1965) has found that utterances which did not so much expand the grammar as explain the content led to greater grammatical improvement.

Comprehension is more difficult to define; behaviour is required as evidence of comprehension, but it is difficult to know whether linguistic behaviour alone is sufficient evidence, or whether non-linguistic behaviour is required. Many linguists accept such responses as 'Put truck window' to the question 'Put the truck where?' as evidence of comprehension. However, control of the linguistic and non-linguistic environment and the possibility of the child indicating comprehension without having to produce language are attractive goals for experimentalists. Like production (see p. 113), comprehension of grammatical features can be experimentally tested in a situation where there is a novel referent and a novel utterance, with only the feature to be tested in its normal form (Herriot, 1968a, 1969a). The other viable alternative, chosen by Fraser, Bellugi and Brown (1963), is to test comprehension of two common sentences differing only in the feature to be tested. For example, the sentences 'The boys draw' and 'The boy draws' differ in the presence or absence of the plural morphemes, and correct selection of one of two pictures, one representing each sentence, is required. This association of utterance with referent is an operational definition of comprehension attractive to behaviourists. However, it might well be objected that comprehension of some sentences requires perception of their deep structure; the logical subject and object of some sentences need to be perceived by the hearer, and perhaps it is permissible to demand their identification by subjects as evidence of comprehension (Herriot, 1969b). Clearly such a procedure is impossible for children.

Moreover, it might also be objected to behaviourists that a verbal definition or paraphrase of the utterance to be comprehended is evidence of comprehension. Generative linguists would claim that a paraphrase can only be accomplished if the deep structure of the original utterance is first perceived, and transformations applied. Psychologists would have to be satisfied that the paraphrase was not rote-learned; and they would not be willing to assume that perception of deep structure or production of paraphrase required psychological application of linguistic transformation rules.

Production is evidenced by utterances which are not imitations, which are grammatical in the sense that they are internally principled, and which bear some relation to non-linguistic features of the environment such that they are comprehensible to a listener.

It is the relations between these three features which are important. The only experiment to investigate *all three simultaneously* is that of Fraser *et al.* (1963). They provided pairs of sentences differing only in the grammatical features to be tested. In the case of all three tasks, the pair of sentences was uttered first; in the imitation task, the three-year-old subjects were required to repeat each sentence after the experimenter; in the comprehension task, they had to select one of two pictures to correspond to each of the sentences; in the production task they had to utter the appropriate sentence from the pair of sentences when presented with one of the pictures. Correct responses were those which reproduced the grammatical features being examined. Imitation was found to be easier than comprehension, which in turn was easier than production. It might be concluded that the former two were necessary conditions of the latter; but such an interpretation is not necessary. Imitation is easiest because it involves a perceptual-motor skill only, without reference being involved; comprehension and production both require awareness of meaning, but production demands utterance while comprehension simply requires pointing.

Taking *imitation and production* alone, Ervin (1964) shows that the imitations of children aged two are not more advanced grammatically than their productions and infers that imitation is not therefore the source of acquisition of new features of language. This finding contradicts that of Fraser *et al.* that imitation *was* easier than production. However, Ervin's subjects were aged two and therefore may have been so limited in their short-term memory that they could not imitate sentences longer than those they could produce. It is true (Slobin, 1964) that children's imitation of *expansions* are grammatically progressive (i.e. are in advance of other examples of their production). Thus, clearly, imitation of this type might give the child opportunities for uttering complex grammatical forms which he would not have otherwise have had. However, one may ask whether it is supposed to be the actual imitative utterance by the child that assists him to form a new rule; it is surely more reasonable to suppose that the child hears his own utterance changed and notes the changes made by his mother, perhaps also perceiving her corrective or tuitional intention. Moreover, these changes will include features which specially refer to the type of situation in which they are uttered; for example, the expansion of 'Daddy briefcase' to 'Yes, that's Daddy's briefcase' will allow the connexion between ownership and the possessive inflexion to be made clear. The actual act of imitation may merely be verbal play; the perception of an exception to one's rule might be the vital feature.

The connexions between *comprehension and production* therefore become of still greater significance. A *behaviourist* would suppose that the fact that comprehension occurs earlier than production implies that experience of utterances in an appropriate context is a necessary condition for producing them in a similar situation. However, the *generative linguists* simply suggest that comprehension and production are both performance features, and that comprehension occurs earlier because there are less factors distorting competence in its case. Therefore, comprehension and production are both considered important because they reveal different 'parameters of conversion' from competence to performance. This option is open because these theorists feel no need to explain the origins of competence.

Several experiments indicating that children can comprehend certain grammatical features have already been described (see pp. 61, 116). However, because they indicate the ability to associate a feature of language (e.g. an inflexion, a form class, or a construction) with a feature of the situation, this does not necessarily prove that the ability was learned in the same way as it was tested. Fraser *et al.* showed that ease of comprehension of different features differed considerably. For example, the affirmative-negative contrast was very easy and so were the tense inflexions and the singular and plural third person possessive pronouns; but the singular-plural contrast marked only by inflexions and the subject-object contrast in the passive voice were far more difficult. Fraser *et al.* explain these findings as being the result of many factors. For example, the passive may be more difficult than the active because it reverses the familiar word order and because it has been heard less frequently by the child; the plural inflexion might be hard because it is perceptually difficult to spot, whereas the tense morphemes offer several cues rather than one only; a final factor mentioned is the length of the utterance presented, the child's short-term memory drastically limiting the comprehensible length. However, it is clear that these explanations do not in any way argue against the generative linguists' position. They would probably maintain that the passive was more difficult because it requires more complex transformations than the active (see also Slobin, 1966a; Hayhurst, 1967; Prentice, 1966), but would admit the other features as being performance factors which prevent underlying competence from being expressed in performance. Indeed, McNeill (1966a) goes so far as to postulate different types of memory span for each of the three types of behaviour (imitation, comprehension and production), and welcomes concentration on comprehension as allowing new evidence for competence.

However, if supposed underlying competence is completely obscured by a performance feature (i.e. if the predictions based on linguistic theory are not supported, but there is a clear performance feature explaining the behavioural differences found), then the argument for learning mechanisms as explanatory devices becomes stronger. Such a situation cannot be discovered in the Fraser *et al.* experiment, where some of the findings, on the contrary, do follow the predictions based on generative theory. However, Herriot (1969a) found that there was an astonishing difference between comprehension of the future tense contrasted with the past tense and comprehension of the same tense contrasted with the present. The referential contrast was between a novel toy about to perform an operation, actually performing it, or in a state of having performed it (at the top of a pole, descending the pole in a novel manner, or at the bottom). Children aged three comprehended both tenses in the former contrast, but in the latter the future was not comprehended till the age of six. The child's attention was fixed on the moving toy (present tense), and the utterance by the experimenter of the future tense could not divert him to point to the stationary toy. Admittedly, however, the argument is merely one of degree – the results show the large influence of performance factors, but do not *contradict* any predictions based on linguistic theory. However, it is possible that the different contrasting situations in which the tenses were tested illustrates the sort of contrast that is important in the situation in which the meanings of the tenses were first learned; for the more discriminable the situational feature, the easier it is to perceive its association with the grammatical feature. Similarly, a clearly discriminable contrast in grammatical features will aid comprehension learning.

Other experiments, too, indicate the effect of various pragmatic features on performance during acquisition. For example, Turner and Rommetveit (1967a) found that sentence reversibility (see p. 71) as well as voice was a factor affecting imitation, comprehension, and production in children; they also showed (1967b) that the emphasis placed on the logical object of a sentence either in the way the referent situation was presented or in the question posed by the experimenter led to the use of the passive construction by the child in response.

In summary, a learning theory of the acquisition of syntax would stress the non-linguistic situation in which language was uttered by the adult. The words or groups of words might be sorted into storage units based on the behaviour with which they were associated. The names of objects, for example, might be associated with manipulating behaviour by the child or pointing and showing behaviour by the adult. Words used to manipulate the child's behaviour, such as prohibitions, may form another such category (see Chase, 1966). These storage units might differentiate out into the categories of deep structure. For example, the category of things one manipulated might differentiate out into a logical object category with a logical subject subcategory. It would be predicted that this differentiation would be assisted by the inflexions and word order cues in the manner described on page 114. In particular, the position of units within larger grammatical units in association with the non-linguistic situation will provide these cues to deep structure (see p. 109).

The emphasis on storage units based on behaviour allows the one word, 'holophrastic' utterances which occur between one year and eighteen months to be explained in terms of the behaviour with which they are associated rather than as a sentence somehow abbreviated. Generative linguists have to suppose that '. . . the single words seem to function in the same way that sentences come to function later on: they cover a complete proposition; for instance, they may stand for a statement such as Daddy is coming down the street' (Lenneberg, 1967, p. 283). A second advantage of the connexion of syntax with behaviour is that it allows a theoretical account to be given of the connexions of language and thinking (see p. 165).

The external environment is particularly important when the names of classes of objects are being learned; for the learning of a class concept, such as dog, requires the experience of more than one example of the class dog before its criterial attributes are abstracted by the child (Brown, 1958). However, even in this case it may well be that the child does not learn so much from the perceptual attributes of the dog as from the behaviour of the adults and of himself towards it, or from the behaviour of the animal itself. Such associations will tend to place the word 'dog' in the logical object *and* logical subject category. This will be not only because the word dog is used in a behavioural context. It will also be because of the position of the word in sentences, because of the inflexions and function words with which it is connected, and because of the other content words with which it co-occurs (see pp. 146–7).

The above account has the advantages that it is based on comprehension, and that it allows for idiosyncratic syntax in early learning; for since behaviour will differ between individuals, so will the categories in which words or phrases are stored. Moreover, the account allows for the insistence of the generative linguists that language acquisition does not consist in the learning of specific visual or auditory cues. It is here suggested that it consists in generalisations based upon such cues; generalisations of syntactic position, modes of behaviour, and inflexional cues which are productive in nature. It is further clear that these generalisations by the child may be hypotheses, in the sense that they are continuously open to revision as new evidence comes in. Finally, it is evident that one may talk about these generalisations as rules; the use of the term 'generalisation' stresses their experiential origin, that of 'rules', their productive nature.

5. ACQUISITION OF THE PHONOLOGICAL SYSTEM

The development of the child's *phonological* system (Lewis, 1951; Fry, 1966) has two very interesting similarities to that of the grammatical system. Firstly, the child appears to have a set of *principles* complete at any given time; and secondly, he depends for his acquisition of these principles upon *hearing* his own and other utterances.

The complete set of phonological principles contains, of course, the *phonemes* of the language which the child is learning. Before the child can learn these abstractions, he must learn to pay particular attention to speech sounds, and to practise and listen to his own speech sounds. The first of these requirements is provided by the mother speaking to her child while giving him pleasure. The second may be fulfilled by the stage of *babbling*. This occurs from about five months until nine months or a year, and consist in the constant repetition of certain sounds e.g. 'dididididi . . .'; one can perhaps infer that the child enjoys listening to these sequences – auditory feedback is a reinforcement. Moreover, the child is practising the articulation of the sounds. They contain many sounds not present in the child's native language, and also do not contain many of the articulations he *will* later require. What is being learned at the babbling stage are certain general skills required for articulation, for example, coordinating the movements of the articulators (lips, palate, tongue, etc.), coordinating the movements of articulators and larynx, repeating the same sound, using the outgoing rather than the incoming airstream, and using it in different ways. Also being learned is the auditory feedback loop between the various articulatory movements which the child can feel and the hearing of the sounds they have produced. This is vitally important since it allows articulatory movements to be modified until they produce a sound which fits a model.

The part played by imitation now becomes apparent, since the mother's utterances (or rather, salient phonological features of them) can provide the model to which the child may approximate more and more closely. Short-term memory will obviously be a limiting factor here, since the child has to retain the model in order to copy it and compare his copy with the original. The extent and specificity of imitation is evident from the degree to which a child copies his mother's regional accent. This account (based on clinical observation) differs from that of learning theorists (based on a priori theories). Mowrer (1954), for example, argues that all the sounds required in speech are uttered by the child in the babbling stage, and the ones required for a particular language are differentially reinforced by the mother. The reinforcement might not only be direct, in the sense that the mother shows pleasure and talks to the child when it makes sounds similar to adult language; it might also be feedback reinforcement, in the sense that the child enjoys hearing himself utter sounds that his mother has uttered (since these are secondary reinforcers).

Mowrer's account pays too little attention to the acquisition of new sounds. More important, it neglects the fact that what are being acquired are not sounds but categories of sounds (phonemes). However, it may immediately be objected, phonemes are by definition only associated with meaningful language; they are items which, when substituted one for another within a word, change that word to a different word. Nevertheless, in addition to the phonemes themselves, it may well be true that the various *distinctive features* of phonemes are learned (see p. 24). It is supposed that the learning of distinctive features is necessary for the learning of phonemes, and therefore it is reasonable to suggest that it is these features that are being acquired during the pre-language stages of development. They vary in the ease with which they may be perceived and articulated. A basic distinction, that between an open vowel and a closed stop consonant, has been distinguished by linguists in the cooing stage, which precedes the babbling stage (Leopold, 1953); other distinctive features, e.g. low versus high vowels, also occur early in the child's articulatory development; but still others, e.g. voiced versus voiceless in stop consonants, may not occur till much later (age two).

Many investigators, however, would only wish to apply phonemic analysis to meaningful utterances of words; but necessary preconditions to the meaningful utterance of words are that the child should have already learned to recognise sounds associated with a particular situation, and that he then should have learned to produce an approximation to those sounds in the situation. Such a performance demands considerable skill in imitating and monitoring one's output to accord with the model; it appears possible that these skills necessarily require the recognition and articulation of some of the distinctive features.

At all events, the earliest words of children usually allow the immediate inference of a phonemic system (although it is still dangerous to infer a phonemic system from *isolated* utterances which may be purely imitative and thereby reveal phonetic, but not phonemic skill). The utterance 'mama' for example, implies a system of two units; the system can be inferred from the fact that there is a distinction between 'm' and 'a' which is not confused with the utterance of one long 'aaaaa'. The utterance of 'dada' and 'baba' add two more units to the system, since substitution of 'd' or 'b' for 'm' will lead to a different word.

The basis for these distinctions are probably the acoustic cues which differentiate the units. Jakobson and Halle (1956) again assume that these cues are the distinctive features, but in fact other cues such as volume or length of sound, or continuing or interrupted nature of sound may well be operative. There is a danger in applying distinctions based on analysis of adult speech to children's systems; this was evident in the description of two and three word sentences in terms of verbs and nouns (see p. 108). It may be supposed that the child needs more and more acoustic cues in order to produce more words (since more words embody more phonemic distinctions). The identity of these new cues depends on the frequency with which a given phonemic contrast occurs in the language to which a child is exposed. The more frequently a contrast is used, the more necessary it is to discover cues to help distinguish the two phonemes involved. Another factor is the ease of perception and articulation of a given contrast; for example, 'p' and 'b' are hard to distinguish perceptually, while 'r' and 'l' and 'f' and 'th' are hard to articulate.

Jakobson and Halle maintain that the development of every child's language follows a certain *sequence* of acquisition of the distinctive features, and claim that this sequence is the reverse of that observed in the dissolution of speech in aphasia (see p. 126). They further note that the distinctions which occur least frequently in the languages of the world are acquired latest (e.g. 'f' and 'th' in English). The assumption of *innate universals* is again tempting, since distinctive feature analysis, it is claimed, can be applied to every language. Further, deaf children can master the phonemic contrasts of English despite considerable hearing loss. However, this may only indicate that there are many different acoustic and articulatory cues which a child can utilise; a deaf child may be more dependent upon information based on the tactile and kinaesthetic self-stimulation resulting from articulation (Fry, 1966.)

The alternative to a set of innate distinctive features is to postulate a set of *experiential* distinctive features. These features will be the cues which the child utilises himself, and will differ in the early stages from child to child. The essential aspect of the concept of distinctive features is that sounds may be compared according to several criteria of which only one need be different for the sounds to be considered to be of different categories. This essential aspect may be a feature of many different systems, which approximate more and more to the adult system as crude perceptual and articulatory distinctions become refined. This process is described as the *acquired distinctiveness* of cues, since cues which were not at first perceived later become used to distinguish phonemes.

This analysis precisely parallels the analysis of the acquisition of grammatical and semantic skills described in the previous section. There, too, it was suggested that the child had at his disposal a set of distinctive features based at the start on his own experience rather than on adult categories; there, too, physiological limitations (e.g. short-term memory) dictated the limits of the system and the cues chosen, just in the same way as perceptual and articulatory limitations affect phonological development.

6. BIOLOGICAL BASES – APHASIA

The use of the term 'innate' by generative linguists refers to a *critical period* theory (in the sense that that term is used by the ethologists) (Hess, 1962). In its extreme form, this states that there is a period in the development of the central nervous system in which it is essential that certain sorts of external stimulation occur if specific mechanisms in the brain are to be triggered off. In the case of language acquisition, such stimulation would be the utterance in the child's presence of connected utterances featuring the linguistic universals; the critical period would be from one and a half to four years; and the specific mechanisms would be the universals written into the brain (LAD, the language acquisition device). However, it is difficult to see how this account can be satisfactory if (on the generative linguists' own admission) all that children hear is sentences expressed in surface structure. For the surface structure would have to be perceived in terms of deep structure for deep structure mechanisms to be activated; yet since such perception is presumably dependent upon the previous activation of the mechanisms, the argument is circular.

An alternative position suggests that at different stages of development of the central nervous system certain very complex skills might include the abstraction of a recurring regularity in different items of input and its application to new instances; the construction of a set of cues (possibly binary in nature) which would permit a distinctive feature analysis of any input item; and the construction of a hierarchical procedure for skilled performance. The difference between the second and the third of these skills is that the second does not imply any sequence of procedure in the application of the distinctive feature analysis; no one feature is temporally or psychologically prior in its application to input or output. The third skill, however, that of hierarchical performance, implies that input and output are differentiated out into different *levels* of unit, each level being a constituent of the level above. This account is taken to be general to all cognitive and non-cognitive skills rather than to be specific to language.

There is a great deal of evidence from the field of *aphasia* and from *maturational* phenomena which support the second position outlined above. Aphasia is 'a non-functional impairment in the reception, manipulation, and/or expression of symbolic content whose basis is to be found in organic damage to relatively central brain structures' (Osgood and Miron, 1963, p. 8). The review which follows aims at showing that the hypothesis of specific innate language features is rendered extremely unlikely by the evidence; and at describing the few reliably recorded connexions between the brain and structural features of language behaviour. The review of aphasia is shorter than the subject merits because a more detailed account would require considerable physiological sophistication.

The history of 'aphasiology' (Lenneberg, 1960) is full of confusions. Useful surveys of the field are to be found in Osgood and Miron (1963), Penfield and Roberts (1959), Schuell, Jenkins and Jimenez-Pabon (1964), Brain (1961*a*), and Lenneberg (1967). A selection of readings is edited by De Reuck and O'Connor (1964). Basically, the confusion is due to different bases of classification (Brain, 1961*b*). Some classifications of different aphasias are based primarily on the language *behaviour* of patients; others are based on the anatomical *locus* of the brain injury causing the aphasia; others, more daring, *correlate* certain loci with certain behavioural deficits. Most classifications have èmphasised anatomical features and omitted completely consideration of physiological *function*; moreover, the descriptions of language behaviour have not taken account of the structural and functional nature of language.

A. *Localisation* of language function in particular parts of the brain is hazardous for several reasons. Firstly, a localisation hypothesis assumes that normal function of a certain part of the brain is a necessary condition of language behaviour; language behaviour could not occur without it. Aphasics seldom lose all their language ability, and may improve considerably after training. Secondly, the traumatic injury, cerebro-vascular accident or tumour never affect one part of the brain alone, and therefore subsequent language impairment cannot be attributed to malfunction of one particular part. Thirdly, injuries affecting the same parts of the brain do not affect the language of some patients at all, but profoundly disturb that of others. This implies that individuals differ considerably in the anatomical locus of the physiological function; and it is the physiological function rather than the locus of the injury which is important. For the brain cannot be regarded as 'a conglomeration of individual "organs" each of which is the centre for a certain isolated mental function' (Luria, 1966, p. 14). Fourthly, the results of surgery differ from those of trauma and cerebro-vascular accident – many fewer cases of aphasia result; this may be due to the previous malfunction of the area excised, but the inference is clear: a strict and detailed localisation of function theory is untenable.

As a result of these difficulties, there is firm agreement only on the following basic facts. Firstly, the *left* hemisphere is the locus of most adult language behaviour (or, putting it operationally, in general it is injuries to the left hemisphere which lead to irreversible impairment). Secondly, the more frontal areas of the left fronto-temporal area are more necessary for *motor*, the more inferior areas for *receptive* language behaviour.

B. The *language impairment* has also been categorised in many ways. *Psychological test batteries* have led to completely contradictory results (although the contradictions are explicable in terms of the techniques of analysis employed). For example, Schuell and Jenkins (1959) applied a Guttman Scale Analysis to their test results, which led to their conclusion that aphasia was unidimensional in nature. The Guttman Analysis requires items and tests to be arranged in order of difficulty; if the subjects fail a test at a certain level of difficulty, but pass all those below that level, it is assumed that there is one function only being measured. Wepman and Jones (1961*a* and *b*), on the other hand, isolate five significant factors, four of which concern difficulties of transmission from perception by one sense modality to production by another (e.g. from visual stimulus to oral response). Their fifth factor is the ability to comprehend language symbols. Osgood and Miron (1963, p. 120 ff.) analysed the clinical literature for descriptions of impaired language behaviour, basing their methods of sampling on Osgood's psycholinguistic model (Osgood, 1963). Thus, for example, they paid particular attention to both word and sentence comprehension, skill and abstraction, etc. They isolated by factor analysis distinctions between skill and symbol, decoding and encoding, vocal and manual output modality, and sentence and word comprehension.

Clinical observation has led to many categories of behaviour, none based on a functional account of language, and none occurring alone in any particular patient. Out of them all, it is possible to isolate difficulties in phonological skill both in perception and production; the breaking of semantic rules within a sentence; searching for particular words; paraphasia (inability to combine phonemes); agrammatism (breaking of grammatical rules); errors of order of words; and specific difficulties in reading and writing. There is a long clinical tradition of discussion about the degree to which other functions are disrupted by an injury which primarily produces aphasia. The view of Jackson (1931), supported by Goldstein (1948) and others, is that there is a general deficit in the ability to abstract, one specific result of which is impairment of language. However, there is a tendency for aphasics to do better on non-verbal tests than non-aphasic brain-damaged patients.

Categories based on *linguistic theory* derive from the hypotheses of Jakobson and Halle (1956). Their proposal that the order of aphasic degeneration was the mirror image of that of acquisition has not been supported; for example, Goodglass and Berko (1960) found that the differential difficulty for aphasics of various inflexions was the result of their different morphological functions, whereas Berko (1958), using a similar test, had found that in the case of children, phonological features probably caused the difficulty.

Jakobson's other major hypothesis, however, that there are two extreme types of impairment, *similarity* and *contiguity* disorders, is better supported. The similarity disorder refers to impairment of paradigmatic function; that is, the selection of an item within a given context, and substitution of one item for another. Contiguity disorder refers to impairment of *syntagmatic* function, that is the sequencing of linguistic units and therefore the construction of larger units from smaller ones. These two types of disorder were taken to be extremes of a continuum, applicable to all levels of performance. Further, they are not taken to be the only relevant dimension: the distinction between decoding and encoding may also be applicable. The similarity-contiguity distinction resembles the representational-integrational dichotomy of Osgood. It accords with many clinical accounts of impaired language behaviour which distinguish difficulty in finding words from difficulty in putting them together. It is also supported by Goodglass and Mayer (1958), who found that agrammatic patients were better at word-finding but worse at repeating phrases and sentences than other aphasics. However, the use of the term 'sequential' to describe syntax is mistaken, as it neglects the transformational and hierarchical nature of syntax. Moreover, the selection of semantic items is probably dependent upon semantic rules which resemble syntactic rules in their hierarchical nature. Investigation of brain-damaged patients' language in terms of generative grammar (see, for example, Marshall and Newcombe, 1967) has only just begun and might result in more clear-cut distinctions than the receptive-productive and substitution-sequencing ones. So might analysis of aphasic utterances as though they were a novel language.

C. Another type of categorisation of aphasia links *specific language deficits with locus of brain damage*. Nielsen (1942) presents an extreme localisation view, but Luria (1947, 1964) is more moderate. He insists that the locus of injury is important only in that it reveals the existence and general area of physiological function. He associates sequencing ability with Broca's area; articulatory skills with the upper parietal area; auditory perception of phonemes with the left temporal area; and ability to synthesise elements into meaningful unity with the premotor area and the frontal lobes. However, he regards focal lesions primarily as disrupting the function of a sensory system, and only secondarily as disrupting the complex language functions. Many sensory systems are taken to contribute in many ways to these more central processes, and therefore the locus of lesions is expected to have only a probabilistic relationship with different types of language disorder. It is interesting to note that Luria's account includes the sequencing versus symbolic and motor versus expressive distinctions; and that he distinguishes between the sensory and motor disorders which are more easy to isolate to particular areas, and symbolic disorders which are more difficult. His approach therefore agrees in this respect with that of Wepman (Wepman, *et al.*, 1960).

In view of the findings in the field of aphasia outlined above, it appears clear that the hypothesis of specific innate language mechanisms may not be in accord with the evidence. For a highly specific innate content might require a specific locus, and this is precisely what is absent even in adult language users. On the contrary, the facts lead one to hypothesise physiological functions involving interactions of many parts of the brain (see Pribram in Miller, Galanter and Pribram, 1960). On the other hand, it might be argued that it is not a specific locus which is required for an innate component, but rather a specific system, which could depend for its adequate functioning on many different parts of the brain. However, in this case, injury to any one part of the brain which subserves the physiological system should irretrievably disrupt language behaviour in childhood; and the extraordinary capacity for recovery in children is well-evidenced.

7. BIOLOGICAL BASES OF ACQUISITION

The hypothesis of a general *critical period* for language learning has more support than the hypothesis of specific innate mechanisms. At the *lower* end of the age range for language acquisition, it would appear that a certain *maturational* level is a necessary condition. Lenneberg (1964, 1967) stresses the following indications of maturational readiness: regular preliminaries to the onset of speech, and regular stages of acquisition; difficulty in suppressing language despite blindness and deafness; and regular relations between the onset of speech and other achievements dependent on maturation (e.g. crawling, walking) in normal and retarded children. Lenneberg (1967) also draws many graphs illustrating the relations between certain indicators of brain development and the onset of language behaviour. However, it should be stressed that there is no specific evidence that a particular brain weight or specific biochemical or electrophysiological changes are necessary conditions for language.

Different evidence is adduced for the *end* of the supposed critical period at around puberty. In adult aphasics, it is thought that language is not relearned, but that any recovery is due to recovery of physiological function. In the case of children aged from four to nine, however, a large majority recover from aphasia, and recovery may take place over several years; this indicates a relearning process – adult aphasics normally recover in less than five months. The younger the child, the more completely the acquisition stage is recapitulated; those injured at the age of two or three even go through the babbling stage again.

The possibility of the relearning of language is connected with lateralisation of function (for a thorough coverage of this topic, see Mountcastle, 1962). When children receive brain injuries before the onset of speech, it does not matter which hemisphere was injured; more than half acquire language normally, and those who are delayed in acquisition suffered in equal numbers left and right hemispherical lesions. When children are injured after the onset of speech and before the age of ten, however, speech disturbances result more often in the case of left hemispherical than of right hemispherical lesions (Basser, 1962). In most cases, recovery from these disturbances occurred. When lesions occurred in infancy, and the hemisphere was later completely removed, no aphasia occurred in the majority of cases; but when the original lesion occurred later in life, there was a resultant aphasia. The inference is clearly that in infancy it is possible for the right hemisphere to take over language function. By puberty, however, language function has polarised to the left hemisphere, and certain other functions to the right (Teuber, 1962). Nevertheless, even in adulthood right hemisphere lesions may disturb some language functions of a conceptualising nature.

Considerable work has been done on the connexion of handedness and aphasia (Zangwill, 1960; Hécaen and de Ajuriaguerra, 1963). This connexion is certainly not simple. In general, it may be said that while nearly all right-handed aphasics have left hemispherical lesions, the converse is not true; in fact, left-handed aphasics more often than not have left hemispherical lesions. The importance of the left hemisphere for language is clearly established, but there remains the possibility that there is bilateral representation of language in at least some left-handers. Some interesting developmental hypotheses may be generated; for example, could localisation of language in the left hemisphere be associated with a corresponding differentiation of other functions and their representation in the right hemisphere?

The hypotheses of a general critical period and lateralisation of function appear to be supported by considerable evidence. However, they do not by themselves offer an explanation for development of language function. Further inferences have to be made; it might be supposed that the lower limit of the critical period is explained by lack of differentiation of the central nervous system; the upper limit might perhaps be explained in terms of decreased plasticity of function, indicated by lateralisation of function (Lenneberg, 1967).

Therefore, in conclusion, it seems necessary to suppose that during childhood, physiological function is sufficiently plastic to relearn language; this implies that there are no specific mechanisms located in particular parts of the brain which are responsible for language acquisition. However, later lateralisation might imply that by adolescence, language function has certain features which differentiate it from other complex functions. General mechanisms in childhood may include hierarchical organisation and transformational operations; the former is evidenced in behaviour by various motor skills (Miller, Galanter, and Pribram, 1960); the latter by cases in which a 'deep structure' similarity is perceived between, for example, two visual patterns which have no physical configurations in common. Perhaps the distinctive nature of the adult language function is connected with the system of semantic categories which has to be built up to achieve rapid retrieval of word items (see p. 99). Or perhaps it is connected with a gradual separation of physiological systems subserving language function into those serving internalised and those serving expressed language (see p. 168).

VI

Language and Thinking

1. INTRODUCTION

The attempt to provide organisation for a field not held together by any theoretical or methodological homogeneity is doomed to failure. This chapter will be organised in terms of human development in cognition, ranging from the comprehension of classes of objects through to the solution of complex problems. A brief account of the development of cognition will precede a discussion of the ways in which language might be connected with this development.

First, however, some questions must be noted which have been asked concerning the possible relationships between language and cognition. Is language a necessary condition of cognition? Cognition a necessary condition of language? Or do the two develop separately and become mutually dependent at a certain stage in development? These questions are not answerable, at least in the form they are put, but they do crudely express some of the theoretical stances adopted by workers in the field. Questions which may be more amenable to experimental solution require greater precision in terminology. One may perhaps meaningfully ask, for example, whether a certain level of development in the comprehension of language is a necessary condition for the attainment of a certain stage of cognitive growth; or whether certain training procedures in linguistic skills assist cognitive growth at some stages more than at others; or whether, on the other hand, it is necessary for certain stages of cognitive growth to be attained before certain language skills become available.

Granted, however, that the right questions are asked, there appear at first sight to be certain factual puzzles which require elucidation. If there is a close connexion between language and thinking, why is grammatical skill almost complete by the age of five (see Chapter V) while formal operational thought (see p. 133) is not normally attained until puberty, and operational thought in general until seven or eight. However, this question is based on the assumption that grammatical

131

skill as analysed by the generative linguists is the foundation of language ability. Other evidence (e.g. Lawton, 1968) indicates that language skills continue to mature through adolescence; and furthermore, no-one knows the age at which children acquire the semantic system. Moreover, the communicative function of language and the constraints this function places on utterances may be as important for cognitive growth as the grammatical structure of the utterance itself. In brief, when considering the connexions between language and cognition, language must not be narrowly defined in terms of its syntactic structure; similarly, cognitive growth must not be solely defined in terms of Piaget's developmental stages.

2. COGNITIVE DEVELOPMENT

Lunzer and Morris (1968) provide a full account of human development, based to a considerable extent on the work of Piaget. Lunzer (1968) also makes clear the connexions between animal behaviour and human development. Cognitive development may best be considered as development in the modes of *regulating one's behaviour*. This refers to the way one constructs the environment when one perceives as well as to the planning of one's overt behaviour.

Behaviour is at first regulated by external stimuli. During the *sensori-motor stage*, the infant responds to sensory input, whether it consists of events outside or inside himself or of his own behaviour. As a result, his behaviour occurs as a linear sequence, since each response acts as a stimulus to the next response (see p. 40). However, hierarchical modes of regulating and organising behaviour soon emerge. These modes of regulating behaviour are the result of the interaction of the organism with its environment and, in particular, of its physical manipulation of that environment. The schemata (see Chapter VII) thus formed accommodate to new experience when such experience is anomalous with their existing nature. Later, the ability to *represent* to oneself the content of experience in a pictorial or symbolic way develops (Bruner, 1964). Such representation allows the manipulation of reality by means of symbols. It therefore permits the planning of future behaviour. This is because transformations may be applied to symbols – their order may be changed, insertions may be made, etc. As a result, alternative sequences of behaviour can be represented.

The possibility of representing to oneself the criteria of one's behaviour may also be the explanation for certain behaviourist results; for example, for the phylogenetic findings of Bitterman (1965) concerning discrimination problems. The results concerning reversal learning in children will be considered more fully later (see pp. 137–8). The point is that the lower down the phylogenetic scale or the earlier on its own developmental scale an organism is, the more likely it is to respond to individual stimulus features in the experimental situation. As a result, when the formation of a learning set or the reversal of a discrimination (see p. 138) is required, the lower or younger organism responds in terms of the stimulus features rather than in terms of the criteria of its choice.

The transition between *pre-operational* and *operational* thinking, which Piaget places at the time when concrete operations become possible (seven or eight years) (Inhelder and Piaget, 1958, 1964), reflects this ability to represent the criteria of one's behaviour to oneself. For example, the well-known conservation of substance tasks require the subject to allow the increased length of the plasticine to counteract the width; the criterion of behaviour is the *reversibility* of the experimenter's action in rolling one ball of plasticine into a sausage. The child realises that he could roll it back into a ball again. The same is true of the classification tasks. To form a correct classification, children have to reflect upon alternative modes of classifying the materials provided. Class intersection (e.g. all red shoes) requires the combination of two such criteria.

Finally, Piaget lays great stress upon the distinction between *concrete* and *formal* operational thinking. Formal operational thought is defined as manipulating the criteria of one's behaviour *within a closed system.* One abstracts a defined set of criteria of behaviour; then one keeps all the other features constant while varying one, as in a scientific experiment. Thus for example, in the pendulum problem, where one has to state what determines the rate of swing of the pendulum, the weight of the pendulum and the position of release may be held constant while the length of the pendulum is varied. Clearly, such behaviour implies the generation of various hypotheses and their retention while each is tested. There are also implied a set of *second-order* relations; that is relations between hypotheses. For one hypothesis may or may not rule out another. In the case of formal reasoning, representation to oneself of the criteria of one's behaviour has made possible the generation of the possible as well as of the real; in other words, behaviour may be envisaged which is possible within the terms of the formal system of hypotheses, but not in the real world.

Clearly, then, Piaget's account of cognitive development lays great stress upon *representation*. Such representation is taken to regulate behaviour by allowing the criteria of that behaviour to be considered, compared and retained. The psychological structures necessary for such representation are taken to be *strategies* and *schemata* (Lunzer, 1968) (see pp. 163–5). Recent research has concentrated on the nature of the stages of cognitive growth – in what sense are they to be treated as stages, and how can one explain intra-individual differences in the solution of problems supposed to require the same level of thinking? Particular stress has been laid on the limitations placed on reasoning by short-term memory capacity (see McLaughlin, 1963); for example, STM obviously limits the number of alternative criteria of behaviour which can be simultaneously retained.

In the light of the above sketch of cognitive development, the connexions between language and thinking may be better investigated in terms of the use of language to represent reality and therefore to regulate behaviour. The different approaches to this question described in the remaining sections of this chapter should not be regarded as being mutually exclusive. Rather than showing either that language is a necessary condition of thinking or vice-versa, they simply embody research which supports certain limited hypotheses; for example, that certain types of language instruction will assist in the regulation of certain types of behaviour, or that certain sorts of behaviour are still possible for those who have not had normal experience of language. There is no coherent theory of the relationship between language and thinking.

3. THINKING AS INTERNALISED LANGUAGE

The phenomenon of *egocentric speech* has been interpreted by Vigotsky (1962) as indicating that language becomes an *internalised* regulator of behaviour. A child at play continuously tells himself what to do, but the older the child the more telegraphic this egocentric speech becomes. Since this is in direct contrast to the rest of the speech of the child, which becomes less telegraphic as he grows older, Vigotsky concludes that self-regulation is becoming covert instead of overt, and that language is the regulator.

This conclusion is supported by an experiment by Luria (1961). When a bulb had to be pressed or not pressed in response to different coloured lights, speech by the experimenter instructing the child not to press was at first merely treated as a general instruction to press. Later in development, the inhibitory function of the semantic feature of negativity gained power, and the child did not press. This development could be assisted, however, by the teaching of a response of letting go the bulb to the command not to press. Next (age five) the child could tell himself out loud what to do and what not to do; and finally, he could do so covertly. The process of internalisation is assumed to have occurred and, in Pavlov's terminology, a *second-signal system* to have been set up.

Luria and Yudovich (1959) gave two monozygotic and culturally deprived twins experience in a nursery with toys and other stimulation. They both improved in terms of the quality and complexity of their constructive and imaginative play. However, when one was given extra language training, he improved considerably faster. But since the two were separated (apparently) at the same time as the commencement of the linguistic training, it is not clear whether or not this improvement was a combined function of the training and the separation (with the consequent abandonment of their own private language).

It is worth noting that the last experiment quoted shows that language *may* aid the regulation of behaviour, not that it is a necessary condition of that regulation. Similarly, the Luria experiment shows the *possibility* of language, external, self-produced, and, presumably, internalised, regulating behaviour. Moreover, the interpretation of egocentric speech as language on the way to being internalised may not be the only possible one. For example, the function of the egocentric speech might not be so much to regulate ongoing behaviour as to remind the child of what he has already planned to do. It is used, in other words, as an aid to memory. In this case the increasingly telegraphic nature of the egocentric speech could be explained in terms of improved language skills: the child needs only to remember one item of a chunk for rehearsal purposes rather than the whole phrase or sentence. Since it may be assumed that chunks of language increase in size and auto-matisation as the child becomes more skilful, then the overt language used as a cue to memory will become more abbreviated.

However, much Russian work has recently been made available (Simon, 1957; O'Connor, 1961; Razran, 1961; and Slobin, 1966c) which indicates that the learning of the name of a class of objects enables very young children to select more instances of that class than when the objects alone were presented. Children aged twelve to eighteen months could even select a new instance of a newly acquired concept. The curiosity value of the referent, and the presence of other referents whose names the subject knows, are important facilitatory factors (Kol'tsova, in Razran, 1961). Moreover, the word describing the class of objects (e.g. 'doll') was presented in a set of sentences treating the doll merely as an object (e.g. 'Here's the doll') to a control group. The experimental group was given sentences which referred to the doll in meaningful connexion with other words (e.g. 'Rock the doll', 'Feed the doll'). The experimental group was more successful at the subsequent task of picking a doll from an array of toys. This latter result was obtained with children aged twenty months at the start of the experiment.

Clearly, these experiments do not try to indicate any internalisation process – they merely show the effect which external speech may have upon behaviour. However, the Russian experimenters insist that this is the first stage in the establishment of the second signal system. Perhaps the finding that the sentences including action words led to the quicker learning of the concept doll supports the suggestion made in Chapter V. This was that the hearing of words in a context of action led to their early comprehension and subsequent production. Such words as 'rock' or 'feed' will therefore be already part of the child's vocabulary. This may be because they can be easily assimilated to the schema (see Chapter VII) for the particular action they denote. As a result, the word 'doll' in the sentence 'Feed the doll' will be learned as the object of a verb representing behaviour for which there are already regulatory mechanisms available.

The complexity of the referent is extended by the Russians to include the relational referents of prepositions and adverbs; the use of the words by the experimenter enables children to comprehend both the specific relationship involved and the general situation expressed by the picture used as referent. Russian differs in the nature of its morphological classes from English. Studies of the acquisition of different classes indicate that regardless of the grammatical complexity of their formation, those classes are uttered first which have the most concrete referents; the largely arbitrary gender system is mastered last.

The Russian results described in the last three paragraphs support the approach of Brown (1958, and see p. 120). His idea is that the earliest learning is of the names of observables, and that the association of names or morphological features (Brown, 1957) with different examples of the class of observables leads to their comprehension. However, Vigotsky himself insists that all thinking is not internalised speech, and the Brown (1957) results (see p. 61) may merely indicate that subjects have learned the verbal tags to concepts they have already acquired by non-verbal means.

It is obvious from this section that language and behaviour are related long before the stage of operational thinking. This does not contradict the theories of Piaget described in Section 2. For Piaget is concerned with the use of language for the purpose of representation; this section has been concerned with the use of language in regulating behaviour in general.

4. THINKING AS A MEDIATED LANGUAGE RESPONSE

American behaviourists have treated internalised language as a *mediating response* (see pp. 85–95). They suppose that verbal mediating responses act as stimuli to induce overt behaviour directly affected by the mediating word rather than by external stimulus conditions. The usual technique using adults (Carmichael, Hogan and Walter, 1932) is to present ambiguous pictorial material paired with one of two words the referents of which are perceptually very close to the material (for example, a hat and a beehive). Subjects' reproductions of the material were affected according to which word was presented with the figure. Bruner, Busiek, and Minturn (1952) found that this was true when the words were presented before the figures, and reproduction was required immediately after their presentation. Herman, Lawless and Marshall (1957) showed that the verbal labels did not need to be overtly presented at all – subjects supplied them covertly to each figure. The task of making free verbal associations to the picture led to the production of lists of words by subjects which closely corresponded to the lists presented by Carmichael *et al.* All this work shows the effect of language labels on recall; in particular, it may be supposed that these labels direct attention to certain features of the stimulus; they also allow mental rehearsal; it will be shown later (see pp. 156–7) that language allows recoding so that many more items are available for retrieval; and it has already been shown (pp. 43–5) that syntactic structure aids recall.

Much work has been done on the mediating function of language for children in various *discrimination* tasks. A thorough survey is provided by Blank (1968). Kuenne (1946) showed that what she termed 'non-verbal' children could only make discriminative choices involving 'near transposition', while 'verbal' children succeeded at 'far transposition' tasks as well. *Transposition* involves the training of a subject to discriminate between items A and B, where A and B are distinguished by some relational difference, e.g. A is bigger than, brighter than B. Then the subject is tested in a discrimination task involving items B and C, where B is bigger than or brighter than C. If the subject selects C in the test phase after having been trained to select B in the training phase, it is clear that he is using a relation as a cue; if he selects B he is merely selecting the stimulus for which he was previously rewarded. Near transposition describes the experimental situation where the test and training stimuli are physically similar, far transposition where they are dissimilar. The success of verbal children at the far transposition task was taken to indicate their use of the mediating concept (smaller than, brighter than). However, the technique has difficulties, since physical difference between training and test stimuli can never be adequately controlled; as a result, subjects may still be generalising their response to features of physical similarity.

Reversal learning obviates this shortcoming; subjects are taught to select according to one feature of the stimulus (e.g. smallness) and then have to shift to its opposite, largeness (since they are now rewarded for doing so). This is known as a *reversal shift*. A non-reversal shift occurs when subjects have to change the criterion of their discrimination behaviour from one feature to another; for example, previously they were rewarded for selecting large v. small squares (the colour being irrelevant). Now they are rewarded for choosing black v. white (size being irrelevant). In this situation a reversal shift would involve choosing white squares rather than black, after having been previously rewarded for choosing black rather than white. Solution of the reversal shift requires that a cue should be selected which had never been rewarded; that of the non-reversal shift that a cue should be selected which had sometimes been rewarded (since the cue had sometimes been present when the previously relevant cue had been selected). If ease of learning of discrimination shifts is a function of the number of rewards that the learner has previously associated with the now correct cue, then non-reversal should be easier than reversal shifts. This is true of younger but not of older (six to seven-year-old) children (Kendler, 1961).

Kendler supposes that this finding may be explained in terms of *verbal mediation* permitting the older child to choose the opposite to his previous choice. She suggests that non-reversal shifts require the institution of a new mediating link, reversal shifts the different use of the old one. The function of the verbal mediator is to direct attention towards the relevant stimulus attributes. The inference of verbal processes does not appear to be necessary however, since animals can be trained to do better on reversal than on non-reversal shifts (Paul, 1965) and subnormals can do reversal problems better than normals of the same mental age (O'Connor and Hermelin, 1959). Furthermore, even if verbal mediation is considered a necessary explanatory device, it remains to be shown how the *right* mediating language is selected to allow the shift to occur. In fact, a specific verbal mediating response (e.g. 'the black one') might well be employed for the training task which is incorrect for the reversal task; and there is no reason to suppose that the antonym 'white' is an immediately available associate. Perhaps the ability to perform *transformations* is a necessary condition of the correct use of language in reversal problems; subjects could then use the instruction '*Not* the black one, the white one'. The ability of subnormals to perform reversal shifts, however, indicates that such a transformational skill is not a necessary condition of successful reversal performance; for subnormals are worse at recall tasks involving transformations than normals, possibly because of their limited short-term memory (Graham, 1968). Furthermore, their imitation, comprehension, and production (see pp. 115–16) are retarded compared with normals (Lovell and Dixon, 1967). The explanation favoured by the present writer is that the mediation involved is not necessarily specifically verbal. Rather, it consists of the child's *reflection upon the criteria of his behaviour* (see Section 2). This clearly should be assisted by language, but not in any simple, labelling manner. Perhaps *attentional* rather than verbal mediational mechanisms are involved (Zeaman and House, 1963); in that case, the reversal learning is a case of switching attention within a stimulus dimension (e.g. colour), non-reversal learning of switching attention between dimensions.

The same hesitations may be expressed concerning the use of a verbal mediation theory to explain children's *learning sets* (Harlow, 1949; Reese, 1963). Children aged five succeed in solving a simple object discrimination by 'one-trial learning' after having solved only one such problem before. In other words, inter-problem as well as intra-problem learning is one-trial. However, *attention* and other factors may explain the superiority over all other species which this performance exhibits. There is no need to suppose that hypotheses as to the identity of the feature vital to successful discrimination or of the various error factors must be couched in verbal terms. Further, it is not clear that the learning sets of children are typical of the acquisition of concepts at all – the child might be perfectly familiar with the variable necessary for a correct solution (e.g. larger than). Concept formation, in other words, may be a very different thing from concept attainment.

The *oddity* problem is more complex than most other learning sets; it requires the selection of the odd man out of three stimuli (Inhelder and Piaget, 1964; Lunzer, 1968). Lunzer and Astin (Lunzer, 1968, p. 293) found that children improved gradually with age, and that verbal hints as to the correct solution did not lead to success immediately.

However, at eight or nine years, children could explain their solution verbally and could turn the tables on the experimenter by acting as experimenter themselves. Lunzer maintains that this indicates that the child is using language to represent his own strategies, not merely as a mediating label. Language, in other words, permits the child to reorganise his behaviour representationally. This explanation accords with the explanation of reversal learning mentioned above: that if verbal mediation processes *are* to be postulated, then they cannot be treated merely as labels of a generalised group of responses. Rather, they must embody the possibility of transformations (the reordering of elements and the insertion of additional morphemes). However, it is again worth noting that the demonstration of the ability to describe verbally the principle of the discrimination and to turn the tables on the experimenter does not prove that verbal rather than other representational processes were necessary for the problem's solution.

The concept of the verbal mediating response has also been used in the design and explanation of several experiments in *adult problem solving*. Typical is the work of Judson, Cofer and Gelfand (1956) (and see Cofer, 1957). They used Maier's (1931) pendulum problem, which required the use of a weight tied to a piece of string to act as a pendulum before the problem could be solved. They found that the prior learning of a word list containing the sequence rope, swing, pendulum, facilitated problem solution. The ordering of the items in this way begs the question – the manipulation of different words as symbols by the subject might be what normally occurs. Furthermore, it is hardly surprising that such verbal clues presented by the experimenter aid solution of the problem. Other experiments, therefore, have stressed the *availability* of the requisite mediating responses to the subject. The verbal responses supposed necessary for problem solution are supposed to be already present in the subject's verbal response hierarchy before the problem is presented (Saugstad, 1955). It is often suggested that it is the uncommon responses which must be available for the solution of many problems. Interestingly, Maltzman *et al*. (1958) found that the elicitation of uncommon verbal responses which did not bear in any obvious way on the problem assisted solution.

These experiments do not indicate that language is *necessary* for problem solution. They do indicate that it can *assist*. Using the three circle problem, which requires the rearrangement of discs on circles making the minimum number of moves, Gagné and Smith (1962) found that those subjects who were required to verbalise during problem solving did better than those who were not. Moreover, those who could verbalise the principle involved at the end of the experiment were also superior. It must be concluded that while experimenter-provided or self-provided verbal cues aid problem solution, they are not necessary for it. Perhaps this is because they assist the subject to assess and compare the criteria of his behaviour.

Purely logical thinking (defined in terms of deductive tasks derived from the logical truth tables) may also be connected with language; although it would seem that there is usually a poor correspondence between natural language and logical thought. Quantifiers such as 'some' and functors such as 'if' seem to have different meanings in language and logic (Johnson–Laird, 1969*a*, 1969*b*).

5. LANGUAGE AND OPERATIONAL THINKING

Piaget's brilliant account of the development of cognition (see, for example, Inhelder and Piaget, 1964) has been based on experiments which often use subjects' verbal responses to experimenter's questions as evidence of thought processes. This experimental approach makes it difficult to manipulate language as an independent variable, or as a response variable with which one can correlate problem-solving behaviour. Furthermore, theoretically Piaget has emphasised the sensori-motor origins of cognitive development and their importance for the later stage of representation by symbols. He therefore regards language as but another symbol system, useful but not necessary for representational thought. Even operational thinking may be viewed as a new coordination of perception and action rather than as a different level of thinking made possible by language (Inhelder *et al.*, 1966).

Bruner (Bruner, Olver and Greenfield, 1966) supposes that 'It is by the interaction of language and the barely symbolically organised experience of the child of two or three that language gradually finds its way into the realm of experience' (op. cit. p. 43–4). This *interaction* Bruner supposes to be possible only when the symbolic organisation of the child is in some degree isomorphic with the structural principles of syntax. He considers that the deep-structure features of language are linguistic expressions of various logical functions; for example, the subject-predicate distinction expresses the proposition that x is a function of y, the verb-object distinction encapsulates the notion of cause and effect, and the modifier-head the intersection between two classes ('red shoes' refers to the intersection of the classes of things red and shoes). The deep structure features of language allow transformations of symbolically organised experience as a result of their linguistic transformational capacity; but first the organisation of experience must develop to include the logical relations which deep structure reflects. This analysis obviously places far greater stress on the part played by language than does Piaget's. However, the emphasis on grammatical structure apart from semantic content appears mistaken. Herriot (1968a) showed that the grammatical structure of a simple affirmative active sentence divorced of content was not comprehended until the age of eight, so the logical relations reflected by deep structure are certainly not apparent to young children. The view that certain words are associated with action schemata and then differentiate out into deep structure banks appears more probable (see p. 119).

Despite the confident detail of these theoretical statements, very few experimental results are available. One field in which nature has controlled one of the variables, language, is that of the psychology of *deafness*. Modern research has shown that deaf children are capable of many types of thinking (Oléron, 1957; Furth, 1966). Furth gave tasks demanding classification, logical classification, visual memory and perception, conservation, and verbal mediation (on the assumption that the reversal tasks employed by Kendler do require verbal mediation). He found that in some cases, deaf children are not inferior to hearing children; but it is worth noting that in nine cases out of twelve, some deaf groups in an experiment *were* inferior to normals. This is particularly true in the conservation experiments, where deaf children were at least one and a half years behind (Oléron found even greater differences). It then depends upon one's assumptions whether one claims that the differences indicate the effect of language on cognition, or that the ability of the deaf to perform cognitive tasks at all still has to be explained.

The deaf used for these experiments were profoundly deaf from before the age of acquisition of language. They therefore had never experienced language in its spoken form. Their ability at solving the problems may have been due to symbolic activity of a non-language type or to the language they had picked up as a result of lip-reading, hand signing, and the reading of books. Their relatively bad performance on conservation problems might be due to the lack of verbal stimulation accompanying action; in particular, to their inability to pick up the semantic rules involved in sentences describing the operations required for problem solution. Thus the hearing child has the opportunity of observing that every time a number is uttered it is followed by a count noun; or that people contrast things looking the same and things really being the same; or that when a substance is transformed from one shape to another, the name of that substance (or a pronoun) is still used to describe it. One says of a lump of plasticine – 'now roll *it* into a sausage.' However, Furth stresses how difficult it was to explain what was required of them to subjects in conservation experiments; and it must be admitted that deaf children are treated differently to normals in other than linguistic ways, and therefore inability to do conservation problems might be due to their lack of experience.

Other research has involved experimentally manipulating the language variable in tasks requiring concrete or formal reasoning. Verbal pre-training aided solution of a concrete operational task (Beilin, Kagan and Rabinowitz, 1966). The problem was to show the point on the side of a container which the water in it would reach when the container is tipped (Piaget and Inhelder, 1956). A set of questions concerning the horizontal nature of the water surface was read to the experimental group before the problem was presented, yes/no answers being required. However, this experiment, like the adult problem-solving described above (p. 140), does not necessarily require active manipulation of language by the subject to solve the problem; and even if active language manipulation were evidenced, this would be shown to aid problem solution rather than be a necessary condition of it.

Bruner and his associates have noted the nature of the expressed language of subjects accompanying their solutions of concrete operational problems. For example, Bruner and Kenney (1966) demanded the reconstruction of a 3 × 3 matrix of glasses in which there were two dimensions, tallest to shortest and narrowest to widest. The position of the glasses was scrambled, and it was found that five-year-olds could reconstruct the matrix as it had been presented. However, when a transformation of position was required, so that the smallest, narrowest glass was at the bottom right rather than the bottom left, only seven-year-olds could perform the task. They used language while they were doing so which did not confound criteria – they did not, for example, say 'That one is tall and that one is narrow'. Nair (1963) noted that those who succeeded in solving the problem of conservation of liquid did not mention in their verbalisations those perceptual features of the situation (e.g. height or width of the vessel) which dominate the errors of non-conservers.

Sinclair (see Inhelder *et al.*, 1966) showed that for conservers, intermediates and non-conservers there were differences in language when their task was to describe dolls holding unequal quantities or objects. Conservers used relational terms – 'One has more than the other' – while non-conservers simply stated that one had got a big bit, the other a small. Conservers used terms only with one opposite, e.g. 'big' and 'small', while non-conservers used the same term with two or more opposites, e.g. 'big' and 'small', and 'large' and 'small'. Conservers, finally, referred to two dimensions in one sentence, e.g. 'He has two, but they are smaller'. Sinclair also found that the non-conservers could obey instructions which employed the structures found in the conservers' utterances. This implies that, as usual, comprehension precedes production. One certainly does not need to infer, with Inhelder, that since a high degree of relation is shown between language and operational thought within a narrow age range, one may be the source of the other; nor that, in this case, operational thought is an acquisition prior to that of coding of event sequences into comparative, coordinated language.

It is clear that language may merely be reflecting cognitive development in all these cases. Just as the non-conserving child talks about the features of the situation he notices, so children not yet capable of forming class concepts will use words to denote their *chain complexes* (Vigotsky, 1962). A chain complex is a system of organising the environment in such a way that items are grouped together merely because they have one perceptual feature in common. This criterion is not constant – different criteria may be used at different points in the selection. Thus, for example, a group of red bricks chosen because of their redness will be augmented by some small bricks because the last red brick selected happened to be small. Clearly, the child is unable to retain in mind the criteria of his behaviour. He uses names in a similar haphazard way: the word 'quah' (Werner, 1948) was first used of a duck in a pond, the water in a glass, and the milk in a bottle. Next, the child applied the word to a picture of a coin with an eagle on it, and then to round (coin-like) objects. The word was clearly being used to describe a chain complex: first, the liquid feature of the situation was pre-potent, then the bird feature, and finally the roundness feature (which had nothing to do with the situation in which the word was first used). However, it is clear that there is no evidence that the paucity or inaccurate usage of language was responsible for the chain complex of thought. It is equally possible (and in this case intuitively more probable) that the language is used in a haphazard way because thinking is haphazard. The child is unable to represent and retain the criteria of his behaviour. It is not known what level of internalised language skill is required to perform this operation, but certainly overt language is pretty well developed syntactically by the age at which children still think in chain complexes.

Another feature of children's activity which shows development from pre-operational to operational thinking is *play* (Piaget, 1951; Lunzer, 1959). Both Piaget and Lunzer stress that play can be practice, or it can be symbolic, Piaget adding the class of rule-governed symbolic play. Lovell, Hoyle and Siddall (1968) found that four-year-old children retarded in language but normal in other respects spent less time on symbolic play than did normally speaking children, and also cooperated less with other children. Hulme and Lunzer (1966) likewise found a correlation between spoken language and play. Though these findings are interesting, it would seem to be more profitable to engage in specific language training and observe its effects on subsequent play.

In conclusion, the writer prefers to attribute the temporal connexions noted in this section between stages in operational thinking and language largely to the effect of short-term memory. It has already been mentioned that the retention of alternative criteria of behaviour, necessary for operational thought, is limited by short-term memory. So, too, are the grammatical and semantic systems of language. In particular, the retrieval system is limited in terms of the number of items available. However, if the retrieval system is organised hierarchically in terms of superordinate and subordinate items, then many more verbal items will be available. This would be because the superordinate items act like chunks, allowing subordinate items to be recoded at leisure (see Chapter IV, Section 10). It might therefore be supposed that increased memory span and development of a semantic system make language at that point a highly suitable way of representing to oneself the criteria of behaviour. But it must also be supposed that the increased short-term memory makes such retention of criteria easier whether language is employed for the purpose or not.

6. SEMANTICS AND COGNITIVE DEVELOPMENT

If a word is experienced within a sentence, its comprehension and appropriate production will be learned more rapidly than if it had been experienced in isolation. This may well be because of the *semantic rules* of sentences; these rules are linguists' formalisations of the fact that certain words may co-occur in a sentence, others may not. The co-occurrence of one word with another may be treated as a clue to the criterial features of the concept supposedly denoted by the first word. Thus, for example, if one learns that 'a puffin flies', one can assume that a puffin is animate and is probably a bird or an insect. Such a view obviously contrasts strongly with the behaviourist view that the origin of meaning is the connexion in experience of language with referent.

The semantic component of the generative linguists' theory is described on pp. 64–6. Some psychologists (e.g. Wales and Marshall, 1966) have suggested that some of the features which are specified in a semantic theory may be the criterial attributes of psychological class concepts. A further consideration of semantic theory is required to evaluate adequately this proposal.

Katz and Fodor (1963) give a concise and brilliant account of semantic theory. They suppose that any item can be described in terms of a series of categories arranged in a hierarchical way; that is, a subsequent category is a sub-category of the previous category. The most inclusive categories are the grammatical form classes; next come the semantic markers; and finally, the distinguishers. The distinction between *markers* and *distinguishers* is that markers refer to features which the item has in common with other items, distinguishers refer to what differentiates an item from all other items. The semantic analysis of 'knife' runs: noun, common noun, count noun, physical object, inanimate, artefact, blade, handle, together with an *evaluation* in terms of use, and a *selection restriction*, indicating the other items with which the item cannot be used (e.g. 'the knife is tired'). Similarly, 'spinster' in the phrase 'my spinster aunt' analyses into: adjective, human, adult, female, who has never married. Adjective, of course, is the grammatical form class in this case, adult a semantic marker, and 'who has never married' is a distinguisher. It is supposed that such features are necessary in order to explain how the native speaker can interpret a sentence. Sentences which contain words which would be ambiguous in isolation (e.g. 'train') but which the context disambiguates are cited as evidence for the existence of these semantic features.

Linguists (e.g. Bolinger, 1965) criticise the theory on the ground that the distinction between markers and distinguishers is arbitrary. Distinguishers may be translated into markers, but only at the expense of multiplying by five the number of markers. Clearly, if the markers are to be the criterial features of concepts, the cognitive load would be prohibitive. However, one valuable suggestion derived from semantic theory is that the semantic markers may be learned from the surrounding verbal context of the sentence. The item 'selection restriction' in the analysis of 'knife' indicated that the word 'knife' could not be used, for example, with the word 'sleeps'. If one experiences the word 'knife' as subject of only those verbs which can take an inanimate subject, one will learn to apply the attribute 'inanimate' to the item 'knife'.

Such a process is complex indeed (in contrast to the supposed learning of a class concept like 'dog' by means of verbal label and physical instances). One must already know the features of the items surrounding the item which denotes the concept one is trying to learn. Since this key item occurs in many different contexts, one will have to know the features of many different items. Thus, for example, in the case of the item 'in-law', one will have to note the presence of the marker 'married' in all those items spoken of as possessing 'in-laws'. Furthermore, one will often have to abstract markers from more than one surrounding item in a context. For example, if one is learning the concept denoted by 'donate', one would have to abstract features denoting possession of a certain item by the logical subject of the sentence and its previous non-possession by the recipient.

Clearly, then, there is an attractive case for supposing that concepts can be learned from the verbal context in which the words denoting them occur. The acquisition of some verbal concepts will lead by geometric progression to the acquisition of more. Such behaviourists as Osgood (1966) allow the type of learning in which the external referent of a verbal item is not experienced, yet the item's meaning is learned. However, it should be noted that this approach severely limits the analysis of meaning proposed in Chapter IV. For it supposes that the meaning of a word is the concept to which it refers. There is no such thing as the meaning of a word, and language is used for many purposes other than reference.

Clark (1968) and Clark and Stafford (1969) have done important exploratory work on adult subjects. Clark showed that when subjects generated sentences as context for different prepositions, some prepositions were substitutable for others, while others were not. Those that were substitutable were most often given as free associates to the words for which they could be substituted; they were also most often judged as meaningfully grouped with them. Correlations obtained between measures suggested that the grammatical class membership of a word primarily determined its meaning (operationally defined as its substitutability); secondly, the words which the prepositions modified directly; and thirdly, the more distant words modified by the prepositions. The distance is measured in terms of the phrase-marker tree – the word modified directly belongs to the immediately larger constituent unit, while words modified more distantly occurred in larger constituents still. Thus, for example, in the sentence 'He fell down the stairs', 'stairs' is the primary word modified by 'down', 'fell' the secondary one. Clearly, at least in the case of prepositions, the grammatical structure points to those words which are most closely related semantically. Clues as to the specific nature of the semantic features criterial to the prepositions were obtained by a close inspection of the words with which the prepositions were allowed to co-occur. 'Down the stairs' is admitted, 'down the day' is not; 'during the day' is admitted, but 'during the stairs' is not. Clark isolates such features of prepositions as movement, direction, position, manner and time. This list is ordered in terms of the degree of commonality which the features have with each other: many prepositions share the features of movement and direction, few those of movement and time. However, even among prepositions connoting e.g. position, other distinctive semantic features need to be postulated; one can say 'between my parents', but not 'among my parents'.

Clark and Stafford (1969) show that verbs also have semantic features, and that those verbs are forgotten first which have most semantic features. Clark and Clark (1968) show that the temporal order of two parts of a sentence, their order of mention, and their main versus subordinate relationship are psychological semantic features. This experiment shows that large scale *grammatical* constructions point to semantic features (see too pp. 69–73). The emphasis on the word as the label for a concept has led to a disregard of the fact that words occur in grammatical constructions, which may also be expected to aid the understanding of sentences. Not only grammatical constructions, but various serial and quantitative features of language have psychological value in refining conceptual organisation. For example, the serial order of many sequences, e.g. 'freshman, sophomore, junior, and senior' (Desoto and Bosley, 1962) affected learning in a paired-associate task, and adverbs such as 'very', 'extremely' (Cliff, 1959; Howe, 1962) have a quantifying function conceptually (see Pollio, 1968, for a review).

A criticism of semantic theory as a psychological theory concerns the *lower levels* of the semantic analysis. It seems extremely improbable that these need to be abstracted and learned for a concept to be acquired. It would require a vast store of distinctive features for such learning to occur, particularly if Bolinger's criticism of distinguishers is justified. One may propose instead that while the grammatical classes and higher order markers (e.g. animate) are distinctive features, lower order markers are not. This would allow the possession of a limited number of distinctive features combinable in many different ways (as in the phonemic system). The function of the lower level markers might be served instead by one's knowledge of the external world (Herriot, 1969a). Putting it crudely, we don't think of saying 'Some whisky is typing' nor 'An elephant is typing', the former because it is linguistically forbidden, the latter because it is forbidden by nature. Moreover, the theory ignores the context of utterance. The criterial features of a word may in one situation be those the dictionary offers – e.g., domesticated, mammalian, quadruped, etc. However, in other situations, the distinguishing feature may be that it drinks water, not petrol, and may as a result be a more efficient mode of transport in certain circumstances! In brief, the criterial features of a word may depend on the perceived alternatives in the situation in which the word is used (Olson, 1969).

Another objection is that the assumption that semantic markers are criterial attributes of concepts ignores much that is known about the *development* of concepts. Much thinking is representational and symbolic in nature and derived from behaviour; the symbol system need not therefore represent nor contain a set of criteria for a concept which are based on the externally obvious features or the semantic features of its referent. The concept may be acquired far more from action schemata derived from experience of the external referent than from features derived from language. Different experience may lead to different concepts for different individuals (although the culturally determined or naturally determined functions of the external referent will limit this individual latitude). Furthermore, one may well employ a concept adequately in certain restricted environments but not in others; Brown (1965) suggests that this might well be due to the fact that even adult concepts may be chain complexes (see p. 144) in many cases. Clearly, then, semantic theory provides suggestive hypotheses concerning the role of surrounding linguistic context in the acquisition of concepts; it does not offer, and should not claim to offer, an explanation of cognitive development.

One might suppose, indeed, that the formation of hierarchical groupings of words in the relationship of superordinate to subordinate is also of the utmost importance. It could lead to the possession of a rapid retrieval storage system (Chapter IV, Sections 9 and 10). Such a system would be likely to facilitate classification behaviour (cars < road vehicles < modes of transport). Brown (1958) showed that older children use more superordinate responses to objects and in the word association task. Significant development of vocabulary therefore requires an added degree of such hierarchical structure, either in differentiating out superordinate into subordinate categories or in integrating subordinate categories into superordinate ones. The mere addition of verbal items to a given level is not significant.

7. COMMUNICATION AND THINKING

It is a plausible suggestion that the requirements of *communication* enforce changes in the child's language which assist his cognitive development. Piaget supposed that egocentric speech differed from speech for others in kind as well as in the situation in which it was uttered. Flavell (1963) has neatly shown the difficulty the young child has in expressing himself in a comprehensible way to others. The experimenter was blindfold, and the child had to direct him to pick up an object placed in the corner of the room. The child was completely unable to perceive that a use of language was required which took into account the other's artificial handicap. He used such expressions as 'it' of the object and 'over there' of direction, without describing verbally what he was referring to. Clearly, one of the requirements of communication is the use of language in the culturally accepted way. Just as Luria and Yudovich's identical twins (see p. 135) improved cognitively when they had to give up their own private language, so a stricter adherence to cultural language norms might lead to less idiosyncratic concepts. Indeed, one of the 'design features' of language mentioned by Hockett (1960) is the fact that language is a cultural product. It names categories of experience which are *functionally* equivalent (e.g. 'food') rather than *perceptually* similar. As a result, the acquisition of concepts, and in particular, the transition from pre-operational to operational thinking, might be assisted by language; for it is a feature of pre-operational thinking that perceptual features rather than functional attributes dominate performance at problem solving.

Certain features of communication situations apart from the cultural constraints of the language itself may affect cognitive development. For example, communication may lead to different behavioural outcomes. Carroll (1964) makes some interesting suggestions about the use of different *sentence types* in a communication situation. One may use an existence-assertion sentence type ('There *is* such a thing as a fairy') if the existence of the referent is in question; a predicate sentence-type if an attribute of the referent is in question; in both these cases, information is being transmitted. Questions are asked when the speaker perceives the hearer as possessing information which he does not possess, while imperatives are used to persuade the hearer to behave in a certain way (but usually when this behaviour is to the hearer's benefit; when it is to the speaker's benefit, the imperative form becomes a request or a polite interrogative). Other, non-sentential, expressions are also associated with various communication situations; greetings indicate recognition and acceptance of the hearer by the speaker, exclamations indicate one's own surprise and are often an effort to draw the attention of the other to the surprising situation. Carroll has confirmed some of these observations in two-person game situations. It is obvious that the assertions concerning the function of different sentence types are statements of probabilities, not axiomatic rules. It would seem plausible to suppose that the use of sentence types in different communication situations would lead to an understanding of those situations. It might also be postulated that the use of certain sentence types in conversation might facilitate acquisition of certain concepts. For example, the repeated asking of 'why' questions and hearing of answers might lead to a quicker understanding of the cause-effect relationship.

The nature and behaviour of the other party in the communication situation may also be a determinant of the nature of the language produced. Hints of this possibility emerge from the verbal operant conditioning field (see pp. 83-4) where the sex, attraction, social status and verbal response of the other party have been shown to be variables affecting production. However, perhaps a more important variable is the degree of comprehension shown by the audience. When this was varied, the speaker's language changed structurally (Loewenthal, 1968). With increased audience understanding, speech became less 'social', more 'private', as indicated by the decreased number of function words.

Other work has been done on the communication of *emotional meaning*. Davitz (1964) found that the same sentence could be read by actors to express admiration, affection, amusement, anger, boredom, cheerfulness, despair, disgust, dislike, fear, impatience, joy, satisfaction and surprise; the moods were usually correctly recognised by untrained raters, and the effects of such features as volume, pitch, speed, 'quality' and 'smoothness' were made clear. Clearly, these are cues to internal rather than external referents; psychologists have paid little attention to these paralinguistic features of speech (but see p. 46) because they have treated language too often as labels for objects. And in English, at any rate, differences in pitch or volume do not indicate different denotative meanings. Further, the communication of emotional meaning may well influence the behaviour of the hearer in a far more marked and overt way than does the communication of information about the external world. Perhaps this is because the hearer perceives the emotive meaning as being part of the communication situation; he must respond to the speaker in a different way as a result of perceiving the emotional meaning. It may also be true that different sounds express emotive meaning ('sound symbolism'). This is a vexed question (Brown, 1958). Various sounds might habitually be used in words which are associated with concepts found unpleasant ('sn', e.g. 'snide') or pleasant ('gl', e.g. 'glad'); bright (long 'ee', e.g. 'gleam') or dull ('oo', e.g. 'doom'). This hypothesis could best be tested by use of the semantic differential.

Argyle and his colleagues have isolated several physical variables in the communication situation which affect the amount spoken in the conversation and by each participant; for example, the distance the participants are from each other and the amount their eyes meet (Argyle and Dean, 1965). For a survey, see Argyle and Kendon (1967).

So far in this section, the possible effects of different features of communication situations in general have been discussed. However, there is also to be considered the fact that communication situations may differ in kind depending on who is engaged in them. In particular, it has been proposed that different kinds of communication situation are typical of different social classes (Bernstein, 1965). A review and critique of Bernstein's work is provided by Lawton (1968). Bernstein is a sociologist, and is primarily concerned with showing the connexions between social structure and individual functioning. At the *sociological* level, he maintains that: 1. the *social structure* of society determines 2. the nature of *social relations* between people, which 3. give rise to different *linguistic codes*. He analyses social structure in terms of middle and working classes, defined by means of educational attainment (among other criteria). He suggests that there are different modes of social relations typical of the two classes, those of the working class being distinguished by the need to maintain rapport and solidarity, those of the middle class by expression of individual differences and long-term goals. As a result, members of the two classes use different linguistic codes, restricted (working) and elaborated (middle).

Bernstein proposes *psychological* correlates of these sociological features. These correlates are in reciprocal relation with the sociological features – society affects the individual, but it is possible for the individual to develop new ways of thinking which affect society's structure. Social structure is supposed to be in reciprocal relation with the *verbal planning* function, forms of social relation with *specific orders of meaning*, and linguistic codes with *speech events*.

Several general points should be made about this theory before the evidence for it is discussed. Firstly, the effects of both linguistic and cognitive development are not treated. External features alone are treated as variables, and these are limited in that experience of the non-human environment is not treated. Secondly, the two codes are spoken of in sociological rather than psychological terms. Predictability is one criterion of code identity, but the predictability is not defined in terms of the units of language (information theory) but in terms of the constraints the social situation exerts on the language uttered; a guide describing the Vatican utters linguistically complex but socially predictable statements. Finally, in general the effect of social features upon codes (sociological level) and that of modes of thinking on speech events (psychological level) is stressed, not the reverse.

Experimental evidence is not plentiful; but the function of theory is as much to generate new hypotheses as to describe obtained data. Whether the theory yields *testable psychological* predictions is another matter. The work reported by Bernstein (1960, 1962a, 1962b) and Lawton (1968) uses social class as the independent and various linguistic performances as the dependent variable. Bernstein found that apprentices were only slightly inferior on the Ravens Progressive Matrices to public schoolboys, but considerably inferior on the Mill Hill Vocabulary Scale; that they used longer mean phrase length, spent less time pausing, and used a shorter word length when engaged in group discussion about capital punishment; and that they used less subordinate clauses, complex verbal stems, adjectives, and uncommon adverbs and conjunctions; they used more sequences termed 'sympathetic circularity' sequences by Bernstein (e.g. 'you know', 'isn't it'). Bernstein thinks these are designed to maintain rapport, but they might simply be filled pauses. The speaker might be searching for a language item but be unwilling to pause in case he is interrupted (Maclay and Osgood, 1959). Lawton, using more median, less extreme samples of socio-economic classes than Bernstein, showed that the differences were greater among fifteen than among twelve-year-olds; and that different tasks (e.g. description versus abstraction) in different situations (e.g. interview versus discussion) were relevant variables. In general, he confirmed Bernstein's findings of class differences, and stressed the difficulty working-class boys had in switching codes when a new situation demanded the use of more elaborated code.

In general, Bernstein's findings are interesting in that they show differences in language behaviour correlated with socio-economic class. However, Bernstein's preoccupations as a sociologist with different patterns of social structure have led him to dichotomise language behaviour into two codes when all the evidence is adduced in terms of differences of degree rather than of kind. More important, the inference is from speech events to linguistic codes; but the existence of linguistic codes is inferred as much from sociological evidence as from behavioural.

And the inference itself is not from behaviour to thinking but from behaviour to a sociological hypothesis concerning predictability within a communication situation. Both of the aspects of thinking mentioned at the psychological level – verbal planning functions and specific orders of meaning – are treated as being dependent upon social, not language variables. Bernstein's position may therefore be summarised as being that of a sociologist who sees language as being a product of a social system and as a means of reinforcing that system and its implied meanings.

A great deal of evidence has been adduced to indicate the effects on language of different *environmental factors* during childhood. Orphanage and non-orphanage children have been shown to differ right through from the age of three months when the sounds made by orphanage children are less frequent and varied (Irwin,' 1948), to adolescence, where their abstract thinking was notably impoverished (Goldfarb, 1945). Clearly, the differences may be due to lack of social contact, non-personal stimulation, and other factors. The linguistic variable is the dependent one in these studies, the independent variable being a complex of factors impossible to differentiate.

Socio-economic class differences are not reflected in linguistic performance until 18 months (Irwin, 1948). Thereafter the effects increase with age (McCarthy, 1930; Day, 1932) when such features as sentence length, complexity, and type are assessed. Association with adults rather than with older children is also important (McCarthy, 1930). Unfortunately, these older studies (reviewed fully by McCarthy, 1954, and see Templin, 1957) failed to control for IQ, and therefore differences in language performance might be due more to hereditary than to environmental factors. Moreover, little effort was made to indicate in which ways impoverished language affected cognitive performance. However, the consensus of opinion appears to favour certain features of middle class as opposed to working class families as being crucial to the language differences. Attitudes to child-rearing and willingness to answer children's questions may be such features; also, of course, the language which working-class adults utter to their children may be itself impoverished (Bernstein).

More modern investigations have employed more sophisticated linguistic measures, and have controlled IQ. Loban (1963) for example, used an index which allows for degrees of subordination of structure (based on constituent analysis). He found that this measure was correlated highly with other measures of language ability (e.g. vocabulary development, reading proficiency) and that all language measures were correlated with socio-economic class. However, inferences as to the effect of these language differences on cognitive performance are all derived from the language performance itself. Other such studies are those of Deutsch (1963), John (1962) and Jensen (1967) (the former two are described by Lawton, 1968). John's analysis is important, for it tries to indicate some of the cognitive processes for which language is important. Middle and working-class negro children differed little on *labelling* tasks, but the middle-class children offered more paradigmatic than syntagmatic word associations; this she took, with other evidence from tasks requiring integrating the relations between objects, to indicate skill at educing *relations*. Furthermore, they more frequently sorted cards into groups representing *categories* (e.g. means of transport) than into other groups, and they more frequently verbalised while doing so. Clearly, this is valuable evidence, although of course the cognitive skills are limited in scope, and language is not used as the independent variable with behaviour requiring cognitive competence as the dependent variable.

In summary, then, the work concerning social class has shown interesting differences in language skills, but has so far failed to show convincingly that these differences are the cause of cognitive differences.

8. LINGUISTIC RELATIVITY

The previous section was concerned with different features of the communication situation. In particular, the fact that different communication situations and language forms may be associated with different social groups was thoroughly discussed. There is also the possibility that differences in language forms may occur between *cultural* as opposed to *subcultural* groups. These cultural groups usually have different languages, and certain differences between the languages might be thought to express cultural differences. Language could then be said to affect cognition insofar as the concepts peculiar to that particular culture are internalised by means of language. It is worth noting that this effect can only be empirically investigated in those cases where a. cultures differ in their concepts and b. these differences are reflected in language. Even then, it might be supposed that other forms of learning led to the acquisition of the concepts concerned. However, where there is a common referent with which both cultural groups might be supposed to be equally familiar, the effect of language differences on cognition might be more confidently inferred. These limitations in the interests of experimental validity are in marked contrast to the richness of the anecdotal evidence presented by Whorf (Carroll, 1956). However, they enabled Lenneberg and Roberts (1956) to demonstrate that different words for colour in different languages lead to different codings of the colour continuum. Carroll and Casagrande (1958) showed that different grammatical features might also affect behavioural regulation. They found that there were special forms of verbs in the language of the Navaho American Indians which denote the shape of the object being dealt with. These added linguistic cues led Navaho children to sort objects into classes according to shape rather than colour more often than English-speaking American children. It is worth noting, however, that if the base-structure features of grammar are universal (Greenberg, 1966), then grammatical differences between languages are not going to exemplify the more important ways in which language structure affects cognition.

To accord with the modest quantity of the evidence, and to generate testable hypotheses, a moderate statement of the 'Whorfian hypothesis' is required. Carroll (1963) offers 'Insofar as languages differ in the ways they encode objective experience, language users tend to sort out and distinguish experiences differently according to the categories provided by their respective language. These cognitions will have certain effects on their behaviour.'

From the efforts to discover cognitively significant differences between languages of different cultures has arisen a technique for investigating the effects of the language conventions of one culture upon the sending and receiving of messages about a certain referent. The emphasis is upon the referent – the ease or difficulty with which statements denoting it may be sent or received; indirectly, therefore, the technique involves the particular language as well, inasmuch as the efficiency of the encoding or decoding process will depend to a large extent upon the efficiency of the denotative function of the language.

The technique employs the Farnsworth–Munsell colour chips, which are equal in brightness and saturation but differ from each other in hue by equal degrees (as defined by just noticeable differences). Since the referent is controlled in this way, it was possible to investigate the degree to which *codability* affects the perception and recognition of the referent. Codability is defined as the ease with which a language tag can be used to distinguish one item from another. Brown and Lenneberg (1954) found that codability was correlated with recognition, when codability was operationally defined in terms of (among other things) the length of time taken by subjects to name any colour and the length of the name given it. Lantz (reported in Brown, 1965) using refined procedures, replicated the finding; she used as her operational definition of codability the ease with which one group of subjects selected colours on the basis of names given them by another group. A third group was given the task of recognising colours after a delay without verbal labels being attached to them at all. Those colours were most easily recognised which were most codable. The more colours which had to be recognised at once, the higher this correlation became.

Within a given linguistic community, therefore, codability is a function of referents; colours or objects are easily codable or not depending on the context in which they are presented (e.g. a red among other reds, or a red among blues) and on the words available in that language. These experiments thus present codability as being constant within the culture and by implication variable between cultures. They are very valuable since they involve the encoder of a message, the message itself, its referent, and the decoder (at least in the form of the technique employed by Lantz). They therefore use one of the very few techniques which can claim to represent the communication situation *as a whole*. However, in order to attain this inclusiveness, the technique has to pay the price of dealing with denotation alone of an external referent.

In conclusion, it must be stated that the present condition of the field of language and thinking is utterly confused. The only way forward is to control language experimentally by means of inducing certain specific language behaviours by the subject while he is performing a task requiring cognitive skill; or by means of training the subject in a specific feature of language and then investigating the changes which such learning has made on his cognitive performance. For example, the technique of expansion combined with imitation (see p. 115) might be used to teach a particular grammatical feature, and the complexity of constructive play then analysed. Perhaps the one unifying feature in this chapter has been the recurrence of the concept of *criteria of behaviour* and the subject's ability to represent to himself these criteria. That language is useful in this performance has been shown; that it is necessary has not. Representation has been shown to be of importance in the later stages of development. It depends upon the previous establishment of modes of regulating behaviour.

VII

Theoretical Conclusions

I. THE NATURE OF THEORY

The *received definition* of theory is that it is a system which describes and explains certain empirical findings and leads to fruitful research. The *historical* origins and development of theory and its abandonment for different theory are far less rational (Kuhn, 1962). The received definition is a respectable statement of faith in psychology as a science; the historical facts often appear little more than good examples of the effects of the generation gap.

The *received definition* is inadequate in the field of the psychology of language for many reasons. Firstly, there is no systematised formulation of a theory of verbal behaviour as a whole. On the contrary, theory has grown around areas of research which each generate their particular problems. As a result, separate bodies of theory have grown up which try to accommodate to and assimilate new findings within particular areas. These efforts at accommodation and assimilation appear to be in the main unsuccessful. Students in the fields of serial learning (Young, 1968), paired-associate learning (Battig, 1968), semantic generalisation (Maltzman, 1968) and verbal conditioning (Dulany, 1968) all find that the effort to adapt existing theory in their fields to experimental results in unavailing. Kjeldergaard (1968) publishes his effort; it contains twenty-six postulates to deal with the field of transfer and mediation in verbal learning; but he admits that it falls a long way short of being 'an exact theory . . . that is capable of mathematical expression'. Indeed, it omits such features of the field as response suppression and the effects of instructions (Mandler, 1968).

There are several reasons for this situation even within the encapsulated fields of verbal behaviour. The most important are the *pre-theoretical assumptions* made by behaviourist psychologists. The use of S–R terminology is an effect more than a cause of these pre-theoretical assumptions. Behaviourists assume, and S–R terminology implies, a commitment to empirical method. Stimulus conditions must be controlled and responses observed before inferences about psychological functioning may be made. This is one assumption made by all behaviourists; some would deny the need to make the inferences. A second assumption is also common to behaviourists and is also denoted, or at least implied, by the use of S–R language. It is that all behaviour, both overt and mediating, is a function of previously experienced stimuli and previously executed responses; environment, not heredity is taken to be of primary importance. A third assumption appears to be implied by the experimental design of much of the behaviourists' work, as well as by S–R language. It is that, originally at any rate, stimuli and responses had to be contiguous in time before behaviour was changed. Paired-associate and serial learning techniques, for example, aim at eliminating previous learning as far as possible in order to investigate the effects of pairing stimuli and responses. Deese (1968) suggests that it is this concentration on the serial nature of behaviour, which is in fact almost an accidental property, which has so limited the scope of experiments. Certainly, it has led to the tendency to define S and R variables only in terms of those events in which they act as the theory says they should (Dulany, 1968). A final pre-theoretical assumption is probably that all theoretical constructs must be logically reducible to observations. An inference about psychological functioning must be an inference about a physiological system which is in principle observable.

In what sense, then, are these pre-theoretical assumptions the cause of the failure of S–R theory to describe the areas within verbal learning? Clearly, the commitment to *experimental control* is a prerequisite of all scientific experiment. The physicalist position of *reductionism* also appears to have little effect on the descriptive power of the theory (although it might be objected that recent physiological discoveries make the inference of internal *r*s appear an over-simplification). It is the combined assumptions of learning by *experience* in general and *temporal contiguity* in particular which make the S–R theorist so eager to obtain experimental manipulation of behaviour to the exclusion of the subject's prior experience and heredity. As a result, situations have been selected for investigation which best provide the opportunity of such experimental control.

The first part of the received definition of theory falls down, therefore, in that there is no single system which describes adequately all or part of the field of verbal behaviour. Since the findings are not adequately described, it is self-evident that they are hardly likely to be adequately explained. If explanation is the formation of theoretical constructs describing inferred processes, then many behaviourists would say that their use of S–R terms was theoretically neutral (Cofer, 1968). However, the actual scientific behaviour of these scientists reveals that there *are* theoretical assumptions implied in their scientific strategies. For example, Cofer himself seeks to 'explain' the facts of free recall in terms of association. Either this is a theoretical construct explaining overt response patterns in terms of internal patterns of association caused by previous temporal contiguity; or it is merely a description of co-occurring events disguised as explanation. In the former case it is empirically falsifiable; in the latter, misleading but a matter of taste. As Kuhn notes, it is a typical defence of the upholders of a failing paradigm to reply to conflicting results by alleging that their theory is not a theory at all.

The second part of the accepted definition of theory suggests that it generates fruitful hypotheses. A count of journal articles to support this view obscures the value judgement which it conceals. It is assumed that the theory describes and explains behaviour which is theoretically important. But in the case of the field of verbal behaviour, this assumption is not justified. The reason is that the experimental behaviour sampled by behaviourists (for example, paired-associate learning) has been chosen for examination as a result of their pre-theoretical assumptions. The experimental tasks chosen were rather more complicated than the operant and classical conditioning procedures from which S–R terminology is derived; as a result, experimental effort has been directed towards adapting S–R terminology to provide a theory to describe and explain these added complications. Had the experimental task been more different from conditioning, a change in terminology might have been forced.

An alternative approach would be to investigate those aspects of normal language behaviour which most lend themselves to experimental investigation. Many of the experiments described in this book derive from this latter approach. It has the advantage that it retains the most important pre-theoretical assumptions of behaviourism, namely, the need for control of the experimental situation, the use of behavioural evidence, and the ultimate physicalist explanation of behaviour. It allows language behaviour to be investigated which resembles language behaviour in everyday life. It allows hypotheses to be tested which are derived from other disciplines (e.g. linguistics). It permits relations between response terms to be the basis of inference as well as between stimulus and response terms (Dulany, 1968). Response terms are the source from which the effect of the experiential history of the subject may be discovered; manipulated stimuli are not. And most important, it permits the inference of psychological processes of differing orders of depth and complexity.

In brief, the discarding of S–R terminology permits more flexible theory to encompass ever more challenging findings. Its retention demands the assumption that S–R 'laws' apply to inferred psychological functions in the same way as they do to observable stimuli and responses. Osgood (1963) is forced to include integration of internal stimuli and responses (*s-s* and *r-r* learning) in his theory, and makes no attempt (1968) to assimilate his speculations about deep structure into S–R terminology. It might be concluded that S–R terminology is only justifiable when used to describe the way in which the experimenter has manipulated the experimental situation; it should not be used as a description or explanation of the subject's behaviour.

In a sense, the preceding critique of the received definition of theory has been based on a view of how *in fact* theoretical paradigms develop and are superseded. For the critique itself is based on certain value judgements; for example, that many of the experimental activities of behaviourists in verbal behaviour have been less than useful because they were investigating phenomena which bore little resemblance to natural language. It is possible that the same sort of value judgements motivate change in psychological theory. Many psychologists see little pay-off in investigating an aspect of paired-associate learning since such investigation will solve only a very limited problem and have little relevance for general theory. The ultimate relevance of paired-associate learning for any general psychological theory is still an article of faith rather than a predictable consequence. Obviously, also, the teaching of psychology affects the later research efforts of students. Work from different countries (e.g. Russia, Switzerland) becomes available to students. As a result, the appeal of different theoretical languages while retaining a basic empirical commitment is great. Moreover, more and more physiology is taught to undergraduate students, with the result that the unlikelihood of simple psychological constructs being adequate when physiological structures are so complex becomes evident to all.

However, such gradual and historically and sociologically explicable processes of change in theory appear unsatisfactory to psychologists. Instead, they rationalise and set up straw models of opposing theory in order to knock them down. This is what is occurring in the present confrontation between behaviourist and generative psychologists exemplified in the exchanges between Garrett and Fodor (1968) and Osgood (1968).

2. A CONFRONTATION

In Chapter III it was made clear that certain basic rationalist principles held by generative linguists were not acceptable as evidence for making psychological inferences. It was also clear, however, from Chapters II, III and V, that there were many experimental results which indicated that subjects treated language not as a sequence of sounds, but in terms of its structure. These aspects of structure include the combination of distinctive features of sound, and probably of meaning; the abstraction of form classes and the units of phrase-structure grammar; and the perception of deep-structure features of language such as the logical subject and object. Clearly, there are different degrees of abstraction from the apparent stimulus and response. Dissatisfaction with definitions of stimulus and response which depend on arbitrarily determined aspects of their physical appearance is evident throughout the field (see, for example, Tulving's (1968) distinction between E units and S units).

Not content with making a value judgement to the effect that S–R language is not useful (the conclusion arrived at in the previous section), many generative linguists claim that S–R theory is *in principle* incapable of describing and accounting for these findings. The basis for such an assertion, however, is an ill-informed view of the nature of S–R theory. They assume that there is only a relatively small number of overt responses permitted by S–R theory, which must therefore be wrong, since the number of different sentences (responses) is infinite. This point of view was stressed by Miller, Galanter and Pribram (1960), Miller and Chomsky (1963), and many since. However, it misses the point – if mediating responses are composed of different distinctive features, then the number of different possible combinations of features makes an immense number of mediating and therefore of overt responses possible.

The strength of the evaluative objection to S–R terminology does not depend on logical arguments based on such linguistic inventions as infinite recursiveness (Bever, Fodor and Garrett, 1968). Rather, it is concerned with the many levels of abstraction revealed by psycholinguistic experiment. The transition from the selection of the logical subject and logical object of a sentence through to its overt expression appears to be governed by simultaneous hierarchical and sequential processes. The hierarchical process requires the insertion of items and the ordering of the whole in terms of surface structure grammar. The sequential aspect involves intra- and inter-phrase sequencing made necessary by the fact that utterances are made in time by a set of behaviours which cannot occur simultaneously. It is the hierarchical process which S–R terminology has difficulty in incorporating, and which, in the case of language behaviour at any rate, seems to be of greater importance. Furthermore, S–R terminology has difficulty in distinguishing the *selection* of deep-structure items from their *transformation* (using the term non-linguistically) into actual utterances.

3. AN ALTERNATIVE

The generative psycholinguists substitute for S–R theory a model derived from transformational grammar. The central component is a grammar as defined by Chomsky, and the merest concessions are made to so-called performance factors by introducing such features as a state of readiness threshold mechanism (see Figure 4). However, as has been said (see Chapter III), such a model assumes that the linguists' theories describe psychological processes. Generative psycholinguists then treat the task of linguists as that of investigating competence assuming that performance features are constant; the task of psychologists as that of investigating performance assuming competence is constant (Bever, 1968).

Furthermore, such a theory is limited to language behaviour alone. This limitation ignores the findings of all psychologists other than psycholinguists, and also inhibits the explanation of the acquisition of deep structure in terms of the behaviour which accompanies utterances (see p. 119).

There is one theory which appears to offer an adequate account of the psycholinguists' findings – that is, an account which describes adequately all findings, including those concerning deep structure. It has the advantages of accounting for behaviour in general; and of being a reductionist theory in the sense that it is taken to represent the functioning of the central nervous system. It has the disadvantage of being framed in terms which are sometimes ambiguous. The theory is that of the *schema* and *strategy* (see Lunzer, 1968). The schema has a long history as a concept in British (Oldfield and Zangwill, 1942) and European (Piaget, 1950) psychology. The strategy is the result of evidence for the hierarchical structure of behaviour derived from diverse fields, owing its inspiration perhaps to Lashley (1951) and its popularity to Miller, Galanter, and Pribram (1960), who call it a plan.

According to Lunzer (1968, pp. 186–7), schema and strategy are to be distinguished as follows.

'The difference is mainly one of emphasis; it is the difference between structure and function. So long as we are describing the actual sequence of events involved in the regulation of behaviour, the language of strategies is quite adequate by itself. However, when we want to describe the connectivity of the various centres which are involved in such strategies, it is more advantageous to use the term schema. The strategy corresponds to the actual operation of the organism at any given time; the schema to its potential for regulated behaviour. The strategy may be likened to the "flow" of current in any phase of the operation of the machine; the schema is the wiring diagram itself.'

Strategies and schemata are hierarchical in nature, and may themselves be sub-strategies or sub-schemata in a hierarchy of strategies or schemata. Schemata may overlap with each other. Sub-strategies may be controlled by an initiating super-strategy, which may exercise different degrees of control over the transition from one strategy to another. Some transitions may be very highly determined, others free-wheeling. As a result of such less determined transitions, schemata associated with the strategies which succeed such a transition will be activated. Transitions may occur from one strategy to another at different levels in the hierarchy of strategies. Different levels of schema may therefore be activated as a result of such transition. Thus schemata are not to be considered as super-strategies, but rather as on the same level as strategies, though fulfilling a different function. Strategies control the organisation of present behaviour at every level, while schemata correspond to 'the functional implications between the possible lines of behaviour at every level' (Lunzer, 1968, p. 189).

Evidently, such a theoretical system is flexible enough to deal with the psycholinguists' findings. *Strategies* are implied by the psychological reality of the phrase-structure analysis of sentences (see pp. 43–52). These are hierarchical in nature, as are strategies. They contain sub-units, for the construction of which sub-strategies are required. The units of a sentence are produced sequentially in time, and the transition from one unit to another may be determined to a greater or a lesser degree. For example, transition at a high level in the hierarchy, from subject to predicate, may be almost obligatory; but there is considerable choice at lower levels of the hierarchy (for example, whether one qualifies a noun with an adjective or not). Both top-to-bottom and left-to-right dependencies are therefore accommodated within the concept of the strategy. It is clear, then, that in its basic nature, the concept is suited to describing the findings of psycholinguistics.

The development of language skills follows the same course as that described by Piaget for the development of schemata. Take, for example, the learning of inflexions. Schemata are formed as a result of continuous interaction between organism and environment. The schema is accommodated to certain salient features in the environment which strike the attention as being inconsistent with one's existing schema. In the case of inflexions, the child may start with an over-simple rule (schema) whereby he produces 's' or 'es' for all plurals. This has to be modified to cope with exceptions which cannot be ignored. The same may well apply to all syntactic rules, for example transformations; it was shown (see pp. 110–12) that when too many positional exceptions to the rule 'negative morpheme first' were perceived, the rule had to be changed and more flexible procedures adopted. It should be noted that accommodation requires the existence of already formed schemata and the presentation of attention-getting and consistent exceptions.

However, perhaps the major discovery of psycholinguists has been the psychological reality of deep structure. Any theory which claims to describe language behaviour adequately must account for it. It is suggested that deep structure is represented in schemata which mediate between non-linguistic and linguistic schemata. It is supposed that deep-structure schemata are activated by non-linguistic schemata and in turn activate more specifically grammatical and linguistic schemata. How such schemata are *acquired* will be discussed; how they are involved in the *production* of language; and how their introduction can clarify the *language and thought* controversy.

Firstly, *acquisition*. An account has already been given of the acquisition of deep structure (see pp. 104–10). In brief, it is supposed that the child hears language items uttered in temporal conjunction with certain types of behaviour. For example, he hears the names of objects uttered while he or his mother is manipulating them. It is hypothesised that perceptual scanning of both linguistic and visual input results in the extraction of certain criterial features of the situation; for example, the manipulating of the object and certain phonological and positional features of the utterance. As a result of this scanning and extraction of cues, verbal items may be stored in terms of the behaviour with which they are associated. Hence, the activation of the schemata which regulate that particular behaviour is likely to lead to the activation of the language schemata based on them. Clearly, however, these language schemata cannot directly regulate language behaviour since they are not grammatically ordered. Rather, they may be the deep-structure basis of language which requires various more specifically grammatical and phonological schemata to be activated by them before language behaviour can result. The suitability of non-linguistic behaviour as the basis for deep structure is clear from the example quoted; a storage bank based on manipulation can clearly develop into a category of logical objects.

The theory also suits the perception and *production* of language by adults. The writer's experiment (Herriot, 1969*b*) has already been cited concerning perception. It showed that when a sentence contained strong cues based on expectation, those cues were employed in preference to grammatical cues. It was concluded that there was a close connexion between specifically linguistic and non-linguistic schemata. Osgood (1968) supposes that the same is true of production. He stresses the importance of content before structure; one decides what one wants to say before how one is going to say it. In particular, there are features of the non-linguistic situation which act as cues to utterance. For example, there might be a situation when a woman bather was rescued on a crowded beach by a boy. The utterance might be 'The tall boy saved the drowning woman'. Take the subject of this sentence, 'The tall boy'. The grammatical construction Article + Adjective + Noun is required because the construction Article + Noun would not distinguish the rescuer from all the other boys on the beach. The physical situation has constrained the grammar; but so too has the requirement of communication. For it is assumed by the speaker of this sentence that the hearer wishes to be able to distinguish the rescuer from other boys. It may thus be inferred that different non-linguistic cues may activate non-linguistic schemata and thence language schemata and language behaviour. These non-linguistic schemata may be expectations about the outside world; perhaps the violation of an expectation is more likely to lead to activation of language schemata; one is apt to mention something unusual. The non-linguistic schemata may also be expectations about the communication situation. These expectation schemata may be activated by, for example, visual cues which suggest that one's audience want information; or are in a position to give one information themselves. This distinction between different types of non-linguistic schemata permits language functions other than that of reference (see Chapter IV) to be explained. The limitation to expectations concerning the physical world would have tended to an over-emphasis on reference.

This same assumption of deep-structure schemata as subordinate to non-linguistic schemata but superordinate to linguistic schemata perhaps sheds light on the *language-thought* controversy (see Chapter VI). It might be supposed that language is indeed being internalised during the period when egocentric speech is decreasing in amount; but the speech does not become the thought. Rather, the difference is merely that the feedback loop from linguistic to non-linguistic schemata becomes internalised. When the child engages in a lot of egocentric speech, it is supposed that the following stages occur; 1. non-linguistic schemata are activated; 2. these activate deep-structure and thence linguistic schemata; 3. this latter activation results in overt speech; 4. the overt egocentric speech acts as feedback cues, activating the linguistic and non-linguistic schemata. They result in overt modified behaviour. It is worth speculating whether in this case language has been a necessary condition for the accommodation of the non-linguistic schemata. When egocentric speech becomes less, it has been observed that it often consists merely of, for example, the logical object of the sentence which would have been uttered in full. Perhaps, therefore, the stages described previously have been changed in the following way: the feedback loop at stage (4) becomes nearly completely internal, because the activated language schemata are suppressed before they result in overt language behaviour. Indeed, they may be suppressed at quite a high level in the hierarchy of schemata, for example, at the level of the deep structure schemata. As a result, deep structure features are the only cues which 'get through' to overt speech.

The above account is only concerned with the regulation of behaviour by means of language and of language by means of behaviour. The latter process is supposed to occur first in development, since it does not demand complex feedback processes. But it should be stressed that the very early connexions between non-linguistic and linguistic schemata postulated in this chapter are not contradictory to the theories of Bruner or Piaget concerning the connexions of language with cognitive development. Bruner wonders why the power-house of language is not harnessed sooner to aid cognition; Piaget replies that cognitive development is according to stages, and that only when a certain stage has been attained can language be used to help. The crucial stage both are concerned with is in fact that of operational thinking. This requires the representation to oneself of the criteria of one's behaviour; in other words, it requires the representation of alternative schemata. This representation of schemata must be distinguished from the regulation of behaviour by non-linguistic and linguistic schemata. It is far more advanced from a developmental point of view.

A final objection must also be considered: that localisation of speech function in the left hemisphere rules out the postulated close connexion between non-linguistic and linguistic schemata. However, it might be supposed that the functions of linguistic schemata as regulators of speech and as regulators of behaviour via feedback might become more and more separated with development. Clearly, their function as regulators of speech requires their full activation, since speech must be fully organised according to the grammatical conventions. Internalised speech on the contrary, might become more and more abbreviated and adopt other symbolic aids. This may be why many aphasics suffer no cognitive impairment whatever.

In conclusion, it might be said that the connexion of linguistic and non-linguistic schemata is the key to the explanation of acquisition and of language and thought; it incidentally brings language behaviour back into a general behaviour theory.

Bibliography

(*J.V.L.V.B.* = *Journal of Verbal Learning and Verbal Behavior*)

1 ABORN, M., RUBENSTEIN, H. and STERLING, T. D. (1959) 'Sources of contextual constraint upon words in sentences', *J. exp. Psychol.*, **57**, 171–180.

2 ARGYLE, M. and DEAN, J. (1965) 'Eye-contact, distance, and affiliation', *Sociometry*, **28**, 289–304.

3 ARGYLE, M. and KENDON, H. (1967) 'The experimental analysis of social performance'. In BERKOWITZ, L. (ed.) *Advances in Experimental Social Psychology*, **3**. New York: Academic Press.

4 ASCH, S. E. and EBENHOLTZ, S. M. (1962) 'The principle of associative symmetry', *Proceedings Amer. Philosoph. Soc.*, **106**, 135–163.

5 ATTNEAVE, F. (1959) *Applications of Information Theory to Psychology*. New York: Holt, Rinehart and Winston.

6 BASSER, L. S. (1962) 'Hemiplegia of early onset and the faculty of speech with special reference to the effects of hemispherectomy', *Brain*, **85**, 427–460.

7 BATTIG, W. F. (1966) 'Evidence for coding processes in "rote" paired-associate learning', *J.V.L.V.B.*, **5**, 177–181.

8 BATTIG, W. F. (1968) 'Paired-associate learning'. In DIXON, T. R. and HORTON, D. L. (eds.) *Verbal Behavior and General Behavior Theory*. Englewood Cliffs, N.J.: Prentice-Hall.

9 BEILIN, H., KAGAN, J. and RABINOWITZ, R. (1966) 'Effect of verbal and perceptual training on water level representation', *Child Devel.*, **37**, 317–329.

10 BELLUGI, U. and BROWN, R. W. (1964) 'The acquisition of language', *Monogr. Soc. Res. Child Devel.*, **29**, 1.

11 BERKO, J. (1958) 'The child's learning of English morphology', *Word*, **14**, 150–177.

12 BERLYNE, D. E. (1966) 'Mediating responses; a note on Fodor's criticisms', *J.V.L.V.B.*, **5**, 408–411.

13 BERNSTEIN, B. B. (1960) 'Language and social class', *Brit. J. Sociol.*, **11**, 271–276.

14 BERNSTEIN B. B. (1962a) 'Social class, linguistic codes, and grammatical errors', *Language and Speech*, **5**, 221–240.

15 BERNSTEIN, B. B. (1962*b*) 'Linguistic codes, hesitation phenomena, and intelligence', *Language and Speech*, **5**, 31–46.

16 BERNSTEIN, B. B. (1965) 'A socio-linguistic approach to social learning'. In GOULD, J. (ed.) *Social Science Survey*, London.

17 BEVER, T. G. (1968) 'Associations to stimulus-response theories of language'. In DIXON, T. R. and HORTON, D. L. (eds.) *Verbal Behavior and General Behavior Theory*. Englewood Cliffs, N.J.: Prentice-Hall.

18 BEVER, T. G., FODOR, J. A. and GARRETT, M. (1968) 'A formal limitation of associationism'. In DIXON, T. R. and HORTON, D. L. (eds.) *Verbal Behavior and General Behavior Theory*. Englewood Cliffs, N.J., Prentice-Hall.

19 BEVER, T. G., FODOR, J. A. and WEKSEL, W. (1965) 'The acquisition of syntax; a critique of contextual generalisation', *Psychol. Review*, **72**, 467–482.

20 BITTERMAN, M. E. (1965) 'The evolution of intelligence', *Scientific American*, **212**, 92–100.

21 BLANK, M. (1968) 'Experimental approaches to concept development in young children'. In LUNZER, E. A. and MORRIS, J. F. (eds.) *Development in Human Learning*, London: Staples.

22 BLUMENTHAL, A. L. (1967) 'Promoted recall of sentences', *J.V.L.V.B.*, **6**, 203–206.

23 BLUMENTHAL, A. L. and BOAKES, R. (1967) 'Prompted recall of sentences', *J.V.L.V.B.*, **6**, 674–676.

24 BOLINGER, D. (1965) 'The atomization of meaning', *Language*, **41**, 555–573.

25 BOOMER, D. S. (1965) 'Hesitation and grammatical encoding', *Language and Speech*, **8**, 148–158.

26 BOUSFIELD, W. A. (1953) 'The occurrence of clustering in the recall of randomly arranged associates', *J. General Psychol.*, **49**, 229–240.

27 BOUSFIELD, W. A. (1961) 'The problem of meaning in verbal learning'. In COFER, C. N. and MUSGRAVE, B. S. (eds.) *Verbal Learning and Verbal Behavior*. New York: McGraw-Hill.

28 BOUSFIELD, W. A., COHEN, B. H. and WHITMARSH, G. A. (1958) 'Associative clustering in the recall of words of different taxonomic frequencies of occurrence', *Psychological Reports*, **4**, 39–44.

29 BOUSFIELD, W. A., WHITMARSH, G. A. and DANICK, J. J. (1958) 'Partial response identities in verbal generalisation', *Psychological Reports*, **4**, 703–718.

30 BRAIN, R. (1961*a*) *Speech Disorders; Aphasia, Apraxia, and Agnosia*. Washington: Butterworth.

31 BRAIN, R. (1961*b*) 'The neurology of language', *Brain*, **84**, 145–166.

32 BRAINE, M. D. S. (1963*a*) 'On learning the grammatical order of words', *Psychol. Review*, **70**, 323–348.

33 BRAINE, M. D. S. (1963*b*) 'The ontogeny of English phrase structure; the first phase', *Language*, **39**, 1–13.

34 BROADBENT, D. E. (1958) *Perception and Communication*. Oxford: Pergamon.

35 BROADBENT, D. E. and GREGORY, M. (1963) 'Vigilance considered as statistical decision', *Brit. J. Psychol.*, **54**, 309–323.

36 BROWN, R. W. (1957) 'Linguistic determinism and the part of speech', *J. Abn. Soc. Psychol.*, **55**, 1–5.

37 BROWN, R. W. (1958) *Words and Things*. Glencoe: The Free Press.

38 BROWN, R. W. (1965) *Social psychology*. New York: The Free Press.

39 BROWN, R. W. and BELLUGI, U. (1964) 'Three processes in the child's acquisition of syntax'. In LENNEBERG, E. H. (ed.) *New Directions in the Study of Language*. Cambridge, Mass.: M.I.T. Press.

40 BROWN, R. W. and BERKO, J. (1960) 'Word association and the acquisition of grammar', *Child Devel.*, **31**, 1–14.

41 BROWN, R. W. and FRASER, C. (1963) 'The acquisition of syntax'. In COFER, C. N. and MUSGRAVE, B. S. (eds.) *Verbal Behavior and Learning*. New York: McGraw-Hill.

42 BROWN, R. W. and HILDUM, D. C. (1956) 'Expectancy and the perception of syllables', *Language*, **32**, 411–419.

43 BROWN, R. W. and LENNEBERG, E. H. (1954) 'A study in language and cognition', *J. Abn. Soc. Psychol.*, **49**, 454–462.

44 BROWN, R. W. and MCNEILL, D. (1966) 'The "tip of the tongue" phenomenon', *J.V.L.V.B.*, **5**, 325–337.

45 BRUCE, D. J. (1958) 'The effect of listeners' anticipation on the intelligibility of heard speech', *Language and Speech*, **1**, 79–97.

46 BRUNER, J. S. (1964) 'The course of cognitive growth', *Amer. Psychologist*, **19**, 1–19.

47 BRUNER, J. S., BUSIEK, R. D. and MINTURN, A. L. (1952) 'Assimilation in the immediate reproduction of visually perceived figures', *J. Exper. Psychol.*, **44**, 151–155.

48 BRUNER, J. S., GOODNOW, J. J. and AUSTIN, G. A. (1956) *A Study of Thinking*. New York: Wiley.

49 BRUNER, J. S. and KENNEY, H. (1966) 'The development of the concepts of order and proportion in children'. In BRUNER, J. S., OLVER, R. R. and GREENFIELD, P. M. (eds.) *Studies in Cognitive Growth*. New York: Wiley.

50 BRUNER, J. S., OLVER, R. R. and GREENFIELD, P. M. (1966) *Studies in Cognitive Growth*. New York: Wiley.

51 CARLIN, J. E. (1958) *Word-association strength as a variable in verbal paired-associate learning*. Ph.D. thesis: Univ. of Minnesota.

52 CARMICHAEL, L., HOGAN, H. P. and WALTER, A. A. (1932) 'An experimental study of the effect of language on the reproduction of visually perceived forms', *J. Exper. Psychol.*, **15**, 73–86.

53 CARROLL, J. B. (ed.) (1956) *Language, Thought, and Reality.* Cambridge, Mass.: The Technology Press and Wiley.

54 CARROLL, J. B. (1959) 'A review of "The measurement of meaning" ', *Language,* **35,** 58–77.

55 CARROLL, J. B. (1963) 'Linguistic relativity, contrastive linguistics, and language learning', *Int. Rev. Applied Linguistics in Language Teaching,* **1,** 1–20.

56 CARROLL, J. B. (1964) *Language and Thought.* Englewood-Cliffs, N.J.: Prentice-Hall.

57 CARROLL, J. B. and CASAGRANDE, J. B. (1958) 'The function of language classifications in behaviour'. In MACCOBY, E. E., NEWCOMB, T. M. and HARTLEY, E. L. (eds.) *Readings in Social Psychology,* New York.

58 CARROLL, J. B., KJELDERGAARD, P. M. and CARTON, A. A. (1962) 'Number of opposites vs. the number of primaries as a response measure in free-association tests', *J.V.L.V.B.,* **1,** 22–30.

59 CAZDEN, C. (1965) *Environmental assistance to the child's acquisition of grammar.* Ph.D. thesis: Harvard Univ.

60 CHASE, R. A. (1966) 'Evolutionary aspects of language development and function'. In SMITH, F. and MILLER, G. A. (eds.) *The Genesis of Language.* Cambridge, Mass.: M.I.T. Press.

61 CHERRY, E. C. (1953) 'Some experiments on the recognition of speech with one and with two ears', *J. Acoustical Soc. America,* **25,** 975–979.

62 CHOMSKY, N. (1957) *Syntactic Structures.* The Hague: Mouton.

63 CHOMSKY, N. (1959) 'Review of B. F. Skinner's Verbal Behavior', *Language,* **35,** 26–58.

64 CHOMSKY, N. (1965) *Aspects of the Theory of Syntax.* Cambridge, Mass.: M.I.T. Press.

65 CLARK, H. H. (1965) 'Some structural properties of some simple active and passive sentences', *J.V.L.V.B.,* **4,** 365–370.

66 CLARK, H. H. (1966) 'The prediction of recall patterns in simple active sentences', *J.V.L.V.B.,* **5,** 99–106.

67 CLARK, H. H. (1968) 'On the use and meaning of prepositions', *J.V.L.V.B.,* **7,** 421–431.

68 CLARK, H. H. and BEGUN, J. S. (1968) 'The use of syntax in understanding sentences', *Brit. J. Psychol.,* **59,** 219–229.

69 CLARK, H. H. and CLARK, E. V. (1968) 'Semantic distinctions and memory for complex sentences', *Quart. J. Exp. Psychol.,* **20,** 129–137.

70 CLARK, H. H. and STAFFORD, R. A. (1969) 'Memory for semantic features in the verb', *J. Exp. Psychol.* (in press).

71 CLIFF, N. (1959) 'Adverbs as multipliers', *Psychol. Rev.,* **66,** 27–44.

72 COFER, C. N. (1957) 'Reasoning as an associative process: the rôle of verbal responses in problem solving', *J. General Psychol.,* **57,** 55–68.

73 COFER, C. N. (1965) 'On some factors in the organisational characteristics of free recall', *Amer. Psychologist*, **20,** 261–272.

74 COFER, C. N. (1966) 'Some evidence for coding processes derived from clustering in free recall', *J.V.L.V.B.*, **5,** 188–192.

75 COFER, C. N. (1967) 'Learning of content and function words in nonsense syllable frames. A repetition and extension of Glanzer's experiment', *J.V.L.V.B.*, **6,** 198–202.

76 COFER, C. N. (1968) 'Problems, issues, and implications'. In DIXON, T. R. and HORTON, D. L. (eds.) *Verbal Behavior and General Behavior Theory*. Englewood Cliffs, N.J.: Prentice-Hall.

77 COLEMAN, E. B. (1963) 'Approximations to English – some comments on the method'. *Am. J. Psychol.*, **76,** 239–247.

78 COOPER, F. S., DELATTRE, P. C., LIBERMAN, A. M., BORST, J. M. and GERSTMAN, I. J. (1952) 'Some experiments on the perception of speech sounds', *J. Acoustical Soc. America*, **24,** 597–606.

79 DAVITZ, J. R. (1964) *The Communication of Emotional Meaning*. New York: McGraw-Hill.

80 DAY, E. J. (1932) 'The development of language in twins. A comparison of twins and single children', *Child Devel.*, **3,** 179–199.

81 DEESE, J. (1961) 'From the isolated verbal unit to connected discourse'. In COFER, C. and MUSGRAVE, B. S'. (eds.) *Verbal Behavior and Learning*. New York: McGraw-Hill

82 DEESE, J. (1962) 'Form class and the determinants of association', *J.V.L.V.B.*, **1,** 79–84.

83 DEESE, J. (1966) *The Structure of Associations in Language and Thought*. Baltimore: The John Hopkins Press.

84 DEESE, J. (1968) 'Association and memory'. In DIXON, T. R. and HORTON, D. L. (eds.) *Verbal Behavior and General Behavior Theory*. Englewood Cliffs, N.J.: Prentice-Hall.

85 DEESE, J. and KAUFMAN, R. (1957) 'Serial effects in the recall of unorganised and sequentially organised verbal material', *J. Exp. Psychol.*, **54,** 180–187.

86 DENES, P. (1955) 'Effects of duration on the perception of voicing', *J. Acoustical Soc. America*, **27,** 761–764.

87 DESOTO, C. B. and BOSLEY, J. J. (1962) 'The cognitive structure of a social structure', *J. Abn. Soc. Psychol.*, **64,** 303–307.

88 DEUTSCH, M. P. (1963) 'The disadvantaged child and the learning process'. In PASSOW, H. (ed.) *Education in Depressed Areas*. New York: Columbia Univ. Teachers College Publications.

89 DONALDSON, M. (1966) 'Comments on McNeill's paper'. In LYONS, J. and WALES, R. J. (eds.) *Psycholinguistics Papers*. Edinburgh Univ. Press.

90 DULANY, D. E. (1968) 'Awareness, rules, and propositional control'. In DIXON, T. R. and HORTON, D. L. (eds.) *Verbal Behavior and General Behavior Theory*. Englewood Cliffs N.J.: Prentice-Hall.

91 EARHARD, B. and MANDLER, G. (1965*a*) 'Mediated associations; paradigms, controls, and mechanisms'. *Canadian J. Psychol.* **19**, 346–378.

92 EARHARD, B. and MANDLER, G. (1965*b*) 'Pseudo-mediation; a reply and more data', *Psychonomic Science*, **3**, 137–138.

93 EHRLICH, S. (1965) *Le rôle de la structuration dans l'apprentisage verbal*, Psychologia Française, **10**, 119–146.

94 ENTWISLE, D. R. (1966) 'Form class and children's word associations', *J.V.L.V.B.*, **5**, 558–565.

95 EPSTEIN, W. A. (1961) 'The influence of syntactical structure on learning', *Am. J. Psychol.*, **74**, 80–85.

96 ERVIN, S. M. (1961) 'Changes with age in the verbal determinants of word association', *Am. J. Psychol.*, **74**, 361–372.

97 ERVIN, S. M. (1964) 'Imitation and structural change in children's language'. In LENNEBERG, E. (ed.) *New Directions in the Study of Language*. Cambridge, Mass.: M.I.T. Press.

98 EVANS, B. and EVANS, C. (1957) *A Dictionary of Contemporary American Usage*. New York: Random House.

99 FEATHER, B. W. (1965) 'Semantic generalisation of classically conditioned responses; a review', *Psychol. Bull.*, **63**, 424–441.

100 FITTS, P. M. (1964) 'Perceptual-motor skill learning'. In MELTON, A. W. (ed.) *Categories of Human Learning*. New York: Academic Press.

101 FLAVELL, J. (1963) *The Developmental Psychology of Jean Piaget*. Princeton: Van Nostrand.

102 FODOR, J. A. (1965) 'Could meaning be an r_m?' *J.V.L.V.B.*, **4**, 73–81.

103 FODOR, J. A. and BEVER, T. (1965) 'The psychological reality of linguistic segments', *J.V.L.V.B.*, **4**, 414–420.

104 FRASER, C. (1966) 'Comments on McNeill's paper'. In LYONS, J. and WALES, R. J. (eds.) *Psycholinguistics Papers*. Edinburgh Univ. Press.

105 FRASER, C., BELLUGI, U. and BROWN, R. W. (1963) 'Control of grammar in imitation, comprehension, and production', *J.V.L.V.B.* **2**, 121–135.

106 FRIES, C. C. (1952) *The Structure of English*. New York: Harcourt Brace.

107 FRY, D. B. (1955) 'Duration and intensity as physical correlates of linguistic stress', *J. Acoustical Soc. America*, **27**, 765–768.

108 FRY, D. B. (1966) 'The development of the phonological system in the normal and the deaf child'. In SMITH, F. and MILLER, G. A. (eds.) *The Genesis of Language*. Cambridge, Mass.: M.I.T. Press.

109 FURTH, H. G. (1966) *Thinking Without Language*. New York: Free Press.

110 GAGNÉ, R. M. and SMITH, E. C. (1962) 'A study of the effects of verbalization on problem solving', *J. Exp. Psychol.*, **63**, 12–18.

111 GARNER, W. R. (1962) *Uncertainty and Structure as Psychological Concepts*. New York: Wiley.

112 GARRETT, M. and FODOR, J. A. (1968) 'Psychological theories and linguistic constructs'. In DIXON, T. R. and HORTON, D. L. (eds.) *Verbal Behavior and General Behavior Theory*. Englewood Cliffs. N.J.: Prentice-Hall.

113 GLADNEY, T. A. and KRULEE, G. K. (1967) 'The influence of syntactic errors on sentence recognition', *J.V.L.V.B.*, **6**, 685–691.

114 GLANZER, M. (1962) 'Grammatical category; a rote learning and word association analysis', *J.V.L.V.B.*, **1**, 31–41.

115 GLEASON, H. A. (1961) *An Introduction to Descriptive Linguistics* (revised edition) New York: Holt, Rinehart & Winston.

116 GOLDFARB, W. (1945) 'Effects of psychological deprivation in infancy and subsequent stimulation', *Am. J. Psychiat.*, **102**, 18–33.

117 GOLDMAN-EISLER, F. (1968) *Psycholinguistics; Experiments in Spontaneous Speech*. New York: Academic Press.

118 GOLDSTEIN, K., (1948) *Language and Language Disturbances*. New York: Grune & Stratton.

119 GONZALEZ, R. C. and COFER, C. N. (1959) 'Exploratory studies of verbal context by means of clustering in free recall', *J. Genet. Psychol.*, **95**, 293–320.

120 GOODGLASS, H. and BERKO, J. (1960) 'Agrammatism and English inflexion', *J. Speech and Hearing Research*, **3**, 257–267.

121 GOODGLASS, H. and MAYER, J. (1958) 'Agrammatism in aphasia', *J. Speech and Hearing Disorders*, **23**, 99–111.

122 GOUGH, P. B. (1965) 'Grammatical transformation and speed of understanding', *J.V.L.V.B.*, **4**, 107–111.

123 GOUGH, P. B. (1966) 'The verification of sentences; the effects of delay of evidence and sentence length', *J.V.L.V.B.*, **5**, 492–496.

124 GRAHAM, N. C. (1968) 'Short-term memory and syntactic structure in educationally subnormal children', *Language and Speech*, **11**.

125 GREENBERG, J. H. (ed.) (1966) *Universals of Language* (2nd ed.) Cambridge, Mass.: M.I.T. Press.

126 GREENSPOON, J. (1955) 'The reinforcing effect of two spoken sounds on the frequency of two responses', *Am. J. Psychol.*, **68**. 409–416.

127 GREENSPOON, J. (1962) 'Verbal conditioning and clinical psychology'. In BACHRACH, A. J. (ed.) *Experimental Foundations of Clinical Psychology*. New York: Basic Books.

128 HARLOW, H. F. (1949) 'The formation of learning sets', *Psychol, Rev.*, **56**, 51–65.

129 HAYHURST, H. (1967) 'Some errors of young children in producing passive sentences', *J.V.L.V.B.*, **6**, 654–660.

130 HÉCAEN, H. and DE AJURIAGUERRA, J. (1963) *Les Gauchers,*

Prévalence Mauvelle et Dominance Cérébrale. Paris: Presses Universitaires de France.

131 HERMAN, D. T., LAWLESS, R. H. and MARSHALL, R. W. (1957) 'Variables in the effect of language on the reproduction of visually perceived forms', *Perceptual and Motor Skills*, **7**, monog. supp. 2, 171–186.

132 HERRIOT, P. (1967) 'Phrase units and the recall of grammatically structured nonsense', *Brit. J. Psychol.*, **58**, 237–242.

133 HERRIOT, P. (1968*a*) 'The comprehension of syntax', *Child Devel.*, **39**, 273–282.

134 HERRIOT, P. (1968*b*) 'The comprehension of sentences as a function of grammatical depth and order', *J.V.L.V.B.*, **7**, 938–941.

135 HERRIOT, P. (1969*a*) 'The comprehension of active and passive sentences as a function of pragmatic expectations', *J.V.L.V.B.* **8**, 166–169.

136 HERRIOT, P. (1969*b*) 'The comprehension of tense by young children', *Child Devel.* **40**, 103–110.

137 HESS, E. H. (1962) 'Ethology; an approach toward the complete analysis of behavior'. In BROWN, R. W., GALANTER, E., HESS, E. H. and MANDLER, G. (eds.) *New Directions in Psychology*. New York: Holt, Rinehart & Winston.

138 HOCKETT, C. (1960) 'The origin of speech', *Scientific American*. **203**, 88–96.

139 HOWE, E. S. (1962) 'Probabilistic adverbial qualifications of adjectives', *J.V.L.V.B.*, **1**, 225–242.

140 HOWES, D. (1957) 'On the relation between the probability of a word as an association and in general linguistic usage', *J. Abn. Soc, Psychol.*, **54**, 75–85.

141 HOWES, D. and OSGOOD, C. E. (1954) 'On the combination of associative probabilities in linguistic contexts', *Am. J. Psychol.*, **67**, 241–258.

142 HULL, C. L. (1930) 'Knowledge and purpose as habit mechanisms', *Psychol. Rev.*, **37**, 511–525.

143 HULME, I. and LUNZER, E. A. (1966) 'Play, language and reasoning in subnormal children', *J. Child Psychol. and Psychiat.*, **7**, 107–124.

144 INGRAM, E. (1968) 'Recent trends in psycholinguistics; a critical notice', *Brit. J. Psychol.*, **59**, 315–325.

145 INHELDER, B., BOVET, M., SINCLAIR, H. and SMOCK, C. D. (1966) 'On cognitive development', *Amer. Psychologist*, **21**, 160–164.

146 INHELDER, B. and PIAGET, J. (1958) *The Growth of Logical Thinking from Childhood to Adolescence*. London: Routledge.

147 INHELDER, B., and PIAGET, J. (1964) *The Early Growth of Logic in the Child*. London: Routledge.

148 IRWIN, O. C. (1948) 'Infant speech', *J. Speech and Hearing Disorders*, **13**, 224–225, 320–326.

149 JACKSON, J. H. (1931) *The Selected Writings, Vol. 2, Speech.* London: Hodder & Stoughton. Reprinted (1958) New York: Basic Books.

150 JAKOBSON, R., FANT, G. and HALLE, M. (1952) *Preliminaries to Speech Analysis* (2nd ed. 1963). Cambridge, Mass.: M.I.T. Press.

151 JAKOBSON, R. and HALLE, M. (1956) *Fundamentals of Language.* The Hague: Mouton.

152 JENKINS, J. J. (1963) 'Mediated associations: paradigms and situations'. In COFER, C. N. and MUSGRAVE, B. S. (eds.) *Verbal Behavior and Learning.* New York: McGraw-Hill.

153 JENKINS, J. J. (1965) 'Mediation theory and grammatical behavior'. In ROSENBERG, S. (ed.) *Directions in Psycholinguistics.* New York: Macmillan.

154 JENKINS, J. J. (1968) 'The challenge to psychological theorists'. In DIXON, T. R. and HORTON, D. L. (eds.) *Verbal Behavior and General Behavior Theory.* Englewood Cliffs, N.J.: Prentice-Hall.

155 JENKINS, J. J. and RUSSELL, W. A. (1952) 'Associative clustering during recall', *J. Abn. Soc. Psychol.,* **47,** 818–821.

156 JENKINS, J. J., RUSSELL, W. A. and SUCI, G. J. (1958) 'An atlas of semantic profiles for 360 words', *Am. J. Psychol.,* **71,** 688–699.

157 JENSEN, A. R. (1967) 'Social class and verbal learning'. In DE CECCO, J. P. (ed.) *The Psychology of Language, Thought, and Instruction.* New York: Holt, Rinehart & Winston.

158 JOHN, V. P. (1962) *The Intellectual Development of Slum Children.* Annual Meeting American Orthopsychiatric Assn.

159 JOHNSON, M. G. (1967) 'Syntactic position and rated meaning', *J.V.L.V.B.,* **6,** 240–246.

160 JOHNSON, N. F. (1965) 'The psychological reality of phrase-structure rules', *J.V.L.V.B.,* **4,** 469–475.

161 JOHNSON, N. F. (1966a) 'The influence of associations between elements of structured verbal responses', *J.V.L.V.B.,* **5,** 369–374.

162 JOHNSON, N. F. (1966b) 'On the relationship between sentence structure and the latency in generating the sentence', *J.V.L.V.B.,* **5,** 375–380.

163 JOHNSON, N. F. (1968) 'Sequential verbal behavior'. In DIXON, T. R. and HORTON, D. L. (eds.) *Verbal Behavior and General Behavior Theory.* Englewood Cliffs, N.J.: Prentice-Hall.

164 JOHNSON, R. C., FRINCKE, G. and MARTIN, L. (1961) 'Meaningfulness, frequency, and affective character of words as related to visual duration threshold', *Canadian J. Psychol.,* **15,** 199–204.

165 JOHNSON, R. L., MILLER, M. D. and WALL, D. D. (1965) *Content analysis and semantic classification.* U.S. Navy Contract No. DA 49–193 MO2490.

166 JOHNSON-LAIRD, P. N. (1968) 'The choice of the passive voice in a communicative task', *Brit. J. Psychol.,* **59,** 7–15.

167 JOHNSON-LAIRD, P. N. (1969a) 'Reasoning with ambiguous sentences', *Brit. J. Psychol.*, **60**, 17–23.

168 JOHNSON-LAIRD, P. N. (1969b) 'On understanding logically complex sentences', *Quart. J. Exp. Psychol.*, **21**, 1–13.

169 JUDSON, A. J., COFER, C. N. and GELFAND, S. (1956) 'Reasoning as an associative process, 2: "Direction" in problem solving as a function of prior reinforcement of relevant responses', *Psychological Reports*, **2**, 501–507.

170 KANFER, F. H. (1968) 'Verbal conditioning; a review of its current status'. In DIXON, T. R. and HORTON, D. L. (eds.) *Verbal Behavior and General Behavior Theory*. Englewood Cliffs, N.J.: Prentice-Hall.

171 KATZ, J. J. and FODOR, J. (1963) 'The structure of a semantic theory', *Language*, **39**, 170–211.

172 KATZ, J. J. and POSTAL, P. M. (1964) *An Integrated Theory of Linguistic Descriptions*. Cambridge, Mass.: M.I.T. Press.

173 KENDLER, T. S. (1961) 'Concept formation', *Annual Rev. Psychol.*, **12**, 447–472.

174 KENT, E. H. and ROSANOFF, A. J. (1910) 'A study of association in insanity', *Am. J. Insanity*, **67**, 37–96, 317–390.

175 KJELDERGAARD, P. M. (1968) 'Transfer and mediation in verbal learning'. In DIXON, T. R. and HORTON, D. L. (eds.) *Verbal Behavior and General Behavior Theory*. Englewood Cliffs, N.J.: Prentice-Hall.

176 KLIMA, E. S. (1964) 'Negation in English'. In FODOR, J. A. and KATZ, J. J. (eds.) *The Structure of Language*. Englewood Cliffs, N.J.: Prentice-Hall.

177 KLIMA, E. S. and BELLUGI, U. (1966) 'Syntactic regularities in the speech of children'. In LYONS, J. and WALES, R. J. *Psycholinguistics Papers*. Edinburgh Univ. Press.

178 KUENNE, M. R. (1946) 'Experimental investigation of the relation of language to transposition behavior in young children', *J. Exp. Psychol.*, **36**, 471–490.

179 KUHN, T. S. (1962) *The Structure of Scientific Revolutions*. Univ. Chicago Press.

180 LADEFOGED, P. and BROADBENT, D. E. (1957) 'Information conveyed by vowels', *J. Acoustical Soc. America*, **29**, 98–104.

181 LADEFOGED, P. and BROADBENT, D. E. (1960) 'Perception of sequence in auditory events', *Quart. J. Exp. Psychol.*, **12**, 162–170.

182 LAMBERT, W. E. and JAKOBOVITS, L. A. (1960) 'Verbal satiation and changes in the intensity of meaning', *J. Exp. Psychol.*, **60**, 376–383.

183 LASHLEY, K. (1951) 'The problem of serial order in behavior'. In L. JEFFRESS (ed.) *Cerebral Mechanisms in Behavior*. New York: Wiley.

184 LAWTON, D. (1968) *Social Class, Language, and Education.* London: Routledge & Kegan Paul.

185 LENNEBERG, E. H. (1960) 'Review of *Speech and Brain Mechanisms* by W. Penfield and L. Roberts', *Language*, **36**, 97–112.

186 LENNEBERG, E. H. (1962) 'Understanding language without ability to speak; a case report', *J. Abn. Soc. Psychol.*, **65**, 419–425.

187 LENNEBERG, E. H. (1964) 'A biological perspective of language'. In LENNEBERG, E. H. (ed.) *New Directions In the Study of Language.* Cambridge, Mass.: M.I.T. Press.

188 LENNEBERG, E. H. (1967) *Biological Foundations of Language.* New York: Wiley.

189 LENNEBERG, E. H. and ROBERTS, J. M. (1956) *The Language of Experience.* Indiana Univ. Publications in Anthropology and Linguistics Memoir.

190 LEOPOLD, W. F. (1953) 'Patterning in children's language learning'. In SAPORTA, S. (ed.) *Psycholinguistics.* New York: Holt, Rinehart & Winston.

191 LEWIS, M. M. (1951) *Infant Speech* (2nd ed.) London: Harrap.

192 LIBERMAN, A. M. (1957) 'Some results of research on speech perception', *J. Acoustical Soc. America*, **29**, 117–123.

193 LOBAN, W. D. (1963) *The Language of Elementary School Children.* NCTE research report No. 1. Champaigne, Illinois.

194 LOEWENTHAL, K. (1968) 'The effects of understanding from the audience on language behaviour', *Brit. J. Soc. Clin. Psychol.*, **7**, 247–252.

195 LOVELL, K., and DIXON, E. M. (1967) 'The growth of the control of grammar in imitation, comprehension, and production', *J. Child Psychol. and Psychiat.*, **8**, 31–39.

196 LOVELL, K., HOYLE, H. W., and SIDDALL, M. Q. (1968) 'A study of some aspects of the play and language of young children with delayed speech', *J. Child Psychol. and Psychiat.*, **9**, 41–50.

197 LUNZER, E. A. (1959) 'Intellectual development in the play of young children', *Educ. Review*, **11**, 205–217.

198 LUNZER, E. A. (1968) *The Regulation of Behavior.* London: Staples.

199 LUNZER, E. A. and MORRIS, J. F. (eds.) (1968) *Development in Human Learning.* London: Staples.

200 LURIA, A. R. (1947) *Traumatic Aphasia.* Moscow: Acad. Medical Science.

201 LURIA, A. R. (1961) *The Rôle of Speech in the Regulation of Normal and Abnormal Behavior.* Oxford: Pergamon.

202 LURIA, A. R. (1964) In DE REUCK, A. V. S. and O'CONNOR, M. (eds.) *Disorders of Language* (CIBA Foundation Symposium) Boston: Little, Brown.

203 LURIA, A. R. (1966) *Human Brain and Psychological Processes.* New York: Harper & Row.

204 LURIA, A. R., and VINOGRADOVA, O. S. (1959) 'An objective investigation of the dynamics of semantic systems', *Brit. J. Psychol.*, **50**, 89–105.

205 LURIA, A. R. and YUDOVICH, F. (1959) *Speech and the Development of Mental Processes in the Child*. London: Staples.

206 LYONS, J. (1968) *Introduction to Theoretical Linguistics*. Cambridge Univ. Press.

207 MCCARTHY, D. (1930) *The Language Development of the Pre-school Child*. Inst. for Child Welfare, Monogr. 4.

208 MCCARTHY, D. (1954) 'Language development in children'. In CARMICHAEL, L. (ed.) *Manual of Child Psychology*. New York: Wiley.

209 MCLAUGHLIN, G. H. (1963) 'Psycho-logic; a possible alternative to Piaget's formulation', *Brit. J. Educ. Psychol.*, **33**, 61–67.

210 MACLAY, H. and OSGOOD, C. E. (1959) 'Hesitation phenomena in spontaneous speech', *Word*, **15**, 19–44.

211 MCNEILL, D. (1963) 'The origin of association within the same grammatical class', *J.V.L.V.B.*, **2**, 250–262.

212 MCNEILL, D. (1966a) 'A study of word association', *J.V.L.V.B.*, **5**, 548–557.

213 MCNEILL, D. (1966b) 'Developmental Psycholinguistics'. In SMITH, F. and MILLER, G. A. (eds.) *The Genesis of Language*. Cambridge, Mass.: M.I.T. Press.

214 MCNEILL, D. (1966c) 'The creation of language by children'. In LYONS, J. and WALES, R. J. (eds.) *Psycholinguistics Papers*. Edinburgh Univ. Press.

215 MCNEILL, D. (1968) 'On theories of language acquisition'. In DIXON, T. R. and HORTON, D. L. (eds.) *Verbal Behavior and General Behavior Theory*. Englewood Cliffs, N.J.: Prentice-Hall.

216 MAIER, N. R. F. (1931) 'Reasoning in humans, 2: The solution of a problem and its appearance in consciousness', *J. Comp. Psychol.*, **12**, 184–194.

217 MALTZMAN, I. (1968) 'Theoretical conceptions of semantic conditioning and generalisation'. In DIXON, T. R. and HORTON, D. L. (eds.) *Verbal Behavior and General Behavior Theory*. Englewood Cliffs, N.J.: Prentice-Hall.

218 MALTZMAN, I. and BELLONI, M. (1964) 'Three studies of semantic generalisation', *J.V.L.V.B.*, **3**, 231–236.

219 MALTZMAN, I., BROOKS, L. O., BOGARTZ, W. and SUMMERS, S. S. (1958) 'The facilitation of problem solving by prior exposure to uncommon responses', *J. Exp. Psychol.*, **56**, 399–406.

220 MANDLER, G. (1966) 'Organisation and memory'. In SPENCE, K. W. and SPENCE, J. T. (eds.) *The Psychology of Learning and Motivation; Advances in Research and Theory*. New York: Academic Press.

221 MANDLER, G. (1968) 'Association and organisation: facts, fancies, and theories'. In DIXON, T. R. and HORTON, D. L. (eds.) *Verbal Behavior and General Behavior Theory*. Englewood Cliffs, N.J.: Prentice-Hall.

222 MANDLER, G. and MANDLER, J. M. (1964) 'Serial position effects in sentences', *J.V.L.V.B.*, 3, 195–202.

223 MARKS, L. E. and MILLER, G. A. (1964) 'The rôle of semantic and syntactic constraints in the memorisation of English sentences', *J.V.L.V.B.*, 3, 1–5.

224 MARKS, M. and JACK, O. (1952) 'Verbal context and memory span for meaningful material'. *Am. J. Psychol.*, 65, 298–300.

225 MARSHALL, J. C. and NEWCOMBE, F. (1967) 'Immediate recall of "sentences" by subjects with unilateral cerebral lesions', *Neuropsychologia*, 5, 329–334.

226 MARTIN, E. and ROBERTS, K. H. (1966) 'Grammatical features in sentence retention', *J.V.L.V.B.*, 5, 211–218.

227 MARTIN, J. G. (1967) 'Hesitations in the speaker's production and the listener's reproduction of utterances', *J.V.L.V.B.*, 6, 903–909.

228 MEHLER, J. (1963) 'Some effects of grammatical transformations on the recall of English sentences', *J.V.L.V.B.*, 2, 346–351.

229 MEHLER, J. and CAREY, P. (1967) 'Role of surface and base structure in the perception of sentences', *J.V.L.V.B.*, 6, 335–338.

230 MEHLER, J. and MILLER, G. A. (1964) 'Retroactive interference in the recall of simple sentences', *Brit. J. Psychol.*, 55, 295–301.

231 MELTON, A. W. (1963) 'Implications of short-term memory for a general theory of memory', *J.V.L.V.B.*, 2, 1–21.

232 MENYUK, P. (1964) 'Alternation of rules in children's grammar', *J.V.L.V.B.*, 4, 748–762.

233 MILLER, G. A. (1956) 'The magical number seven, plus or minus two; some limits on our capacity for processing information', *Psychol. Review*, 60, 81–97.

234 MILLER, G. A., (1962) 'Some psychological studies of grammar', *Amer. Psychologist*, 17, 748–762.

235 MILLER, G. A. (1964) 'The psycholinguists', *Encounter*, 23, 29–37.

236 MILLER. G. A. (1965) 'Some preliminaries to psycholinguistics', *Amer. Psychologist*, 20, 15–20.

237 MILLER, G. A. and CHOMSKY, N. (1963) 'Finitary models of language users.' In LUCE, D. R., BUSH, R. R. and GALANTER, E. (eds.) *Handbook of Mathematical Psychology*. New York: Wiley.

238 MILLER, G. A., GALANTER, E. and PRIBRAM, K. H. (1960) *Plans and the Structure of Behavior*. New York: Holt Dryden.

239 MILLER, G. A., HEISE, G. A. and LICHTEN, W. (1951) 'The intelligibility of speech as a function of the context of the test materials', *J. Exp. Psychol.*, 41, 329–335.

240 MILLER, G. A. and ISARD, S. (1963) 'Some perceptual consequences of linguistic rules', *J.V.L.V.B.*, **2**, 217–228.

241 MILLER, G. A. and MCKEAN, K. O. (1964) 'A chronometric study of some relations between sentences', *Quart. J. Exp. Psychol.*, **16**, 297–308.

242 MILLER, G. A. and NICELY, P. E. (1955) 'Analysis of perceptual confusions among some English consonants', *J. Acoustical Soc. America*, **27**, 338–352.

243 MILLER, G. A. and SELFRIDGE, J. A. (1950) 'Verbal context and the recall of meaningful material', *Am. J. Psychol.*, **63**, 176–185.

244 MINK, W. D. (1963) 'Semantic generalisation as related to word association', *Psychological Reports*, **12**, 59–67.

245 MIRON, M. S. and OSGOOD, C. E. (1967) 'The multivariate structure of qualification'. In CATTELL, R. B. and HAMMOND, K. R. (eds.) *Handbook of Multivariate Experimental Psychology*. New York: Rand McNally.

246 MORAY, N. (1959) 'Attention in dichotic listening; affective cues and the influence of instructions', *Quart. J. Exp. Psychol.*, **11**, 56–60.

247 MOUNTCASTLE, V. B. (1962) *Intrahemispheric Relations and Cerebral Dominance*. Baltimore: Johns Hopkins.

248 MOWRER, O. H. (1954) 'The psychologist looks at language', *American Psychologist*, **9**, 660–694.

249 NAIR, P. (1963) 'An experiment in conservation'. Cambridge, Mass.: In Center for Cognitive Studies Annual Report.

250 NIELSEN, J. M. (1942) *Agnosia, Apraxia, Aphasia*. New York: Paul B. Hoeber.

251 NOBLE, C. E. (1952) 'An analysis of meaning', *Psychol. Review*, **59**, 421–430.

252 NOBLE, C. E. (1963) 'Meaningfulness and familiarity'. In COFER, C. N. and MUSGRAVE, B. S. (eds.) *Verbal Behavior and Learning*. New York: McGraw-Hill.

253 O'CONNOR, N. (ed.) (1961) *Recent Soviet Psychology*. London: Staples.

254 O'CONNOR, N. and HERMELIN, B. (1959) 'Discrimination and reversal learning in imbeciles', *J. Abn. Soc. Psychol.*, **59**, 409–413.

255 OLDFIELD, R. C. and ZANGWILL, O. (1942) 'Head's concept of the schema and its application in contemporary British psychology'. Parts 1, 2 and 3, *Brit. J. Psychol.*, **32**, 267–286; **33**, 58–64 and 113–129.

256 OLÉRON, P. (1957) *Research on the Mental Development of Deaf-mutes*. Paris: National Centre For Scientific Research.

257 OLSON, D. (1969) 'Language and thought: aspects of a cognitive theory of semantics'. Paper presented at the Conference on Human Learning, Prague.

258 OSGOOD, C. E. (1961) 'Comments on Professor Bousfield's paper'. In COFER, C. N. and MUSGRAVE, B. S. (eds.) *Verbal Learning and Verbal Behavior*. New York: McGraw-Hill.

259 OSGOOD, C. E. (1963) 'On understanding and creating sentences', *Amer. Psychologist*, **18**, 735–751.

260 OSGOOD, C. E. (1966) 'Meaning cannot be an r_m?' *J.V.L.V.B.*, **5**, 402–407.

261 OSGOOD, C. E. (1968) 'Toward a wedding of insufficiencies'. In DIXON, T. R. and HORTON, D. L. (eds.) *Verbal Behavior and General Behavior Theory*. Englewood Cliffs, N.J.: Prentice-Hall.

262 OSGOOD, C. E. and MIRON, M. (1963) *Approaches to the Study of Aphasia*. Urbana, Illinois: Univ. Illinois Press.

263 OSGOOD, C. E., SUCI, G. J. and TANNENBAUM, P. (1957) *The Measurement of Meaning*. Urbana, Illinois: Univ. Illinois Press.

264 PAUL, C. (1965) 'Effects of overlearning upon single habit reversal in rats', *Psychol. Bull.*, **63**, 65–72.

265 PENFIELD, W. and ROBERTS, L. (1959) *Speech and Brain Mechanisms*. Princeton, N.J.: Princeton Univ. Press.

266 PETERSON, M. J. (1965) 'Mediated Meaningfulness?' *Psychonomic Science*, **5**, 61–62.

267 PIAGET, J. (1950) *The Psychology of Intelligence*. London: Routledge & Kegan Paul.

268 PIAGET, J. (1951) *Play, Dreams, and Imitation in Childhood*. London: Heinemann.

269 PIAGET, J. and INHELDER, B. (1956) *The Child's Conception of Space*. London: Routledge & Kegan Paul.

270 POLLIO, H. R. (1968) 'Associative structure and verbal behavior'. In DIXON, T. R. and HORTON, D. L. (eds.) *Verbal Behavior and General Behavior Theory*. Englewood Cliffs, N.J.: Prentice-Hall.

271 PRENTICE, J. L. (1966) 'Semantics and syntax in word learning', *J.V.L.V.B.*, **5**, 279–284.

272 RAZRAN, G. (1949a) 'Semantic and phonetographic generalisation of salivary conditioning to verbal stimuli', *J. Exp. Psychol.*, **39**, 642–652.

273 RAZRAN, G. (1949b) 'Some psychological factors in the generalisation of salivary conditioning to verbal stimuli', *Am. J. Psychol.*, **62**, 247–256.

274 RAZRAN, G. (1961) 'The observable unconscious and the inferable conscious in current Soviet psychophysiology; interoceptive conditioning, semantic conditioning, and the orienting reflex', *Psychol. Review*, **68**, 81–147.

275 REED, G. F. (1968) 'Skill'. In LUNZER, E. A. and MORRIS, J. F. (eds.) *Development in Human Learning*. London: Staples.

276 REESE, H. W. (1963) 'Discrimination learning set in children', *Advances in Child Devel. and Behavior*, **1**, 115–145.

277 REISS, B. F. (1946) 'Genetic changes in semantic conditioning', *J. Exp. Psychol.*, **36**, 143–152.

278 REUCK, A. V. S. and O'CONNOR, M. (eds.) (1964) *Disorders of Language*, C.I.B.A. Foundation Symposium, Boston: Little, Brown.

279 ROSENBERG, S. (1965) 'The influence of grammatical and associative habits on verbal learning'. In ROSENBERG, S. (ed.) *Directions in Psycholinguistics*. New York: Macmillan.

280 ROSENBERG, S. (1966) 'Recall of sentences as a function of syntactic and associative habit', *J.V.L.V.B.* **5**, 392–396.

281 RUSSELL, W. A. and JENKINS, J. J. (1954) *The complete Minnesota norms for responses to 100 words from the Kent-Rosanoff word association test*. Technical Report No. 11, Contr. No. N8 onr –66216, Office of Naval Research and University of Minnesota.

282 RUSSELL, W. A. and STORMS, L. H. (1955) 'Implicit verbal chaining in paired-associate learning', *J. Exp. Psychol.*, **49**, 267–293.

283 SAUGSTAD, P. (1955) 'Problem-solving as dependent on availability of functions', *Brit. J. Psychol.*, **46**, 191–198.

284 SAVIN, H. B. and PERCHONOCK, E. (1965) 'Grammatical structure and the immediate recall of English sentences', *J.V.L.V.B.*, **4**, 348–353.

285 SAVIN. H. B. and PERCHONOCK, E. (in press) Quoted in WALES, R. J. and MARSHALL, J. C. (1966) 'Psycholinguistic Performance'. In LYONS, J. and WALES, R. C. (eds.) *Psycholinguistics Papers*. Edinburgh Univ. Press.

286 SCHUELL, H. and JENKINS, J. J. (1959) 'The nature of language deficit in aphasia', *Psychol. Review*, **66**, 45–67.

287 SCHUELL, H., JENKINS, J. J. and JIMENEZ-PABON, E. (1964) *Aphasia in Adults*. New York: Harper and Row.

288 SHIPLEY, W. C. (1933) 'An apparent transfer of conditioning', *J. General Psychol.*, **8**, 382–391.

289 SIMON, B. (1957) (ed.) *Psychology in the Soviet Union*. London: Routledge & Kegan Paul.

290 SKINNER, B. F. (1957) *Verbal Behavior*. New York: Appleton-Century-Crofts.

291 SLOBIN, D. (1964) *Imitation and the Acquisition of Syntax*. Paper presented at the Second Research Planning Conference of Project Literacy.

292 SLOBIN, D. (1966a) 'Grammatical transformations and sentence comprehension in childhood and adulthood', *J.V.L.V.B.*, **5**, 219–227.

293 SLOBIN, D. (1966b) 'Comments on "Developmental Psycholinguistics"'. In SMITH, F. and MILLER, G. A. (eds.) *The Genesis of Language*. Cambridge, Mass.: M.I.T. Press.

294 SLOBIN, D. (1966c) 'Abstracts of Soviet Studies of Child Language'.

In SMITH, F. and MILLER, G. A. (eds.) *The Genesis of Language.* Cambridge, Mass.: M.I.T. Press.

295 SOKOLOV, A. N. (1961) 'Investigations of the problem of verbal mechanisms of thinking', *Psychological Science in the U.S.S.R.*, I, 669–703. Washington: U.S. Joint Publications Research Service.

296 SOLARS, A. K. (1960) 'Latency of instrumental responses as a function of compatability with the meaning of eliciting verbal signs', *J. Exp. Psychol.*, **59**, 239–245.

297 SOLOMON, R. L. and POSTMAN, L. (1952) 'Frequency of usage as a determinant of recognition threshold for words', *J. Exp. Psychol.*, **43**, 195–201.

298 SPIELBERGER, C. D. (1965) 'Theoretical and epistemological issues in verbal conditioning'. In ROSENBERG, S. (ed.) *Directions in Psycholinguistics.* New York: Macmillan.

299 STAATS, A. W. and STAATS, C. K. (1959) 'Meaning and "m", correlated but separate', *Psychol. Review*, **66**, 136–144.

300 STAATS, A. W., and STAATS, C. K. (1963) *Complex Human Behavior.* New York: Holt, Rinehart & Winston.

301 SUCI, G. J. (1967) 'The validity of pause as an index of units in language', *J.V.L.V.B.*, **6**, 26–32.

302 TEMPLIN, M. C. (1957) *Certain Language Skills in Children.* Inst. for Child Welfare, Monogr. 26.

303 TEUBER, H. L. (1962) 'Effects of brain wounds'. In MOUNTCASTLE, V. B. (ed.) *Intrahemispheric Relations and Cerebral Dominance.* Baltimore: Johns Hopkins Press.

304 THORNDIKE, E. L. and LORGE, I. (1944) *The Teacher's Word Book of 30,000 Words.* New York: Columbia Univ. Press.

305 TREISMAN, A. M. (1960) 'Contextual cues in selective listening', *Quart. J. Exp. Psychol.*, **12**, 242–248.

306 TREISMAN, A. M. (1964) 'Verbal cues, language, and meaning in selective attention', *Am. J. Psychol.*, **77**, 206–219.

307 TREISMAN, A. M. (1965) 'Verbal responses and contextual constraints in language', *J.V.L.V.B.*, **4**, 118–128.

308 TULVING, E. (1968) 'Theoretical issues in free recall'. In DIXON, T. R. and HORTON, D. L. (eds.) *Verbal Behavior and General Behavior Theory.* Englewood Cliffs, N.J.: Prentice-Hall.

309 TULVING, E. and PATKAU, J. (1962) 'Concurrent effects of contextual constraint and word frequency on immediate recall and learning of verbal material', *Canadian J. Psychol.*, **16**, 83–95.

310 TULVING, E. and PEARLSTONE, Z. (1966) 'Availability versus accessibility of information in memory for words', *J.V.L.V.B.*, **5**, 381–391.

311 TURNER, E. A. and ROMMETVEIT, R. (1967a) 'The acquisition of sentence voice and reversibility', *Child Devel.*, **38**, 649–660.

312 TURNER, E. A. and ROMMETVEIT, R. (1967b) 'Experimental

manipulation of the production of active and passive voice in children', *Language and Speech*, **10**, 169–180.

313 UNDERWOOD, B. J. and SCHULZ, R. W. (1960) *Meaningfulness and Verbal Learning*. Philadelphia: Lippincott.

314 VIGOTSKY, L. S. (1962) *Thought and Language*. New York: Wiley.

315 WALES, R. J. and MARSHALL, J. C. (1966) 'The organisation of linguistic performance'. In LYONS, J. and WALES, R. J. (eds.) *Psycholinguistics Papers*. Edinburgh Univ. Press.

316 WASON, P. C. (1961) 'Response to affirmative and negative binary statements', *Brit. J. Psychol.*, **52**, 133–142.

317 WASON, P. C. (1965) 'The contexts of plausible denial', *J.V.L.V.B.*, **4**, 7–11.

318 WAUGH, N. C. (1961) 'Free versus serial recall', *J. Exp. Psychol.*, **62**, 496–502.

319 WEPMAN, J. M. and JONES, L. V. (1961a) *Studies in Aphasia; an Approach to Testing*. Univ. Chicago Education-Industry Service.

320 WEPMAN, J. M. and JONES, L. V. (1961b) *The Language Modalities Test for Aphasia*. Univ. Chicago Education-Industry Service.

321 WEPMAN, J. M., JONES, L. V., BOCK, R. D. and VAN PELT, D. (1960) 'Studies in aphasia; background and theoretical formulations', *J. Speech and Hearing Disorders*, **25**, 323–332.

322 WERNER, H. (1948) *Comparative Psychology of Mental Development*. Chicago: Follett.

323 WHITMARSH, G. A. and BOUSFIELD, W. A. (1961) 'Use of free associational norms for the prediction of generalisation of salivary conditioning to verbal stimuli', *Psychological Reports*, **8**, 91–95.

324 WICKELGREN, W. A. (1966) 'Phonemic similarity and interference in short-term memory for single letters', *J. Exp. Psychol.*, **71**, 396–404.

325 WILLIAMS, J. H. (1964) 'Conditioning of verbalisation; a review', *Psychol. Bull.*, **62**, 383–393.

326 YATES, A. J. (1963) 'Delayed auditory feedback', *Psychol. Bull.*, **60**, 213–251.

327 YELEN, D. R. and SCHULZ, R. W. (1963) 'Verbal satiation?' *J.V.L.V.B.*, **2**, 372–377.

328 YNGVE, V. (1960) 'A model and an hypothesis for language structure', *Proceedings Am. Philosoph. Soc.*, **104**, 444–466. A popular account is (1962): 'Computer programs for translation', *Scientific American*, **206**, 6, 68–76.

329 YOUNG, R. K. (1968) 'Serial learning'. In DIXON, T. R. and HORTON, D. L. (eds.) *Verbal Behavior and General Behavior Theory*. Englewood Cliffs, N.J.: Prentice-Hall.

330 ZANGWILL, O. L. (1960) *Cerebral Dominance and its Relation to Psychological Function*. Edinburgh: Oliver & Boyd.

331 ZEAMAN, D. and HOUSE, B. J. (1963) 'An attention theory of

retardate discrimination learning'. In ELLIS, N. R. (ed.) *Handbook of Mental Deficiency: Psychological Theory and Research*. New York: McGraw-Hill.

332 ZIPF, G. K. (1935) *The Psycho-biology of Language*. Boston: Houghton Mifflin.

Appendix

Below are listed some of the volumes of readings and conference reports available. After each is a list of the numbers of those items in the bibliography of this book which are to be found in part or in whole in them.

DE CECCO, J. P. (ed.) (1967) *The Psychology of Language, Thought, and Instruction.* New York: Holt, Rinehart & Winston. 40, 48, 54, 110, 115, 157, 169, 171, 234, 236, 238, 251, 290, 314.

DIXON, T. R. and HORTON, D. L. (eds.) (1968) *Verbal Behavior and General Behavior Theory.* Englewood Cliffs, N.J.: Prentice-Hall. 8, 17, 18, 76, 84, 90, 112, 163, 170, 175, 215, 217, 221, 261, 270, 308, 329.

JAKOBOVITZ, L. A. and MIRON, M. S. (eds.) (1967) *Readings in the Psychology of Language.* Englewood Cliffs, N.J.: Prentice-Hall. 4, 19, 24, 32, 40, 62, 63, 73, 96, 103, 159, 171, 210, 234, 236, 240, 248, 251, 259, 290, 299, 319.

LENNEBERG, E. H. (ed.) (1964) *New Directions in the Study of Language.* Cambridge, Mass.: M.I.T. Press. 39, 97, 187.

LUNZER, E. A. and MORRIS, J. F. (eds.) (1968) *Development in Human Learning.* London: Staples. 21, 275.

LYONS, J. and WALES, R. J. (eds.) (1966) *Psycholinguistics Papers.* Edinburgh Univ. Press. 89, ~77, 214, 315.

OLDFIELD, R. C. and MARSHALL, J. C. (eds.) (1968) *Language.* Harmondsworth, Middlesex: Penguin Books. 25, 31, 37, 45, 102, 105, 185, 187, 214, 236, 241, 307, 317.

OSGOOD, C. E. and MIRON, M. S. (eds.) (1965) *Psycholinguistics* (2nd ed.). Indiana Univ. Press. 232.

ROSENBERG, S. (ed.) (1965) *Directions in Psycholinguistics.* New York: Macmillan. 153, 279, 298.

SAPORTA, S. (ed.) (1963) *Psycholinguistics; A Book of Readings.* New York: Holt, Rinehart & Winston. 11, 36, 43, 54, 62, 131, 141, 151, 183, 189, 192, 242, 243, 263, 290, 314, 322.

SMITH, F. and MILLER, G. A. (eds.) (1966) *The Genesis of Language.* Cambridge, Mass.: M.I.T. Press. 108, 213, 293, 294.

The following important publications are in press, or too recently published to be consulted by the author.

FODOR, J. A., JENKINS, J. J. and SAPORTA, S. *An Introduction to*

Psycholinguistic Theory. Englewood Cliffs, N.J.: Prentice-Hall (in press).

MILLER, G. A. and MCNEILL, D. 'Psycholinguistics'. In *Handbook of Social Psychology* (revised ed.). New York: Addison-Wesley (in press).

ROSENBERG, S. and KOPLIN, J. H. (1968) *Developments in Applied Psycholinguistic Research*. New York: Macmillan.

Author Index

Aborn, M., 42, 169
Ajuriaguerra, J. de., 129, 175
Allerton, D., 5
Argyle, M., 152, 169
Asch, S. E., 98, 169
Astin, J. C., 139
Attneave, F., 40, 169
Austin, G. A., 79, 171

Bachrach, A. J., 175
Basser, L. S., 129, 169
Battig, W. F., 95, 96, 158, 169
Begun, J. S., 50, 70, 71, 172
Belloni, M., 88, 180
Bellugi, U., 105, 107, 110, 115, 116, 169, 171, 174, 178
Berko, J., 34, 113, 114, 127, 169, 171, 175
Berkowitz, L., 169
Berlyne, D. E., 94, 95, 169
Bernstein, B. B., 152, 153, 154, 169, 170
Bever, T. G., 46, 58, 109, 162, 163, 170, 174
Bitterman, M. E., 132, 170
Blank, M., 137, 170
Blumenthal, A. L., 74, 75, 170
Boakes, R., 75, 170
Bock, R. D., 186
Bogartz, W., 180
Bolinger, D., 146, 148, 170
Boomer, D. S., 46, 170
Borst, J. M., 173
Bosley, J. J., 148, 173
Bousfield, W. A., 88, 89, 90, 92, 93, 96, 97, 170, 186
Bovet, M., 176
Brain, R., 125, 170
Braine, M. D. S., 53, 60, 105, 108, 109, 112, 170, 171
Broadbent, D. E., 26, 29, 46, 171, 178

Brooks, L. O., 180
Brown, R. W., 27, 31, 61, 72, 98, 100, 105, 107, 110, 114, 115, 116, 120, 136, 149, 152, 156, 169, 171, 174, 176
Bruce, D. J., 5, 29, 171
Bruner, J. S., 79, 132, 141, 143, 167, 171
Bush, R. R., 181
Busiek, R. D., 137, 171
Butcher, H. J., 5

Carey, P., 75, 181
Carlin, J. E., 87, 171
Carmichael, L., 137, 171, 180
Carney, E., 5
Carroll, J. B., 82, 92, 150, 151, 156, 171
Carton, A. A., 82, 172
Casagrande, J. B., 156, 172
Cattell, R. B., 182
Cazden, C., 115, 172
Chase, R. A., 119, 172
Cherry, E. C., 29, 172
Chomsky, N., 9, 14, 27, 39, 40, 46, 52, 54, 56, 57, 58, 61, 63, 64, 65, 66, 73, 102, 103, 115, 162, 163, 172, 181
Clark, E. V., 148, 172
Clark, H. H., 35, 50, 70, 71, 147, 148, 172
Cliff, N., 148, 172
Cofer, C. N., 36, 53, 97, 140, 160, 170, 171, 172, 173, 175, 177, 178, 182, 183
Cohen, B. H., 97, 170
Coleman, E. B., 42, 173
Cooper, F. S., 27, 173

Danick, J. J., 88, 170
Davitz, J. R., 151, 173

Day, E. J., 154, 173
Dean, J., 152, 169
De Cecco, J. P., 177, 188
Deese, J., 29, 36, 42, 96, 98, 99, 159, 173
Delattre, P. C., 173
Denes, P., 27, 173
Desoto, C. B., 148, 173
Deutsch, M. P., 155, 173
Dixon, E. M., 139, 179
Dixon, T. R., 7, 169, 170, 173, 175, 177, 178, 180, 181, 183, 185, 186, 188
Donaldson, M., 103, 173
Dulany, D. E., 158, 159, 160, 173

Earhard, B., 88, 174
Ebenholtz, S. M., 98, 169
Ehrlich, S., 98, 174
Ellis, N. R., 187
Entwisle, D. R., 36, 174
Epstein, W. A., 34, 43, 174
Ervin, S. M., 35, 105, 110, 113, 117, 174
Evans, B., 79, 174
Evans, C., 79, 174

Fant, G., 25, 177
Feather, B. W., 85, 174
Fitts, P. M., 21, 174
Flavell, J., 150, 174
Fodor, J. A., 7, 46, 62, 68, 93, 94, 95, 109, 146, 161, 162, 170, 174, 175, 178, 188
Fraser, C., 72, 103, 105, 108, 110, 116, 117, 118, 171, 174
Fries, C. C., 36, 174
Frincke, G., 30, 177
Fry, D. B., 28, 120, 123, 174
Furth, H. G., 142, 143, 174

Gagné, R. M., 140, 174
Galanter, E., 100, 128, 130, 162, 163, 176, 181
Garner, W. R., 28, 175
Garrett, M., 7, 62, 68, 161, 162, 170, 175
Gelfand, S., 140, 178

Gerstman, I. J., 173
Gladney, T. A., 50, 175
Glanzer, M., 36, 175
Gleason, H. A., 11, 30, 34, 37, 175
Goldfarb, W., 154, 175
Goldman-Eisler, F., 46, 175
Goldstein, K., 126, 175
Gonzalez, R. C., 53, 175
Goodglass, H., 127, 175
Goodnow, J. J., 79, 171
Gough, P. B., 70, 72, 75, 175
Gould, J., 170
Graham, N. C., 139, 175
Greenberg, J. H., 156, 175
Greenfield, P. M., 141, 171
Greenspoon, J., 83, 175
Gregory, M., 29, 171

Halle, M., 25, 36, 122, 123, 127, 177
Hammond, K. R., 182
Harlow, H. F., 57, 103, 139, 175
Hartley, E. L., 172
Hayhurst, H., 5, 118, 175
Hécaen, H., 129, 175
Heise, G. A., 28, 181
Herman, D. T., 137, 176
Hermelin, B., 138, 182
Herriot, P., 43, 50, 51, 71, 72, 116, 118, 142, 148, 166, 176
Hess, E. H., 124, 176
Hildum, D. C., 27, 171
Hockett, C., 150, 176
Hogan, H. P., 137, 171
Horton, D. L., 7, 169, 170, 173, 175, 177, 178, 180, 181, 183, 185, 186, 188
House, B. J., 139, 186
Howe, E. S., 148, 176
Howes, D., 82, 83, 176
Hoyle, E., 5
Hoyle, H. W., 145, 179
Hull, C. L., 40, 176
Hulme, I., 145, 176

Ingram, E., 61, 176
Inhelder, B., 133, 139, 141, 143, 144, 176, 183

Irwin, O. C., 154, 176
Isard, S., 182

Jack, O., 42, 181
Jackson, J. H., 126, 177
Jakobovitz, L. A., 92, 178, 188
Jakobson, R., 25, 36, 122, 123, 127, 177
Jeffress, L., 178
Jenkins, J. J., 47, 52, 60, 77, 82, 86, 88, 92, 96, 125, 126, 177, 184, 188
Jensen, A. R., 155, 177
Jimenez-Pabon, E., 125, 184
John, V. P., 155, 177
Johnson, M. G., 70, 177
Johnson, N. F., 7, 43, 44, 45, 48, 49, 54, 70, 98, 177
Johnson, R. C., 30, 177
Johnson, R. L., 92, 177
Johnson-Laird, P. N., 70, 141, 177, 178
Jones, L. V., 126, 184
Judson, A. J., 140, 178

Kagan, J., 143, 169
Kanfer, F. H., 83, 84, 178
Katz, J. J., 56, 61, 146, 178
Kaufman, R., 42, 173
Kendler, T. S., 138, 142, 178
Kendon, H., 152, 169
Kenney, H., 143, 171
Kent, E. H., 83, 178
Kjeldergaard, P. M., 82, 158, 172, 178
Klima, E. S., 110, 111, 178
Koltsova, V., 135
Koplin, J. H., 189
Krulee, G. K., 50, 175
Kuenne, M. R., 137, 178
Kuhn, T. S., 17, 158, 160, 178

Ladefoged, P., 26, 178
Lambert, W. E., 92, 178
Lantz, M., 156, 157
Lashley, K., 40, 163, 178
Lawless, R. H., 137, 176
Lawton, D., 132, 152, 153, 155, 179

Lenneberg, E. H., 27, 30, 31, 120, 125, 128, 129, 130, 156, 171, 174, 179, 188
Leopold, W. F., 122, 179
Lewis, M. M., 120, 179
Liberman, A. M., 25, 173, 179
Lichten, W., 28, 181
Loban, W. D., 154, 179
Loewenthal, K., 151, 179
Lorge, I., 41, 82, 185
Lovell, K., 139, 145, 179
Luce, D. R., 181
Lunzer, E. A., 5, 100, 132, 134, 139, 140, 145, 163, 164, 170, 176, 179, 183, 188
Luria, A. R., 89, 125, 127, 128, 134, 135, 150, 179, 180
Lyons, J., 7, 11, 173, 174, 178, 180, 184, 186, 188

McCarthy, D., 154, 180
Maccoby, E. E., 172
McKean, K. O., 66, 182
McLaughlin, G. H., 134, 180
Maclay, H., 46, 153, 180
McNeill, D., 35, 98, 100, 103, 104, 106, 107, 108, 110, 111, 112, 118, 171, 180, 189
Maier, N. R. F., 140, 180
Maltzman, I., 85, 88, 89, 94, 140, 158, 180
Mandler, G., 42, 88, 99, 100, 158, 174, 176, 180, 181
Mandler, J. M., 42
Marks, L. E., 73, 181
Marks, M., 42, 181
Marshall, J. C., 7, 67, 127, 146, 181, 184, 186, 188
Marshall, R. W., 137, 176
Martin, E., 51, 69, 181
Martin, J. G., 46, 181
Martin, L., 30, 177
Mayer, J., 127, 175
Mehler, J., 68, 69, 73, 74, 75, 181
Melton, A. W., 98, 174, 181
Menyuk, P., 110, 181
Miller, G. A., 17, 21, 23, 25, 28, 40, 41, 42, 43, 51, 59, 61, 63, 66, 67, 68, 69, 73, 74, 98, 100,

Miller, G. A.—*contd.*
128, 130, 162, 172, 174, 180,
181, 182, 184, 185, 188, 189
Miller, M. D., 92, 177
Mink, W. D., 87, 182
Minturn, A. L., 137, 171
Miron, M. S., 92, 125, 126, 182,
183, 188
Moray, N., 29, 182
Morris, J. F., 132, 170, 179, 183,
188
Mountcastle, V. B., 129, 182, 185
Mowrer, O. H., 93, 121, 182
Musgrave, B. S., 170, 171, 173,
177, 182, 183

Nair, P., 143, 182
Newcomb, T. M., 172
Newcombe, F., 127, 181
Nicely, P. E., 25, 182
Nielsen, J. M., 127, 182
Noble, C. E., 82, 87, 182

O'Connor, M., 125, 179, 184
O'Connor, N., 135, 138, 182
Oldfield, R. C., 100, 163, 182, 188
Oléron, P., 142, 182
Olson, D., 60, 149, 182
Olver, R. R., 141, 171
Osgood, C. E., 7, 46, 47, 48, 49, 51,
52, 54, 60, 61, 70, 71, 76, 78,
82, 88, 89, 90, 91, 92, 93, 94,
95, 99, 125, 126, 127, 147, 153,
161, 166, 176, 180, 182, 183,
188

Passow, H., 173
Patkau, J., 42, 185
Paul, C., 138, 183
Pavlov, I. P., 135
Pearlstone, Z., 98, 100, 185
Penfield, W., 125, 179, 183
Perchonock, E., 68, 69, 75, 184
Perl, N., 5
Peterson, M. J., 87, 183
Piaget, J., 104, 132, 133, 137, 139,
141, 142, 143, 145, 150, 163,
165, 167, 176, 183
Pollio, H. R., 92, 148, 183

Postal, P. M., 56, 61, 178
Postman, L., 29, 185
Prentice, J. L., 118, 183
Pribram, K., 100, 128, 130, 162,
163, 181

Rabinowitz, R., 143, 169
Razran, G., 89, 135, 183
Reed, G. F., 21, 183
Reese, H. W., 139, 183
Reiss, B. F., 85, 184
Reuck, A. V. S., 125, 179, 184
Roberts, J. M., 156, 179
Roberts, K. H., 51, 69, 181
Roberts, L., 125, 179, 183
Rommetveit, R., 119, 185
Rosanoff, A. J., 83, 178
Rosenberg, S., 49, 52, 53, 54, 177,
184, 185, 186, 188, 189
Rubenstein, H., 169
Russell, W. A., 82, 86, 87, 92, 96,
177, 184

Saporta, S., 179, 188
Saugstad, P., 140, 184
Savin, H. B., 68, 69, 75, 184
Schuell, H., 125, 126, 184
Schulz, R. W., 82, 92, 186
Selfridge, J. A., 40, 41, 42, 182
Shipley, W. C., 85, 184
Siddall, M. Q., 145, 179
Simon, B., 135, 184
Sinclair, H., 143, 144, 176
Skinner, B. F., 114, 172, 184
Slobin, D. I., 69, 70, 71, 104, 110,
117, 118, 135, 184
Smith, E. C., 140, 174
Smith, F., 172, 174, 180, 184, 185,
188
Sokolov, A. N., 27, 185
Solars, A. K., 91, 185
Solomon, R. L., 29, 185
Spence, J. T., 180
Spence, K. W., 180
Spielberger, C. D., 84, 185
Staats, A. W., 93, 185
Staats, C. K., 93, 185
Stafford, R. A., 147, 148, 173
Sterling, T. D., 169

Storms, L. H., 86, 87, 184
Suci, G. J., 46, 90, 91, 92, 177, 183, 185
Summers, S. S., 180

Tannenbaum, P., 90, 91, 183
Templin, M. C., 154, 185
Teuber, H. L., 129, 185
Thorndike, E. L., 40, 82, 185
Treisman, A. M., 29, 37, 185
Tulving, E., 42, 96, 97, 98, 99, 100, 162, 185
Turner, E. A., 119, 185

Underwood, B. J., 82, 186

Van Pelt, D., 186
Vigotsky, L. S., 134, 136, 144, 186
Vinogradova, O. S., 89, 180

Wales, R. J., 7, 67, 146, 173, 174, 178, 180, 184, 186, 188

Wall, D. D., 92, 177
Walter, A. A., 137, 171
Wason, P. C., 70, 186
Waugh, N. C., 96, 186
Weksel, W., 109, 170
Wepman, J. M., 126, 128, 186
Werner, H., 144, 186
Whitmarsh, G. A., 88, 97, 170, 186
Whorf, B. L., 156
Wickelgren, W. A., 25, 186
Williams, J. H., 83, 186

Yates, A. J., 31, 186
Yelen, D. R., 92, 186
Yngve, V., 51, 54, 69, 70, 186
Young, R. K., 158, 186
Yudovich, F., 135, 150, 180

Zangwill, O. L., 100, 129, 163, 182, 186
Zeaman, D., 139, 186
Zipf, G. K., 30, 187

Subject Index

acoustic, 25–7, 122–3
acquired distinctiveness, 123
acquisition, 102–124, 128–130, 165–6
ambiguity, 60
anticipation, 23
aphasia, 124–8
approximations to English, 40–3
articulation, 24–7, 30–2
attention, 139
automatisation, 22
autonomic responses, 89
availability, 98
awareness, 13–14, 84

babbling, 121–2
behaviourism, 18–19, 79–101, 117, 158–63

categories, 95–101, 145–9, 156
chain complex, 144
click technique, 45–6
clustering, 95–7
codability, 156–7
cognitive development, 132–4
commitments, 51, 69
communication, 150–5
competence, 14, 52, 56–8, 61–2, 68, 102–4, 163
comprehension, 69–70, 110, 115–18
concrete operational thought, 133
conservation, 143–4
constituent, analysis, 37–40
content words, 36–7
context, 19, 27–30, 108–110, 119
contextual generalisation, 53, 108–109
critical period, 124, 128–30

deafness, 142–3
decoding hypothesis, 43–4

deep structure, 39, 62–3, 68, 74–6, 104–10, 119–20, 141–2
delayed auditory feedback, 31
depth (Yngve), 51
dichotic stimulation, 29
differentiation, 106–7
discrimination, 137–41
distinctive features, 24, 122–4

egocentric speech, 134–5
elaborated code, 152
emotional meaning, 151–2
expansions, 115–17

feedback, 22, 31, 121
form class, 32–7, 53–4
formal operational thought, 133
free recall, 95–7
freedom of occurrence, 38–9
function words, 36–7

generative grammar, 39–40, 56–78, 102–14, 117–18

hierarchy, 11, 16–17, 21–2, 43, 48–50, 124, 149, 163–5

imitation, 115–17, 121
immediate constituents, 38
inflexions, 33, 113–14
information theory, 28–9
internalisation, 134–6
interrogatives, 110–12
introspection, 13

language
    as a system, 11–14
    as inter-personal behaviour, 15–16
    as personal behaviour, 14–15
    v. speech, 11

language acquisition device, 102–103, 124
lateralisation of function, 126, 129–130
learning of language, 114–20
linguistics, 11–14, 24–5, 30, 32–4, 37–40, 56–66, 102–4, 162–3
linguistic relativity, 155–7
localisation of function, 125–8

maturation, 128–30
meaning, 17, 55, 69–73, 76–7, 79–101
meaningfulness, 29, 82–3, 87
mediation, 47, 85–95, 137–41
morpheme, 12, 32–3
morpho-phonemics, 31
motor theory of speech perception, 25

negatives, 70, 110–12

oddity problem, 139–40
open class, 105–6
operant conditioning, 83–4, 114–15
operational thought, 132–4, 141–5
orienting reflex, 89

paradigmatic, 34–6
passives, 70–1
pauses, 46–7
performance, 56–8, 163
phoneme, 11–12, 24–7, 120–4
phrase structure grammar, 39–40, 50
pivot class, 105–6
play, 145
pragmatics, 71–2
prepositions, 147–8
problem solving, 140–1
production, 116–18, 166
productivity, 13, 31, 34, 106–7

redundancy, 31, 34
regulation of behaviour, 132, 166–8
representation, 85, 89–95, 132–3, 157
restricted code, 152

retrieval, 97–101
reversal shift, 138–9
reversibility (cognitive), 133
reversibility (semantic), 71, 119
rules, 39, 62

schema, 134, 163–8
second signal system, 135–6
selection restrictions, 64–5, 146–7
semantics, 12, 45, 47, 64–5, 69–74, 145–9
semantic differential, 29, 91–3
semantic generalisation, 85–7
semantic satiation, 92
sentence types, 69–72, 150
sequential dependencies, 40–5, 48–50, 52
short-term memory, 23, 51, 69, 134
skill, 21–4, 31–2, 34, 54
social class, 152–5
speech perception, 24–30
S-R theory, 18, 158–63
storage, 98–100
strategy, 134, 163–8
subcategorisation rules, 64–5
subjective organisation, 95–7
surface structure, 39, 62–3, 75–6
syntagmatic, 35–6
syntax, 12, 37–40, 45, 47, 62–4, 73–4

tachistoscopic recognition, 29–30
temporal contiguity, 159–60
theory, 158–68
thinking, 131–57, 166–8
transformations, 63–4, 66–73, 110–112, 139
transitional error probability, 43–5
transposition, 137–8

ultimate constituents, 38
universals of language, 106–7, 123

verbal mediation, 85–9, 137–41

word association, 34–5, 82–3, 96–7